Tales of
the North
Atlantic

Tales of the North Atlantic

HAL LAWRENCE

McClelland and Stewart

McClelland and Stewart Limited
The Canadian Publishers
25 Hollinger Road
Toronto, Ontario
M4B 3G2

Canadian Cataloguing in Publication Data

Lawrence, Hal, 1920-

  Tales of the North Atlantic

ISBN 0-7710-4730-4

1. Canada. Canadian Armed Forces – History.
2. Canada – History, Naval – 20th century.* I.Title

VA400.L38 1985   359 '.00971   C85-099656-2

Printed and bound in Canada by John Deyell Company

Contents

This book is written for number 1 son, Richard,
of
The Royal Canadian Corps of Sea Cadets
and
The Canadian Guards,
heir to the traditions of his father, grandfather, and great-grandfather.

Acknowledgements

The debt I owe to many people for helping me tell tales of the sea and of the Royal Canadian Navy can be acknowledged but never fully repaid; my gratitude is beyond measure. There are, for instance, all those whose sea stories I have been reading since I was a boy; these have become part of my being and echoes from them are a resonance in my stories. There are also those who have told me their tales; as I repeat them I can see again the faces and hear again the voices – the faces mostly smiling and the voices mostly merry. To these men I am indebted – and to their wives; for, aside from the partings that passing years inflict, their girlfriends I met over forty years ago are their wives today and are intrinsic to their yarns.

My Gibraltar has been the scholarship and the moral and practical support of the professional historians. Dr. Gilbert Norman Tucker (deceased), our first naval historian in Naval Service Headquarters, Ottawa, in the 1940s, laid the foundations of research and writing on the Royal Navy in Canada from the late 1700s through to the Royal Canadian Navy in the early 1950s. Mr. Ted Russell, a seaman himself, was Tucker's successor; he continued the research and expanded it. Dr. Alec Douglas, the current Head of the Directorate of History and also a seaman, has inherited the burgeoning body of accumulated knowledge and expanded it greatly in the national and international fields. He has encouraged graduate students to write theses on maritime subjects and many have been completed under his aegis; he has expanded oral research to complement the written word – Captain Mack Lynch's *Salty Dips* is one example; he has founded the Canadian Nautical Research Society and is tireless in speaking at symposia of naval learned societies at home and abroad. To me he is a patient cornucopia of nautical knowledge and historical methodology. His staff have also been most helpful – especially Elsie Roberts, Dr. Marc Milner, Mr. Dave Kealy, and Mr. Philip Chaplin. I must also thank two other authors, Bill McNeil and Barry Broadfoot, for helping me by commenting on my text.

Dr. Jim Boutilier, Head of the Department of History at Royal Roads Military College, Victoria, made me at home in HMCS *Royal Roads* and was an amiable scourge with his editor's eye. He and Dr. Reg Roy and Dr. Michael Hadley of the University of Victoria welcomed me to the academic community here. These, then, are scholars whose research and writing complements and provides a solid background for a mere spinner of salty dips like myself. I thank Liz Grambart at the University of Victoria Library for the help she has given me with photo research.

On the naval side, Captain Casey Cameron and Captain Colin Shaw, Royal Canadian Navy (Retired), of the Maritime Museum of British Columbia, and Marilyn Gurney Smith of the Naval Museum in Halifax, Nova Scotia, gave support and access to our nautical in- heritance. Two Admirals are the prime movers of these tales. In ex- pressing my gratitude to Vice-Admiral Nigel Brodeur and Rear- Admiral Robert Yanow I only make public once again their known devotion to naval history. Their friendship and that of their wives, Anne and Valda, and the knowledge of their support, has cheered me in many a frustrated and lonely hour. Admiral Yanow and his prede- cessors as Maritime Commander, Pacific, Gordon Edwards and Bill Hughes, have made me welcome during these past six years in the naval community of British Columbia which I departed twenty-seven years ago. Today's serving officers have been unfailingly hospitable and have given me some assurance that I am not yet *quite* an ancient mariner with a long grey beard and glittering eye, who forces passers- by to listen. Commander Bob Luke is one of the most jovial of these; he also found for me a dimly-remembered quote I had been seeking for years.

In writing a previous work I saw a lot of the art and craft of turning an often incoherent manuscript into a readable book. I therefore owe a great deal to my (then) editor – Jan Walter. Of course, on the profes- sional as well as the personal side, I owe all to the support of my wife. I say "of course" only in the sense that she has always been my main support.

Author's Preface

I have spent sixty-five years of my life in the service of the sovereign. My father was a career soldier, having joined as a Boy Sapper in 1908, and thus I was born in the Royal Engineer's Barracks in Chatham, England, where the young Lord Kitchener had swanked it as a subaltern. My father went from the Royal Engineers to the Royal Canadian Engineers, from which, two wars and thirty-eight years later, he was retired as Lieutenant-Colonel, mutinously murmuring about the unbearded youths trying to run the army today.

That I am a royalist perhaps goes without saying. I am told that this trait first became evident when I was four. At that time, the dashing, handsome Prince of Wales was causing all feminine hearts to beat quicker. The Beau Brummell of the twenties, he had started a run on check suits and jackets. I was attired in a similar outfit, Mother being no exception to the adoring and emulating female population. The Prince attended some military affair resplendent in black and white, cap at a rakish angle, and I, apparently thinking that wearing the same attire constituted a basis for some friendly gesture on my part, slipped through the cordon of soldiers and advanced at the marching pace I had observed on the parade ground, left arm swinging in a soldierly fashion, right hand extended in greeting. My offered hand was grasped and I received a royal pat on the head before a shocked guardsman was able to steer me back to a wide-eyed mother.

I went to the RE garrison school at age five. My first headmaster was Regimental Sergeant-Major White. Like all RSMs he was a magnificent brute: six-foot-one, two hundred pounds, florid-faced behind a fierce six-inch moustache waxed to a point at either end, his brass buttons, rank badges, belt buckles, and cap badge glittering like twelve small suns. His swagger stick and Sam Browne belt were boned to a

9

lustrous mahogany and his boots – well, his boots! How many hundreds of hours had his batman polished, re-polished, chamoised, boned, and artistically silked the final product? Had he and the Kaiser ever come face to face during the Great War, the Kaiser would have instinctively handed over his sword. A stentorian voice had he, and large mottled hands with fingers like marlinspikes. He strode the playground before and after classes, during recess and lunch hour, watching with infinite benignity over his sixty youngsters. He had large, warm, brown eyes and the only subject he taught was poetry. I know now that *all* RSMs are not like that, but I was five.

One day I took a nasty spill from my bike, grazing both knees and one hand on the gravel. Grit-embedded and blood seeping, I sat up, my breath coming in gulps, hands clenched, shaking. He was at my side in an instant, down on one knee, me hoisted on the other. "It's all right to cry if you want, Harold. In a few years it will not be permissible, but it's all right at your age."

Sergeant-Major White and my father had emerged from a particularly beastly war only seven years previously. The Engineers had fought the Turks in the Dardenelles and the Germans in France and Belgium. They had covered the retreat of the British Expeditionary Force at the Battle of Mons. Le Cateau, Passchendaele, Verdun: the Engineers had seen them all. My father spoke of beginning short rest periods by prying the lice out of his legs with a knife. He spent two months in the line in wet clothes. The Engineers preceded an attack by building bridges – usually under fire: they were last out in a retreat as they blew up bridges – usually under fire – so as to delay the enemy. Once, when overrun, my father's field company battled its way out in hand-to-hand fighting with pistol and rifle and bayonet. Yet I saw only the gentle side of these men's natures. Up to about age ten I would hear bits of their stories (that bit about bayonet fighting, for instance, and the lice) as I sat quietly in the corner of the mess while they exchanged banter at the bar, or in the locker room of the RE tennis club. But it was mostly the good times they talked of, with much affection and laughter. When my time came, I would be like them, I vowed.

My time came when I was eighteen. I joined the Royal Canadian Navy as a midshipman. My first teachers, the naval equivalents of Sergeant-Major White, were Chief Petty Officers Gunner's Mates. To me their ferocity was quite unnerving. How could anyone be so furious just because I had turned left instead of right and wandered off their wretched parade ground, head steadfastly erect, arms swinging to the ordained height, and feet at the correct cadence of one hundred and twenty paces to the minute? A bleak outlook was seen for me if I didn't buck up: "When you come to attention you stamp your feet like a bloody pongo. When you swing your arms you look like the little wooden soldiers my old mum gave me when I was a nipper. Your past must of been dreadful. Your present is not satisfactory at all. The future I see for you is gloomy. You must buck up, young sir, *promise me you'll buck up.*" (His eyes bulging, face turning puce, forehead veins throbbing.) And how could the cold stare of the Staff Officer (Operations) – a certain Lieutenant-Commander Lay – cause me to fear punishments yet unnamed for sins I had not yet committed? And, yet, after working hours, there was amongst us the same good fellowship I had seen in the RE mess in Chatham.

Mother and I were my father's camp followers at barracks after barracks, camp after camp, schools of military science – the Royal Military Colleges in Kingston and Sandhurst I remember best. When I was fifteen my father was on the teaching staff at RMC, Kingston. On Saturday mornings the riding master taught equitation to children of the staff. Sergeant Saxon looked as though life, manifested under the guise of gentlemen cadets and horses, was constantly trying to defeat him – and might yet succeed. His voice sounded like a reed in a winter wind and his usual expression assured us he had been weaned on a pickle. He was strict, like all others of the breed. To start with he would not allow us to have saddles and I frequently fell off my massive beast, as my skinny legs could not hold me on its enormous barrel. The sawdust of the riding shed was not as hard as the playground of the garrison school but it was a lot farther to fall from a horse than from my bicycle and I was being bumped up and down as I never was on my bike.

"Get *up*, lad, get *up*. You're not hurt; catch your mount and get up. You've got tears in your eyes. At *your* age. Get *up*, lad."

Soon I was a Boy Signalman in a reserve squadron of the Royal Canadian Corps of Signals. We wore bandoliers, riding britches, puttees, boots, and spurs. We carried not a swagger stick but a riding crop. We were paid fifty cents a day. If I had had it I would have paid *them* to be allowed to wear that uniform. I was in the army Canadian Officers Training Corps at age seventeen when I was at Saint Mary's College in Halifax. But I had lost my heart to the navy when I was eight in Chatham, England. Chatham has had a Naval Barracks and Dockyard since the time of Henry VIII, and one rare day in June I saw

HMS *Hood* gliding up the Medway River – dormant power, serene, the symbol of hundreds of years of Britain's sea power. From then on, for me heaven and earth were in tune. That sea change is with me still. In Halifax, on a similar June day in 1939, I began my twenty-eight years in the navy. I was retired twenty years ago but we of the Band of Brothers still meet from time to time. Today's serving officers and men are unfailing in their courtesy and show us many kindnesses.

This may seem a circuitous way of approaching stories of the sea, but I wanted to impart something of the heart of the teller of these tales and something of the hearts and minds of those men and women whose tales they are. We are all cast from the same mould, cut from the same cloth. The dichotomy between the fighting man and that same man as father, husband, friend, is strange but definite. I saw a little of Sergeant-Major White sixty years later in Vice-Admiral Harry G. DeWolf, CBE, DSO, DSC, CD, Chief of Naval Staff in the late 1960s. On duty he was a terror – my oath he was! If you were going to brief "Hard-Over Harry," you'd better be sure your facts were right. If you had prepared a memo for him to sign it had better be impeccable in syntax and logical in presentation and sense or it would be hurled across the desk in your face. If, at sea, anything was not as it should be, may God help you; it is certain that nobody else could. Similarly, Rear-Admiral H. Nelson Lay, OBE, CD, when his destroyer was approaching the enemy coast, found a lookout asleep on watch and told him that according to the Naval Discipline Act his crime was punishable by death: "I ought to order you to be shot." These two men and a dozen others stopped many a career if they felt the good of the navy or the efficiency of the ship required it.

And, although I didn't realize it until many years later, these men shared the same gentleness and humour that I had first seen in the Royal Engineers over fifty years before. Admiral DeWolf, in 1982, when talking to me of one of his bygone staff officers, said, in wonder, "He seemed to be *afraid* of me." Admiral Lay has told me how, after finding that lookout asleep and telling him that the penalty could be death, he only sentenced him to three months in prison. He told me, "I think I had to do that. The whole ship was endangered." This mildness seemed strange to me. Again the dichotomy: I thought ninety days a light punishment, but the Admiral still thinks of that wretched ordinary seaman of forty-five years ago.

This book's title may be *Tales of the North Atlantic* but *Scuttlebutt* would have been equally appropriate. All these stories have been around for forty, fifty, sixty years. Some go back centuries. Do we exaggerate when we spin our salty dips? No! We heighten for artistic effect. Did it really happen just that way? Of course it did! And if it didn't, it should have. Do our memories perhaps become faulty as we all approach seventy or eighty or ninety? About what we did last week or last year, maybe, but not about our youth, our glorious youth. And for those of us who survived it *was* a glorious youth. Despite the gales and the guns roaring and the scream of bombs and the cries of dying men, we were a happy breed. Somehow we had learned that happiness is more a matter of duty and discipline and morality than it is of security and comfort. Few of us knew of this Sanskrit poem,

> Look well to this day,
> For it is life,
> The very life of life.
> In its brief course lie all
> The realities and verities of existence,
> The bliss of growth,
> The splendour of action,
> The glory of power.
>
> For yesterday is but a dream,
> And tomorrow is only a vision,
> But today, well lived,
> Makes every yesterday a dream of happiness
> And every tomorrow a vision of hope.
>
> Look well, therefore, to this day.

But that's mostly how we lived – yesterday forgotten, today the bliss of growth and the splendour of action as we succeeded to higher and higher ranks and more responsibility, the excitement of the battle, and the glory of just being in charge.

For the men with whom I served I feel rancour towards few, affection for most, and love for some. You will notice the debt I owe to the Chief and Petty Officers who taught me so very much. They passed on not only their technical knowledge but their whole attitude toward the austere life we lived (austere in the professional sense only; in all else we lived with zest and humour). And I had their unfailing loyalty and support when they served under me. When I was Commander of the Eleventh Escort Squadron and Senior Officer in Command, I still saw in my Chief Petty Officers much of Sergeant-Major White and Sergeant Saxon; they kept me up to the mark and looked after my interests much as the NCOs of my childhood and youth had done.

I said in a preface to a previous work, ". . . and now that it is finished I know what it is about. It is a love story, rather it is a series of love stories." So it is with this book. These are love stories of ships and of men I knew so well, and of other ships and men I only heard of but whose history gave a meaning and a continuity to my path through this life. For me and for the people you will meet in these pages, the navy was a religion as much as a profession, just as for my first headmaster and my first riding master and my father, the Regiment was a religion.

As I approach what is euphemistically called the autumn of my life, I find that one of my rewards is vivid remembrance of indiscretions I do not regret. I remember the moments of terror but also the hours and days and years of tranquil happiness. May what I have written recall those times for those who shared them with me. This book is therefore dedicated to those men I have had the honour to serve with in the Royal Navy and the Royal Canadian Navy, Boy Seaman to Admiral. We are all sailors of the queen.

Hal Lawrence

Feast of Saint Barbara, 1985.

The Birth of
The Royal Canadian Navy

It is upon the Navy, wherein, under the good Providence of God, the Wealth, Safety, and Strength of this Realm do chiefly attend.

Preamble to The Articles of War, Charles II, 1661

The last warship of the Royal Navy's North Pacific Squadron departed the Esquimalt base in 1906. The dockyard was closed. For nearly two hundred years the RN had patrolled Canadian waters, keeping intruders out and our sea lanes open. It had been no small feat: there were 2,000 miles from the Atlantic up the St. Lawrence through the Great Lakes to Lake Superior to cover, as well as 34,000 miles from Halifax up the Atlantic coastline, through the Arctic archipelago and south, down the Pacific seaboard to Victoria. The navy ranged further afield as need arose, the cost borne by Great Britain. Since Canada had proclaimed itself an independent dominion in 1867, the British began to think this unreasonable, and in 1897, the Colonial Secretary, Joseph Chamberlain, suggested that the prosperous colonies should begin to bear some of the cost of their own naval defence. The First World War was looming in the ensuing years, and at a naval conference our prime minister, Sir Wilfrid Laurier, said to Chamberlain, "If you want our aid, call us to your councils." This has a fine ring of rugged Canadian independence to jingoistic historians who often forget Mr. Chamberlain's answer: "Come in. By all means, come in. But pay as you enter."

In 1910, Canada formed the Royal Canadian Navy. That year, HMCS *Niobe*, a heavy cruiser, arrived in Halifax from the United Kingdom, and HMCS *Rainbow*, a light cruiser, arrived in Esquimalt. On November 7, 1910, the Union Jack was lowered at Esquimalt and the new RCN Union Jack was hoisted. The Royal Canadian Navy – about eight hundred officers and men – was in business. For four years the dockyard at Esquimalt had had only a caretaker and two watchmen; no artisans. This was to present problems of the first magnitude – well, maybe of the second magnitude, judge for yourself.

In the mid 1940s I served for three years in destroyers based in this dockyard, first as Gunnery Officer to Lieutenant-Commander John Charles in the *Crescent*, then as Flotilla Gunnery Officer to Commander O. C. S. Robertson in the *Cayuga*. In the late 1950s I was again there serving as Staff Officer (Gunnery) to the Flag Officer, Pacific Coast, Rear-Admiral Hugh Pullen. During those years I knew Bill MacLaurin, a civilian Senior Technical Officer with, by 1955, forty-five years experience with the navy. Ministers of marine, admirals, and historians have all written about the passing on of the traditions and customs and folklore of the Royal Navy to the Royal Canadian Navy. They have discoursed upon matters of state, political differences, and the fractiousness of politicians. But here is how it looked to Bill, at that time an Engine Room Artificer in *Rainbow*.

By April 1911, *Rainbow* was due for her annual refit and docking, but there were no artisans in the dockyard. The Engineer Commander mustered the ship's artisans aft and said that there was no money to put work out to contract, that while under RN regulations ship's artisans got extra money for working in dockyards this was not so under RCN regulations, but the ship had to stay seaworthy and he intended that his engine-room would be so. "May I please have volunteers?" There was only one possible answer; the hands set to work with gusto. Anything out of ship's routine is a skylark. Tools were mustered and chamfered, the steam boiler was fired up and given a water-pressure test, the compound steam engine for driving overhead shafting was overhauled, and, in six days, the smithy, foundry pattern, coppersmith, and shipwright shop were in operation again.

The refit started with a bang – not a metaphorical bang but a literal bang. When molten metal was poured for the first casting, the moulder forgot to dry the sand in the mould box, which created a build-up of steam pressure and – BANG! Alarm, consternation, youbloody-fool yells from foremen; sand, molten metal, and wood flying here and there; but nobody was hurt.

To save time, the midday meal was served in the Stone Frigate – the barracks ashore – and not on board. Victualling allowance was twenty-five cents per man per day so there was no seven-bell tea for the hands in the dockyard. But the dockyard manager's Guernsey cow roamed at will in the lush grass between the buildings. Chief Stoker Dick Fernandez knew that growing boys need their milk, and daily he induced this amiable old animal into the blacksmith shop – no seven-bell tea, but milk all round. But the owner became worried about Bessie's drop in production and called in the vet. How do we keep him from finding out? Get more milk-making food into her. So, daily, she was coaxed through a narrow back door into the victualing storeroom where she devoured cabbage and whatever else struck her fancy. Soon the victualing storesman became puzzled by his rapidly declining stock. The cow's owner and the storesman got their answers one day when Bessie was left unattended in the storeroom. Hands at her forrard end, hauling, and hands at her after end, shoving, could not get her out the narrow door.

Rum and tobacco have been for centuries the *de facto* if not the *de jure* coinage of the naval realm. There being no horses or carts at Esquimalt, everything had to be man-handled and jack-assed up the hill from the ship to the factory. Besides being back-breaking work, it took up a lot of time that could have been better spent by the skilled artisans. In 1910, when the provincial prison in Victoria burned to the ground, the powers-that-be suddenly thought, why not accommodate some of the prisoners in the dockyard gaol? The warden, Bob Bradley, a retired Chief Boatswain's Mate (RN), ex-HMS *Shearwater*, a member of the RCN Chief and Petty Officers' Club, set to work. Recruiting was brief, that much is known, perhaps only a few minutes; and the RCN had its first pressed men. Whether coinage changed hands is not known.

A soft answer turneth away wrath but so does a quick answer. In 1912 the Governor General, the Duke of Connaught, was to inspect the Esquimalt workshops and all hands were set to work on every single machine, whether or not a particular one was needed that day. Sparks flew, torches burned, fires flared, molten metal flowed, overhead shafting twirled, lathes hummed, hammers hammered, and chisels rang.

The Duke, complete with courtiers, swept in. One very young and junior Engine Room Artificer hadn't yet started up.

"What do I do, Chief?" he whispered.

"Chuck a piece of metal in that there lathe and bloody well take a heavy cut."

And smoking hot metal chips started flying. But where did the Governor General stop? Of course. At this lathe.

"And what are we making here, my good man?"

The operator looked stunned and the Chief moved smoothly in.

"This lad is rough-cutting this here metal quill preparatory to sizing for pump piston rings, sir."

"I see."

"Instant and willing obedience to orders" is the hortatory phrasing of Their Lordships, Commissioners of the Admiralty, and the exhortation is followed by the more pragmatic "under the penalty of death or some such other punishment as shall be hereinafter mentioned." The threat is, of course, real, so how do we account for the cheerful optimism of Jack? The Game: see what you can get away with. If you're caught, tough titty. The good-natured vendetta of the lower deck against the wardroom is one of the chief sources of amusement to both. It has variations – square-rig (sailors) against fore-and-aft rig (Chief and Petty Officers) – but it is all the Game. You don't get willing obedience with threats.

Sailors have their perks, sanctified by long if officially unacknowledged custom and usage. When I became Captain of my first ship my liquor supply was never locked, nor was my cabin – custom. My steward, Elepheson, was omnipresent and I lacked nothing. I got things I never asked for and some to which I was not entitled – custom. Sometimes when I came back on board after an evening ashore and decided to pour myself a nightcap, I noticed the level of the bottle was a little lower, about three ounces, a tot. Steward's perks – custom (and in another sense, usage).

It was the same in *Rainbow* when Walter Hose was Captain in 1911-17. He told me this story when he was a retired Admiral in his nineties. One of the duties of the bugler boy was to keep gleaming the emergency handsteering wheels abaft the quarterdeck. The forward wheel was artistically decorated around the perimeter, in bold letters on white background, with the battles engaged in by previous ships of this name: *Cadiz, Spanish Armada, Trafalgar,* etc.

A gleaming white duck cover with blue trim protected this shrine from wind and weather. The First Lieutenant had several times complimented the bugler on the well-washed cover.

"Good work, Boy Bugler. Keep it up."

"Aye aye, sir."

One Sunday, Captain Hose complimented the First Lieutenant on the gleaming white-and-mahogany after steering wheels, brightwork glinting in the sun.

"Thank you, sir."

"But," added the Captain (always poking around, he was), "isn't there a cover? May I see that fitted please?"

In a flash it was on – spotless.

"Very good, Number One."

"Thank you, sir."

In the best tradition of the Service, the First Lieutenant would later pass on the praise to the Boy Bugler. He would never realize that he should have taken the praise for himself. There was a detachment of Royal Marines on board, and through the medium of a marine batman, the Bugler had been slipping the wheel-cover into the First Lieutenant's laundry, paid for out of his personal account.

In battle, the Royal Marine Sergeant was responsible, as Captain of the Turret, for the aftermost turret. This entailed drilling the turret's crew so that his ship would hit first, hit hard, and keep on hitting, with never a missed broadside from *his* turret. Also he was responsible for the scrupulous cleanliness – maniacal cleanliness, the troops said – of the RM barracks. (Bootnecks don't live in messdecks like mere matelots.) The general well-being and deportment of the RM detachment was his personal pigeon at all times. Ashore, he was responsible to the Major of Marines as Second-in-Command of the landing party, for spearheading the assault on the beaches of any of His Britannic Majesty's enemies; for disciplining unruly wogs from black through all the delicate gradations of colour to white (wogs start at Calais!); for impressing lesser breeds without the law by parading a platoon of imperturbable mein, clock-like precision, and impeccable dress (pith helmets and webbing pipe-clayed to a spiritual white the Virgin Mary herself would envy, brass work polished to a dazzle, boots boned, brushed, and chamoised to a supple glow far exceeding that of patent-leather dancing pumps.) He was also responsible for the receipt and delivery of the ship's mail and for reminding the navigating officer to wind the ship's chronometers and staying with him until that task had been completed. In addition to this awesome list, the RM Sergeant's knowledge of the art of stealthy work, field training, the lie of the land, grenade-lobbing, and the esoteric principles of enfilading fire far surpassed anything that would be known to a yo-heave-ho-and-a-bottle-of-rum sailor.

Food in the lower deck was seldom bad – mostly good filling stuff: kippers, potatoes, veg. The meat was alright, but after the first week at sea the troops were often down to salt pork, perhaps plum duff occasionally. As I say, good filling stuff, but not satisfactory to a hand with any gastronomic sensibilities.

Chicken coops were rigged in His Majesty's Canadian ships before the advent of refrigeration. The chickens were bought by the officers and the junior steward fed them daily. On a long trip, when the ship's company was down to salt pork and hardtack, they made tempting targets. Jigging a chicken off the galley range with a fish hook was often contemplated but was put aside as being too dangerous. But Jack will always find a way. The Game.

One Able-bodied Seaman found his way by feeding the chickens daily with scraps from his mess: hardtack crumbs, bacon rinds, anything. Once trust had been established and the chicken would eat out of his left hand, he would throttle it to prevent squawks and his right hand would pierce the brain with a sewing needle set in a wine-bottle cork. A shipmate casually taking the air nearby would act as a lookout. The murderer would then leave the dead chicken with her living mates. This operation took perhaps three seconds.

When the junior steward arrived for the routine feeding he would usually throw over the side any chickens that had succumbed to close confinement or natural causes. Jack, keeping a close eye on *his* chicken, would protest to the steward about such waste when a hungry seaman could use the bird. (The stewards were never hungry; they ate the officer's food.) "Me and me mates could use something besides salt pork. A bit of fowl would go good."

"Well, if you want to risk eating diseased chicken, take it."

The first Naval College of Canada opened in the Halifax dockyard on January 1, 1911, and in the first class of twenty-two was Cadet John Grant. "We didn't have many facilities," he told me, "No rugby ground, no cricket field, but we played grass hockey on the hard ground of the dockyard. The academic side was the usual but we had also a tremendous amount of practical engineering. The Parsons turbine, for instance; we'd take out the rotor blades and the stators, generally take it apart and put it back together. But when we first went to sea it was in a coal-burning, triple-expansion reciprocating engine and I didn't see turbines until I went to destroyers in the RN. At the Naval College we did our sea training in the schooner *Diane*."

After two years at the college, Grant and twenty of his Canadian classmates were sent to Great Britain to join the cruiser *Berwick*. Perhaps the "wild colonial boys" came as a bit of a shock to the RN Sub-Lieutenant of the Gunroom of *Berwick* and to Captain Sir John Clinton-Baker; the "civilized" midshipmen from the RN Naval College went to *Cornwall* or *Cumberland*. Be that as it may, Grant says, "It was a very happy, a very *lively* gunroom." They got the usual treatment for the minor misdemeanours – there were certainly no major ones – which was six strokes on the backside with the Sub's cane. "But we never considered it was harsh treatment; we thought it was very just, I think."

Berwick did her work-ups with the Home Fleet, which, in 1913, was of mammoth size. The inevitability of war with Germany had been evident to the First Sea Lord, Admiral of the Fleet Sir Jackie Fisher, for many years and he had scrapped hundreds of obsolete warships, "too old to fight and too slow to run away." The new dreadnoughts were there as well as the older ships which fought in the Battle of Jutland with Admiral Sir David Beatty and his battle cruiser squadron and Sir John Jellico. Then she sailed for Bermuda, headquarters of the North America and West Indies Station.

While at a dance in Barbados, Grant had an experience reminiscent of the lines from Byron's *Childe Harold's Pilgrimage*, "There was a sound of revelry by night. . . ." He was called away on an emergency which turned out to be nothing like Byron's picture of the night before the Battle of Waterloo, however. Upriver from Coatzacoalcos in Mexico – a hundred or so miles south of Veracruz – was a British mining company which had been paying protection to the local bandits. Possibly they had missed a couple of installments, but they were under fire either from their own bandits or the opposition, and *Berwick* was sent there "to protect British citizens and British interests." One Lieutenant-Commander, one Midshipman (Grant), and two armed sailors were sent about half-a-day's steaming up the river to the mine site, and the opposition melted into the countryside. If this seems laughable today it is good to remember that, had this force been killed, a platoon could have been sent, then a company, then a battalion. Whether Britannia ruled the waves would soon be disputed but in

1913, around the world, she certainly did rule the waves and a lot of the world's shorelines too. Just two officers and two sailors brought this microscopic ripple of dissension in a trouble-torn country to a close. But behind these four was the whole might of the British Empire.

The British Consul in Coatzacoalcos was so delighted he threw a king-size bash for the victors. Grant remembers that one of his term mates returned to ship on his hands and knees, "I don't remember whether this was a necessary mode of procedure or whether he was just demonstrating that it was the end of a good day and he was happy."

When war was declared, *Berwick* was back in Halifax with the squadron of Rear-Admiral Sir Christopher Craddock, which was patrolling the east coast of North America, mostly to prevent German merchant ships making a run for home. Grant was transferred to *Suffolk*, another ship in the squadron. Four of Grant's shipmates were midshipmen: Hathaway ("very fine looking, modest, very nice, played the piano for our sing-songs, a promising young officer"), W. A. Palmer ("very brainy, used to be top of the class apparently without having to work"), Arthur Silver ("rather like Hathaway, very well-known Halifax family, keen fisherman and famous for his art in casting"), and Malcombe Cann ("a good mess mate from Yarmouth, Nova Scotia). These four were sent to the old armoured cruiser *Good Hope* when Sir Christopher transferred his flag to her and wanted four more senior midshipmen. *Good Hope*, with the cruiser *Monmouth*, the light cruiser *Glasgow*, the armed merchant cruiser *Otranto*, and the old battleship *Canopus*, sailed to the Falklands, around Cape Horn, and up the west coast of South America to Valparaiso, Chile. Off this coast Sir Christopher was to engage the squadron of Vice-Admiral Graf von Spee who had been obliged to retreat from Chinese waters by the combined forces of the Royal and the Japanese navies (the Japanese were our allies in that war). Spee led his force – the armoured cruisers *Scharnhorst* and *Gneisenau*, the light cruisers *Nürnberg* and *Leipzig* – across the Pacific to Chilean waters; there he was joined by the light cruiser *Dresden*. On November 1, 1914, when the two squadrons met, *Canopus*, Sir Christopher's old battleship, intended to provide heavy fire support, was three hundred miles astern, unable to keep up. The battle was just no contest. Von Spee held his fire until he had Craddock's ships silhouetted against the setting sun, then opened up at 12,000 yards. The superior German gunnery sank *Good Hope* and

22

Monmouth and the rest withdrew to the south. This became known as the Battle of Coronel. Afterwards, von Spee rounded Cape Horn and headed northeast for home, but a little over a month later, on December 8, in the first Battle of the Falkland Islands, he and all his force were destroyed by ships of the local forces plus two battle cruisers sent post-haste from the Home Fleet.

But from our ships sunk at the Battle of Coronel there were no survivors. Midshipmen Hathaway, Palmer, Silver, and Cann became the first casualties of the Royal Canadian Navy. Midshipman John Grant went on to an adventurous time in the remaining years of the war, but there was a certain suitability to his appointment, from 1942 to 1945, as Captain of HMCS *Royal Roads*, our newest Naval College. There, the Coronel Library honours the memory of these first of our young Canadian naval officers to die in the service of their country.

All the wartime classes left the Naval College of Canada and went to the Royal Navy to do their midshipmen's training. The first I met was Lieutenant-Commander Louis Joseph Maurice Gauvreau, RCN, a native of Quebec and the Seigneur de Villery. He had been in Canada's Naval College in the first class of 1911. His son Bob and I played rugger together on the team at St. Mary's High School in Halifax in 1936 and his daughter Maureen would sometimes invite me to escort her to dances for the youngsters at Admiralty House. We were about sixteen. "Cappy" Gauvreau (he ended the war as Captain) would tell us stories of the Great War. I remember one about the Battle of Jutland where he was a "gofer" (go for this, go get that) in a destroyer. "A large shell, about 8-inch judging by the hole, came in a port bulkhead and went out a starboard. It didn't explode, probably because it was armour-piercing shell aimed at one of our battleships. A destroyer's thin skin wouldn't ignite the fuse. Now if it had hit something *solid*, like a winch. . . ."

I also met Lieutenant-Commander Teddy Orde. He had been at the Naval College at the time of the Halifax explosion. The SS *Mont Blanc* was going through the narrows between Halifax Harbour and Bedford Basin when she collided with the SS *Imo*. *Mont Blanc* carried picric acid and TNT. She blew up, laying waste the whole of the north end of the city, including the Naval College. Many cadets were injured by flying glass and Orde lost an eye. When I knew him he had a glass eye; as a matter of fact I was told that he had three, although I only ever saw two: his ordinary one and the one that he would sometimes don for late-night parties, which had the naval ensign in place of the pupil. The third, I was told, was bloodshot, to match his good eye when he had been imbibing too freely the night before.

Then there was Commander Jeffries, who, besides his Great War medal ribbons, had a white ribbon for service in north Russia in 1918-19. Fighting ashore he was, for the tsarists, of course. From these and many others I heard tales of the navy similar to those of the army I had heard from my father and his comrades.

Sub-Lieutenant John Grant joined HMS *Beaver* in the Harwich force escorting cargo ships carrying beef from the Hook of Holland to England and mine-sweeping at high speed in the Channel ahead of the Fleet. At the beginning of 1917 the German battle cruisers had shown up off Constantinople so *Beaver* went to the Dardanelles. On the way through the Mediterranean the British cruisers and about twenty-four destroyers bombarded the Italian fleet at Durazzo, on the Albanian coast. The German submarines were based there and had gone up to the Adriatic. The object was to ruin the base and they did. Grant was the Gunnery Officer and "came to a headland which blotted out my view of the inner harbour. So I shifted fire to horse-drawn artillery which was going up the mountain to get better range, hoping not to hit the horses. In fact, I hoped I wouldn't hit anything even though I was trying to, because our fire power was quite overwhelming and I thought it a bit unfair."

Later, *Beaver* went to Sulina at the mouth of the Danube, then upriver to Galati, Rumania, where the Captain and he were invited to wait upon the Queen. The Bolsheviks and the Loyalists were sniping at each other and rifle fire was constant at ports like Odessa and Sevastapol – "where the Russian Black Sea Fleet lay deserted, not a soul on board." The Bolsheviks were running wild and looting the countryside, "Terrible poverty; people getting shot just for the clothes on their backs. We gave a great deal of our clothing away – and suffered for it later. We took over the telegraph line. Imagine a Sub-Lieutenant and two Able Seamen taking over the Eastern Telegraph Company to keep communications open. The radio station had been destroyed.

"A Colonel Boyle, a Canadian from the Yukon, had equipped a machine gun regiment at his own expense and taken his men to France. He had been able to rescue a lot of Rumanian prisoners of war and get them back to Rumania. That made all Canadians popular there."

At the end of the war, Grant was returned to Canada, a Lieutenant by now, and appointed to the Naval College, which had, because of the damage of the explosion, moved to Esquimalt.

Alfred Charles Wurtele had no naval ancestors but his father had joined the Royal Military College, Kingston, in 1876, the year it opened. (His regimental number was 1.) Alfie joined the Naval College in August 1913. After graduation, he joined HMS *Leviathan* under Captain Marcus Rowely Hill, called by the troops "Makes us really ill." Next came the battle cruiser *Renown* in the Grand Fleet of Admiral Jellico, making sweeps into the Atlantic and waiting for the German High Seas Fleet to come out. "But I was invalided home to Canada – medically unfit. I had a case of poison ivy and the British doctors didn't know how to treat it. I was cured in Canada and returned." Then there was HMS (later HMCS) *Shearwater*, an hermaphrodite rig of steam and sail – jib, staysail, and a trisail on the mizzen. With the little two-bladed propellor going and a following wind she could make ten knots. Barry German, RCN, was the First Lieutenant, "a marvellous fellow, good officer, good tennis player; he had only one arm. Lost the other in a motorcycle accident; it was wonderful to see how quickly he could swarm up a ladder." After he passed his examinations for Sub-Lieutenant in 1917, Wurtele was sent to HMS *Swift* in Great Britain.

"She had just had her stern blown off and her Sub-Lieutenant blown up so they were short-handed. When we were fixed up we were on the Dover patrol, mostly screening the monitors." From 1916 onwards the Germans had mounted shore batteries from Calais to Cap Gris Nez with guns so large they could fire across the English Channel to such ports as Dover, Sandgate, New Romney, and a little north towards Deal. But these were mounted on railroad tracks and hard to pinpoint. The smaller guns were fixed and it was against these that the monitors were sailed. A monitor is not really a ship; it is a propelled gun platform. A hull, engines, compass, and two guns. Speed eight knots, sometimes ten; length about four hundred feet; draught about ten feet; just over three hundred sailors, mostly to man the guns. "HMS *Terror* and *Erebus* and two Greeks, *Glatton* and *Gorgon*, had 15-inch; *General Wolf* had 18-inch – she used to try to bombard Ostend on the southern Belgian coast from ten or twelve miles off. I saw *Glatton* blow up in Dover. That was hair-raising! It was sabotage. There was flame all the way fore and aft. We sent away a boat and picked up survivors but a great many were killed."

Wurtele was at sea off the enemy coast on the eleventh of November 1918, but he got a ringside seat at the surrender of the German High Seas Fleet. At the beginning of the war this had had fifteen dreadnaught battleships, four battlecruisers, thirty-two pre-dreadnaught battleships, nine armoured cruisers, twelve light cruisers, and eighty-eight destroyers. Rear-Admiral Hipper had bombarded Yarmouth, West Hartlepool, Scarborough, and Whitby in December 1914. Admiral Scheer led them to battle at Jutland against Admiral Jellico's Grand Fleet on May 31, 1916. After that the High Seas Fleet – not the whole fleet, just bits and pieces of it – sortied again only three times, twice in 1916 and once in 1918. Now they steamed out into the North Sea to Rosyth under the guns of the Grand Fleet.

"It was well organized. The Germans had their guns trained fore and aft. Our fleet had their guns trained on the German ships all the time. *Swift* was a destroyer leader and we patrolled around the Germans. Then they anchored in the stream and we patrolled them making sure their boats were hoisted, and so on. The German sailors were very despondent; they had a miserable time there. However, they were due for it.

"Then I went to the cruiser *Cleopatra* in the Baltic; this was 1919. After a while there we heard that Canada was taking over the cruiser *Aurora* and the destroyers *Patriot* and *Patrician*. Sure enough, I went to *Patrician* in 1920 and we brought her to Esquimalt. I remember the rig for entering harbour for the hands was number one uniforms and sennet [straw] hats. So, from 1913 to 1920 I learned a few things and saw a bit of the world."

Alured P. Musgrave's naval antecedents go back a bit. His father joined the Royal Navy in the 1880s and went to *Britannia*. "One of his term was the Prince of Wales, he who became King George V. I remember a little story of how my father was sketching (he was good at it), and the Prince leaned over his shoulder and smirched the sheet. My father swung around and slugged him. I would have thought that one could get put in cells for less than slugging the future king. Nothing happened, of course. Later, he served in RN ships in Esquimalt in the nineties."

Musgrave joined our Naval College in May of 1914. "I remember Commander Nixon there. He was a wonderful man. When he was hearing defaulters we learned not to give long contrived stories as to why we had erred. He'd say, 'Why?' and we'd give a shorter version. 'Why?' and we'd cut it more so it seemed silly even to us. We learned it was best just to say 'guilty'; we were, usually, and it saved time. He'd just stop your pocket money or give you extra drill. We got little leave, anyway."

Musgrave was appointed midshipman in 1917 and went to the cruiser *Roxburg*. From there he went to *Minotaur* in the Home Fleet, mostly doing the northern patrol up to Iceland seeking any German ships that might get into the Atlantic or Norwegian convoys. These convoys ran from the Orkneys to Bergen. Two cruisers and four destroyers for a screen. "We and our sister ship, *Shannon*, would go out with our destroyers. We were just bait, really, to see if the German heavy units could be coaxed out, although I suppose the convoy cargos were needed. Just below the horizon were ships of our battle squadron. They would come up if we ran into any Germans but the only one we saw was a submarine, and we didn't see her, we saw her torpedo which passed between us.

"Then we went with the fleet to Invergordon for the surrender of the German High Seas Fleet. That was quite a sight. We went out in two lines: battleships, battle cruisers, cruisers, destroyers. We met the Germans steering the opposite course, coming up between us. We turned 180 degrees, slowed, and we were on either side of them, guns trained on them.

"Funny the things you remember. Drafting of sailors was stable in those days. You knew your hands. We had been in commission since 1912, out on the China Station at first, Weihaiwei. We had one hand who had joined as a Boy Seaman and he went Able Seaman, Leading Seaman, Petty Officer, Chief Petty Officer, to Gunner in that ship. A brilliant fellow. He got drafted ashore after she finally paid off, couldn't handle it. Didn't know what was going on, really. Drank himself to a discharge, I heard.

"We colonials had trouble with the RN midshipmen; they were younger than us, from Dartmouth Naval College, but senior to us; they joined at age fourteen. There were eight of them and six Royal Naval Reserve. The Sub-Lieutenant of the gunroom would beat us at the drop of a hat. Six cuts across the bum, you bent over a table. What for? For looking sideways at him, anything. We got sick of this and we eight Canadians threw all the RN and RNR out of the gunroom and barricaded ourselves in. We RCN midshipmen were up in front of the Captain, of course, but he saw the problem. We were too old to be browbeaten by youngsters. So he cancelled all seniority in the gunroom; or rather, we were all the same, whatever *that* was."

After the war, Musgrave was sent to a trawler as a Sub-Lieutenant. She was on fishery patrol. This didn't suit him at all.

"I decided that I didn't like the navy and I put in my resignation and asked that it be forwarded to Ottawa. I was just feeling bolshie; at that age one is very intolerant. It was forwarded. But it arrived the day after our Chief of the Naval Staff, Rear-Admiral Sir Arthur Kingsmill, had left and before the new CNS, Commodore Walter Hose, took over. There seemed nobody in charge but a clerk. He stamped it "Approved." I went into business here in Victoria and didn't return to the RCN until 1939."

Niobe was a lightly armoured cruiser of 11,000 tons, built in 1899. She could make seventeen knots and had sixteen 6-inch guns, twelve 12-pounders, five 3-pounders, and five 2-pounders, two 18-inch torpedo tubes; complement, about 700. Her Captain in 1910 was a native of British Columbia, Commander W. B. Macdonald, RN. She reached Halifax on October twenty-first and was met by the fishery protection vessel, Coast Guard Ship *Canada*. She was manned by an RN crew that was to be replaced by RCN.

Rainbow was a lightly armoured cruiser of 3,600 tons built in 1891. She could make twelve knots and had two 6-inch, six 4-inch, eight 6-pounders, two 14-inch torpedo tubes; complement, about 270. Her captain in 1910 was Commander J. D. D. Stewart, RN. She sailed from Portsmouth to Esquimalt via the Strait of Magellan – fifteen thousand miles. She steamed into harbour on November seventh.

Recruiting posters told Canada that Boy Seamen could enter from age fourteen, Seamen from age fifteen, Stokers from age eighteen. The period of service was seven years from age eighteen. Canada was in prosperous times and pay was set higher than in the Royal Navy; some British sailors transferred. By 1912, 350 young Canadians had joined their navy. Both ships plied up and down their coasts showing the flag, *Niobe* rather blotting her copy book by going aground on Cape Sable and having to be towed off by *Cornwall* (which was damaged on an uncharted rock doing so). By 1914, five cadets who had started their training in *Canada* in 1909 were Sub-Lieutenants; nineteen Midshipmen were serving in *Berwick*; thirteen cadets of the class of 1912 were joining the Fleet; and the rest were still at the Naval College. The money to run the navy had dropped from $1.7 million in 1910 to $1.2 million in 1912 to $1 million in 1913 to $.6 million in 1914. Enrollment in the Naval College had dropped from twenty-eight in 1911 to four in 1914. In that year the total strength of the Royal Canadian Navy was 350 and that of the Royal Canadian Naval Reserve was 250. The RCN was not in good shape on the eve of war.

On July 29 the warning telegram was received from Admiralty; war was imminent. Prime Minister Sir Robert Borden was in Muskoka; he returned to Ottawa August 1. All hands were recalled from leave and the navy was empowered to enrol volunteers. *Niobe* and *Rainbow* were to ammunition to wartime capacity, store, coal, and ship warheads on torpedoes. On August 2 all wireless stations were taken over by the navy and the RNR called out. The RCNVR was ordered to report to Esquimalt dockyard. The Victoria *Times* said:

> Esquimalt presented an animated appearance. . . . Its busy streets reminded one of the days, not far back, when the British fleet made Esquimalt its home port. Throughout the afternoon and well on into the evening, many Victorians and a number of people visiting this city took the street cars to the naval town to look over what may be the scene of an engagement.

On August 3 the port of Esquimalt was closed to all except naval vessels. *Rainbow* sailed on her first war patrol. On August 4 German troops entered Belgium. Britain sent an ultimatum to Berlin. At midnight it had not been answered. The war telegram was received from Admiralty. But in 1914 the waging of war was more gentlemanly than in 1939 (when a U-boat sank the unarmed liner *Athenia* the first day), and a period of ten days' grace was given for German merchant ships to leave Canadian ports. Aemilius Jarvis of the Navy League of Canada told Ottawa that he had fifty former RN ratings who would serve in *Niobe*. On August 7 the ten days' grace was rescinded.

On the east coast, the North American squadron of Rear-Admiral Sir Christopher Craddock's cruisers was based at Bermuda and Halifax. These were his flagship, *Suffolk*, leading *Bristol*, *Berwick*, *Essex*, and *Lancaster*; later the battleship *Glory* joined. It was with these that *Niobe* patrolled. Her first voyage was to escort the Royal Canadian Regiment to relieve the British garrison in Bermuda. Her complement shows the growing pains of the infant RCN just four years after being born. Of her officers, 16 were RN, 18 were RCN (mostly junior), and 10 were reserves. In the lower deck, 194 were RN, 28 RCN, and 441 reserves. *Niobe* was sent to the Strait of Belle Isle to intercept a German cruiser reported there. The *Dresden* and the *Karlsrühe* were known to be in these waters. No show. But from Cartagena to Boston, ninety-one enemy ships had sought sanctuary in east-coast harbours. Until the autumn of 1915 *Niobe* was part of the blockading squadron off New York and none escaped. But the North Atlantic winter was fierce, she was old and tired, and she put in to Halifax to refit. So decrepit was she found to be that this was not done and from then on she served as a depot ship.

On the west coast were HMCS *Rainbow*, HMS *Shearwater*, and HMS *Algerine*. To the war here was added a personal touch. In the Mexican Civil War some time earlier various governments had established squadrons to help their nationals. At Mazatlan, Mexico, the crews of SMS *Nürnberg* and later *Leipzig*, *Algerine*, and the Japanese *Idzumo* saw much of each other, no doubt upon the premise of "know thine enemy," but also, we may be sure, because a party is always welcome and the brotherhood of the sea is a very real thing and transcends differences of opinion between governments.

On August 2, Commander Hose had received a signal telling him that *Leipzig* had cleared Mazatlan and he was to sail south "and guard trade routes north of the equator." On August 3 he sailed. All in Esquimalt dockyard who saw her sail were in no doubt that, if the adversaries met, then they were now seeing the last of *Rainbow*. *Leipzig* was thirteen years younger and six knots faster; although her guns were 4-inch as opposed to *Rainbow*'s 6-inch, they were modern. Also, incredible as it may seem now, *Rainbow* had no high-explosives, but ancient shells filled with gunpowder. She was a training ship and only half up to a wartime crew. The Victoria *Times*, however, was not as pessimistic, "The *Rainbow*, a faster boat and mounting two six-inch guns, is more than a match for the German boat." Later the same day, Hose was told that war had been declared. The enthusiasm of the Victoria *Times* was matched by that of National Defence Headquarters in Ottawa when a staff officer with a fine sense of glory sent the signal:

Received from Admiralty. Begins – "NÜRNBURG and LEIPZIG reported August 4th off Magdalena Bay steering north." – Ends. Do your utmost to protect Algerine and Shearwater, steering north from San Diego. Remember Nelson and the British navy. All Canada is watching.

Commander Hose was to coal in San Diego. On August 4, *Leipzig* was in fact in Magdalena Bay, just south of California; Captain Haun's orders told him to join up with Admiral von Spee, then leaving far eastern waters for the west coast of North America. *Nürnburg* had coaled in Honolulu and joined von Spee; this was not known to *Rainbow*. On August 11, *Leipzig* sighted the approaches to the Golden Gate. Haun had asked that coal, lubricating oil, and stores be sent to him at sea. The German consul met him offshore and told him that the Americans were unfriendly and that *Rainbow*, *Algerine*, and *Shearwater* were looking for him. That we were looking for Haun bothered him not a jot or a tittle; he knew our armament.

But if he was to be a commerce raider he needed coal. He entered San Francisco, took on board five hundred tons, and departed within twenty-four hours. He steamed north perhaps as close as eight hundred miles off Cape Flattery, the entrance to the Juan de Fuca Strait and to Esquimalt. *Rainbow* steamed south. They never met. *Leipzig* joined von Spee's squadron and went with him to the Battle of Coronel.

Rainbow entered San Francisco wanting five hundred tons of coal. No. Hose was told that neutrality laws required that he take only enough to get to a British coaling station, and he got fifty tons. On August 11, 12, and 13, *Nürnburg* and *Leipzig* were still reported to Hose as being off San Francisco. The air was filled for many days with much false information. *Rainbow* returned to Esquimalt. On September 3 *Newcastle* had departed Esquimalt to seek *Leipzig* but she had steered a westerly course into the Pacific to meet von Spee off Easter Island. After Coronel she was sunk with most of the others at the Falklands.

From 1914 to 1917, *Rainbow* patrolled from Panama to the British Columbia coast. In her as well as in *Niobe* the difficulties of manning an infant navy were apparent. In 1914 she had 8 RN officers, 5 RCN, and 2 RCNVR. In the lower deck 45 were RN, 139 were RCN, and 52 were RCNVR. By 1917 the Japanese navy had taken responsibility for the whole of the north Pacific. To keep *Rainbow* seaworthy would require an extensive refit. In view of a mounting enemy offensive on the east coast and a shortage of trained men, *Rainbow* was paid off and used as a depot ship.

Commander Hose and most of his crew moved to the Atlantic patrols. In 1916, before America entered the war, the German U-53 and the cargo submarine *Deutschland* visited US ports. *Deutschland* was large even by Second World War standards, 1,700 tons; most sea-going boats of that war were about 700 tons. She loaded crude rubber and industrial metals for a Germany blockaded by Allied ships. Her range was seventeen thousand miles on the surface at six knots; a handy cruising speed was twelve knots. Her sister boat, the U-151, carried two 5.9-inch guns, two 22-pounders, machine guns, and four torpedo tubes. Submerged she could do fifty miles at a speed of seven knots. Thus she was a "diving boat" rather than a true submersible. But she was formidable enough as a surface raider. In June 1918, U-156 under Kapitänleutnant von Oldenburg sank ships from Newport to Boston before moving north and sinking the British *Dornfontein* off Nova Scotia in August, followed by *Luz Blanca*. Then he sank the schooners *Nelson A. Holland* and *Agnes B. Holland*. These sinkings were leisurely affairs. In accordance with the procedures of the day he stopped the *Gladys M. Hollett*. The form was to give the crew time to take to their boats taking with them all they wished – not much in a nineteen-foot dory. Then the U-boat would take what stores she required, and sink the vessel by scuttling charges. Schooner captains were sometimes given an official receipt for their vessel, sometimes invited on board for a drink before they set out to row ashore – a hundred, two hundred miles. Of course, they were usually picked up before they had to cover the full distance.

U-156 developed a particularly good *ruse de guerre*. She captured the steam trawler *Triumph*, manned her, armed her, and sailed in among other ships that recognized her as "friendly." She got seven schooners and the 4,700-ton *Diomed* this way. She was followed by Kapitänleutnant Otto Droscher's U-117 which laid three mine fields and sank nine fishing vessels and three steamers in American waters before moving north. Off Newfoundland he sank three more schooners. One, on August 30 was the *Elsie Porter*, out of Le Havre with a German-speaking crew. Droscher let the crew escape on the dorys before sinking her but kept her captain, Edward Esenhaur, on board for interrogation and a drink. Some hours later he stopped the *Potentate* – another German-speaking crew – and invited her captain on board for interrogation. Then, after inviting both captains to the wardroom for refreshments, he set them adrift.

Walter Hose was appointed Captain of Patrols and put in charge of the forty or fifty small boats (it varied early on) that tried to cope with these predators from Newfoundland to Nova Scotia – a thousand-mile beat. By the summer of 1918 the number was 116 vessels – 87 belonging to Admiralty but built in Canada, the remaining 29 Canadian.

These were the first Canadian warships to face an attack on Canada. They were built in Canada, manned by Canadians, commanded by an officer of the Royal Canadian Navy. Towards the end they were supported by air patrols from Halifax and Sydney, six from each station. They did as well as could be expected, these patrols. They may even have acted as a deterrent to the Germans. "Nevertheless," as naval historian Gilbert Tucker says in *The Naval Service of Canada*, "the bricks which the Israelites were forced to make without straw were not necessarily the best in Egypt."

He has a point. Since her earliest days, Canada has provided soldiers for whatever was necessary: the American Revolution to defend our borders, from the War of 1812 for a similar purpose. In 1918 (and again in 1939) soldiers were sent overseas within a month or so of war being declared; this army grew from 3,000 to 650,000. The RCN grew from 600 to 9,600. For over two hundred years soldiers had been known across our land, sailors only on our waterways. There was a public constituency supporting soldiers; the Royal Canadian Regiment, for instance, since 1883. This nation-wide tradition was lacking for sailors. Building a force where a man has to fight in an alien element takes longer, much longer.

In the naval and political climate of the early 1900s, when the battleship was queen of the seas and Admiral Fisher and Admiral Tirpitz were in a race to see which of them could build the most, a deep-sea blue-water navy seemed natural for Canada to achieve. *Rainbow* and *Niobe* were obsolescent when we got them and intended only as training ships. The First World War proved that we were a small-ship navy. In the climate of the 1930s, the battleship was still queen and Admiral Sir Dudley Pound and Admiral Raedar still believed in a deep-sea blue-water navy. It is one of the ironies of history that the small craft of the Atlantic patrols in the First World War and the corvettes and frigates of the Second World War proved more suitable to Canadians. A more bitter irony (for Germany) is that had Admiral Raedar listened to Kommodore Karl Dönitz and built U-boats instead of battleships and cruisers, the outcome of the 1939 to 1945 war could well have been different.

These are the fancies of an historian but indispensible to understanding our sea heritage. What Admiral Morison has written of the sea operations of the USN and Captain Roskill of the RN, Canadians like Gilbert Tucker, Alec Douglas, Marc Milner, and Michael Hadley do for the RCN – proper historians, these; not yarn-spinners. For in time of war we see through a glass darkly; in the retrospect of peace we see more clearly what might have been.

What is clear to me is the courage and devotion to duty of our naval ancestors. "Cappy" Gauvreau, Teddy Orde, and the two score young officers and a hundred men who served in the Royal Navy. Lieutenant Stanley Nelson was killed in action in HMS *Indefatigable* in the battle of Jutland; Lieutenant William Maitland-Dougall in HM submarine D 3; Midshipmen Silver, Palmer, Cann, and Hathaway at Coronel. I know their sense of duty and in the ones I got to know, their sense of fun.

I first met Admiral Hose in the 1950s when I was on the staff of the Flag Officer, Naval Reserves – I looked after the cadets in thirty universities from Memorial in Newfoundland to the University of Victoria (a thousand of them; now *that's* a back-up of trained officers in case of war!). I was asked to speak to the cadets at a dinner at the naval division in Windsor, Ontario, HMCS *Hunter*. Walter Hose was on my right and I, with the port passed several times and in a flight of impassioned oratory, pointed with a sweep of my arm, "And there, to starboard, were fifty more U-boats. . . ." I struck him. He tumbled backwards. Alarm and consternation all round. A rush to pick him up. He rose, unaided, ancient greenish dinner jacket awry, port on his boiled shirt, medals askew. A breathless hush as I held his chair and he re-seated himself with more calm than expected. "I hope you don't make a practice of hitting Admirals, young man."

Every Wednesday at noon he made his call to the wardroom of *Hunter*. All the ship's officers were busy enough around town at their various professions but they all took time off to lunch there Wednesdays. One day I heard this gem of practical wisdom. "Engage von Spee? Of course, but we would have come a cropper. To know where he was, exactly, at *that* time, would have been *Rainbow's* main contribution. *Newcastle* could have given *Leipzig* what for. But we were under complement and not really worked up. My main armament was my wireless, and *that* only had a range of two hundred miles."

A few years later I was driving a squadron in the Great Lakes and had the honour of giving the Admiral lunch on board. The First Lieutenant had invited us to the wardroom first for him to meet the officers. His reception was polite, in the extreme. I was furious that my officers would be so gauche and, well, they almost *stared* at him, in respectful silence, of course. "Don't look at me as if I was a display in a naval museum. May I have a gin, please?" Walter Hose died in his nineties having spent more time on pension than he had in the navy. This was a great source of satisfaction to him. The day his death was announced, the Ministry of Finance in Ottawa declared a half holiday.

I still see John Grant; he is more limber than one would expect at ninety. He visits *Royal Roads* occasionally. When Pip Musgrave was Captain of our Signal School at St. Hyacinthe during the war, one of his Signal Lieutenants was John Charles. They and their wives dine at the Union Club occasionally. I dined with Alfie Wurtele – and two hundred and fifty other serving and retired officers of the RCN – at *Royal Roads* in May of this year, our seventy-fifth anniversary. For the forty years since Wurtele retired he has been busy, for many years as Reeve of Esquimalt. Men still stop him and say, "You won't remember, sir, but I was an Able Seaman under you when you were a Lieutenant. . . ." In good health and respected by all, he can be seen at the Admiral's garden party, the Lieutenant-Governor's garden party, meetings of the Royal United Services Institute, the Naval Officers Association, the New Year's Levee. . . . The present Admiral, Bob Yanow, was host to fourteen retired Admirals that night, five of whom had held his position before him.

In the Beginning

Their sayings and doings stir English blood like the sound of a trumpet; and if the Indian Empire, the trade of London, and all the outward and visible emblems of our greatness should pass away, we should still leave behind us a durable monument of what we were in these sayings and doings of the English admirals.

Robert Louis Stevenson, 1881

Canada's motto, "From Sea to Sea" is not strictly accurate, but I suppose it is now too late to change it. "The Seas Surround Us" would be closer to the truth. To our south, the St. Lawrence River and the Great Lakes make a path into our heartland for two thousand miles. Our sea coast from the Atlantic Ocean through the Arctic to the Pacific Ocean measures, if we log it from cape to cape, twenty-three thousand nautical miles. If we measure the shoreline of all our peninsulas, inlets, and bays, we arrive at the figure of thirty-four thousand nautical miles – five million square miles of territorial waters. The richness of our nautical past and the insistance of today's tensions makes us a maritime people.

From the first hollowed-out log a hundred thousand years ago to the hundred-foot, oar-driven hulls of the Pharaohs of six thousand years ago, to the warship biremes and triremes of the Phoenicians of only two thousand years ago, and right up to today, the moving of men and materials over water has taken more labour than any other human endeavour. But to those who know her, the sea is not a barrier but a highway. Lief, son of Eric the Red, in the year 1000, sighted the coast of Labrador. He named it Helluland, which describes what it looks like but which actually means "Land of Rocks." He went south to what became Nova Scotia and New England but found our forests claustrophobic and never came back.

Under the aegis of the houses of Tudor and of Lorraine and Guise, the ships of imperial France and England brought mariners, explorers, and settlers to this empty continent. Well, empty for all practical purposes – from the Atlantic to the Pacific, from the Gulf of Mexico to the Arctic, there were three million Indian and Inuit, but with the gift of aplomb that superior weapons bestow, these native peoples were shouldered aside. The French and the English navies had a series of brouhahas from the 1400s to 1700s when the French fortress of Louisbourg in Nova Scotia was captured by British soldiers landed from the ships of Admiral Boscawen. A fleet of twenty-five transports and thirteen warships sailed from France under Admiral La Jonquiere to retake Louisbourg and, in a running fight with the ships of Admiral Anson, were fought to a standstill and five transports were captured. French naval power waned. After the capture of Quebec by General Wolfe and Admiral Saunders, the French navy went home for all time. The Royal Navy stayed.

We in the Royal Canadian Navy call the Royal Navy "The Old Firm," just as they do in the Royal Australian Navy, the Royal New Zealand Navy, the Royal Indian Navy, the Royal South African Navy, and in other naval forces of the old Empire. The Empire became the Commonwealth and some of those countries chose to leave, but the connection with the mother navy is still strong; they left, after all, only a few years ago when one considers the five hundred years since The Old Firm began, for all practical purposes, to run the naval affairs of the world. Foreign navies were patterned on the Royal Navy. The German *Kriegsmarine*, I have been told by officers who served prior to the Great War, seemed anxious to get a word of praise from RN officers when their ships were in company. And right up to the eves of both wars there was a great deal of social to-ing and fro-ing between the ships' companies all over the world. The Italian navy has a sad apocryphal story told about it; but like all apocryphal stories it conveys the vital truth of the matter. In the thirties an Italian officer suggested to an RN officer – they were drinking together in Taranto – that perhaps what he had heard about the RN efficiency might not be true.

"Not true? Good Heavens! My dear fellow, why not?"

"You always seem to be out practising."

Yes, practising and fighting for five hundred years. Henry VII, who ruled from 1485 to 1509, was the founder of the Royal Navy. In 1982, in the tradition of King Henry's Admirals, Chief of Defence Staff Sir Terence Lewin, Admiral of the Fleet, sent his navy of 114 ships – 37 RN and 77 Merchant Marine – steaming 8,500 miles to the Falkland Islands to show that the Royal Navy still had teeth. An old firm indeed.

Some will say that King Alfred, who ruled from 871 to 899, was the founder of the Royal Navy but this is not really so. He was, however, the first king to see that Britain's enemies must be met at sea; he was the first great English naval leader. An archeological dig at Sutton Hoo in East Anglia brought up a thirty-eight-oared ship of Alfred's period, leading to the theory that some of his ships might have had up to sixty oars and a small square sail. Across the North Sea and the English Channel they sailed with ease but not far out into the Atlantic. The connection between the Royal Navy and the Merchant Navy started then; when the ships were not needed for war they were rented to merchants to export and import goods. Conversely, Alfred either rented or impressed merchant-built ships when he needed them for war. (As did Queen Elizabeth II through Terence Lewin in 1982.) But King Alfred's navy withered after his death and the lessons had to be learned all over again nearly six hundred years later.

Before Henry VII, some of the great English kings – Edward III or Henry V, for example – built warships, but this was *a* Royal Navy. *The* Royal Navy started with Henry VII in 1490 and fought last in 1982 in the Second Battle of the Falklands.

Thus began, five hundred years ago, the Royal Navy's *Tales of the North Atlantic* (not to mention the rest of the globe) with its explorations, scientific discoveries, ignominious defeats, and glorious victories. This background is, I think, necessary in order that landsmen may understand the pre-eminence of the Royal Navy in this book. The traditions of the Royal Canadian Navy, its customs and background, sense of fun and sense of duty, come to us by right of inheritance from mother to daughter. And seventy-five years of growth, from our first faltering paddle in the shallows around Canada's shores to our confident strokes in the deeps of the North Atlantic (not to mention the rest of the globe), have added a few idiosyncratic Canadian customs and traditions, but we never, and we are proud of this, "threw out the baby with the bath water." What suited the Canadian ethos we kept, but we added our own customs and traditions. My bloody oath, we did!

Henry VII built the *Regent* and the *Sovereign*. He was a business man, was our Henry, and both these were merchant ships, but they carried 225 guns to ensure that their cargoes reached their destination. The money rolled in. Henry died with a million pounds of gold in his treasury – and those were the days when a pound was a pound, you might well add. A frugal government he ran, some say miserly, a trait of his borne ruefully by patient sailors. What else could they do? The British sailor wants only to be left alone to practise his profession. This governmental characteristic is one of those passed on from Britain to Canada. Our government has run its navy with frugality, some say parsimony. How else can we explain our periodic inability to pay or feed our sailors, the lack of fuel to sail our ships? And worse, how explain our current lack of ships? If professional competence was the first cachet of the British sailor of the 1400s, and rueful patience the second, the same can be said of the Canadian sailor of the 1900s, whose government perhaps has not a million pounds. Henry's "a penny saved is a penny earned" attitude was extraordinary in those days of profligate monarchs. Perhaps, with the prosperity that a good navy brought to his people, a prosperity which continued throughout the reigns of his son Henry VIII, of Elizabeth I, of Charles II, and even beyond, Henry VII was the source of Napoleon's sneer that the English were "a nation of shopkeepers." They were, but they were sailors as well, as Admiral Lord Nelson showed the French in 1805 at the Battle of Trafalgar.

Henry VIII loved the sea and built ships that made his father's look like fleet tenders. He built *Henry Grâce à Dieu* (which the insular British nicknamed *Great Harry*) and the *Mary Rose* (which foundered off the Isle of Wight and which was raised last year under the aegis of Commander the Prince Charles, RN). Henry VII built four ocean carriers; Henry VIII built eight-five.

In 1492, Columbus made a landfall at San Salvador. In 1497, Vasco da Gama rounded the Cape of Good Hope, struck out northeast and made a landfall on the coast of India at Calicut. The world was opened up to the Royal Navy – regrettably by foreigners; Henry VII had refused to support Columbus. He did, however, support John Cabot. In 1496, he issued letters patent granting to

Our well-beloved John Cabot, citizen of Venice, to Lewis, Sebastion and Santius, sonnes of the said John, full and free authority, leave and power upon theyr own proper costs and charges, to seeke out and finde whatsoever isles, countries, regions or provinces of the heathen and infidels, which before this time have been unknown to all Christians.

At five o'clock of a Saturday morning, the twenty-fourth day of June in the year of Our Lord 1497, Cabot and the eighteen-man crew of the King's ship *Mathew* made a landfall on the northern tip of Cape Breton. Cabot explored the coast from there to the north, named the islands of St. Pierre and Miquelon, and took his departure back to England from Cape Race, whence east-bound merchant ships and warships have always since departed. On Sunday, August 6, *Mathew* dropped anchor in Bristol. Henry VII awarded Cabot ten pounds "for having found the new isle," the new found land. In the years that followed, the fishing fleets of Bristol, Le Havre, La Rochelle, and Lisbon arrived annually for the cod run; they still do. From 1500, Canada's coast was no longer *terra incognita*.

Queen Elizabeth I loved the navy for its colour and dash but also for much the same reason as her father and grandfather had – the profits were spectacular! Her privateers, pirates to the Spaniards, were a speculative business financed by her and by syndicates. Sir Francis Drake's famous voyage in 1580 paid a dividend of 4,700 per cent. Piracy and patriotic compound interest formed a happy marriage. Out of her share, the queen paid off the entire national debt. The £42,000 of Drake's profits went to the Levant Company, out of whose profits the East India Company was founded. That company's profits, during the seventeenth and eighteenth centuries, started England's foreign trade. (John Maynard Keynes once calculated that the £42,000 of Drake's booty would have accumulated by 1930 to the actual aggregate amount of Britain's foreign investment, £4,200,000,000 – a hundred thousand times greater than the original investment.)

Britain's prosperity brought the search through the uncouth northern seas for the Northwest Passage to India. After Captain John Cabot* came Jacques Cartier in 1534 to explore Quebec and inland up the St. Lawrence to Mount Royal, Donnacona. He saw the westward path up the St. Lawrence and the Ottawa rivers. Samuel de Champlain reached Lake Huron in 1612. The *coureur-de-bois* Jean

---

* I belong to The Company of Master Mariners of Canada. Captain John Cabot – a direct descendant – is Area Master for British Columbia.

Nicolet found Lake Michigan; the dissidents Pierre Radisson and Médard Chouart des Groseillers went north of Lake Superior to Hudson Bay. By 1710, freight canoes, a hundred or more, plied the Great Lakes; by 1800, they had been replaced by a thousand or more schooners. Henry Hudson of our Hudson Bay, John Davis of our Davis Strait, Martin Frobisher of our Frobisher Bay, probed north and west; William Baffin of our Baffin Island reached 77 degrees 45 minutes north in 1616. In 1789, Alexander Mackenzie became Canada's first rapid-transit proponent on the river that bears his name, travelling from Lake Athabaska to its arctic delta – three thousand miles – in 120 days. In 1850, Captain McClure sailed in HMS *Investigator* into Canada's Arctic from the west, got as far as the strait that bears his name, was iced in, and continued on foot and sleds eastward until he and his men were picked up by HMS *Resolute* and *Intrepid* and returned to England from the east.

Yes, we have been a maritime people for a long time. In fact, one of the expeditions searching for Sir John Franklin and his men was mounted in 1848 by Commander W. A. S. Pullen, RN, ancestor of the Rear-Admiral Hugh Pullen, RCN, who appears in these pages. Hugh's brother, Captain Tommy Pullen, RCN, commanded the navy's arctic patrol vessel HMCS *Labrador* and furthered arctic exploration in the 1950s and 1960s. Pullen and others charted anew Canada's arctic coastline, changing the charts of Canada's north. Tommy Pullen still sails the Arctic as Ice Master for scientific expeditions and for various petroleum companies. The Pullen family have amassed in the RN, the RCN, the Merchant Navy, and the Coast Guard since 1700, a total of 451 years of service. And that is but one Canadian family.

From the 1500s on, Canada's west coast saw war between the white-winged sloops, frigates, corvettes, and line-of-battle ships of Russia, Spain, and Britain. Spain had founded missions as far north as Yerba Buena (San Francisco) and wanted to extend her rule northwards. Don Mañuel Quimper sailed into Esquimalt Harbour under the naval flag of imperial Spain in *Princessa Real* (the captured British sloop *Princess Royal*) in 1790 and named it Puerto de Cordova after the forty-sixth Viceroy of New Spain. He erected a cross at Valdez y Bazan, where one day the third Royal Canadian Naval College, Royal Roads, would be founded. During these years, several Spanish ships were based in Nootka Sound.

The Tsar of all the Russias had had a foothold on this continent since 1728, when, after discovering the strait that divides Asia and America, Vitus Bering, with Tchirikow, had sighted Alaska. Russian fur traders and whalers began to probe south. Canada's position was its usual one – a sparsely-populated country between great powers. The Royal Navy showed the flag with the arrival of Captain Cook in 1778 in Nootka Sound. In 1790, the Nootka Sound Convention said that the coast between Alaska and San Francisco was open to the peaceful commerce of England and Spain. Captain Vancouver discovered Puget Sound and circumnavigated Vancouver Island. Alexander Mackenzie made his way through the Rockies to the Pacific Ocean, Simon Fraser came down the river that bears his name, and David Thompson reached the Columbia River. By 1826, there were thirteen trading posts on the west coast. By 1856, the naval dockyard had been established in Esquimalt.

In 1837, the Pacific Station was shown for the first time in the Navy List with the appointment of Rear-Admiral of the White C. B. H. Ross, RN, as Commander-in-Chief. His squadron patrolled the seven thousand miles from Cape Horn to Cape Flattery to Point Barrow in northern Alaska. In the war with Russia between 1854 and 1856, his ships attacked Petropavlovski on the southeast coast of Kamchatka. Between 1837 and 1910, when the RCN took over, followed thirty-six Royal Navy Commanders. In November of 1910, our first light cruiser, HMCS *Rainbow*, glided gracefully into the sparkling waters of Esquimalt Harbour against a background of dark greens of fir and spruce and the yellow of the broom and gorse. Since then, through thirty-three Commanders of the Royal Canadian Navy from Commander Walter Hose to Rear-Admiral Robert D. Yanow of 1985, Canada's west-coast interests have been served.

Our east-coast navy has a similar story. In 1749 England had a most unseemly monarch in George II, a greedy, strutting, and noisy man whose heart was still in Hanover. Bonnie Prince Charlie, the last of the Stuarts, the Pretender to the Throne, the "King over the Sea," had fled to France where he was given sanctuary because of his value as a nuisance to the British Whig government, themselves rascals, a wealthy, brilliant, rakish aristocracy. The pious, steady middle-class was impotent still; a wretched populace had many soldiers discharged and sailors on the beach with the peace of Aix-la-Chapelle. Louisbourg, Nova Scotia, had been won from the French in 1745 with the blood of British soldiers and sailors, and now England returned it to the French in exchange for France's recognition of the House of

Hanover. Good news for the King – the end of the Pretender. Good news for the merchants – unmolested trade. Good news for the people – "Peace in our time."

But the colonies in America howled. Nova Scotia was pointed like a dagger at the heart of Boston. Right up to the time of their tea party, New Englanders were loyal, if not to a stupid king, then to the mother country. There must be a garrison between them and the French, preferably in Halifax, and settlers, preferably Protestant to offset the papish French Acadians settled on the Bay of Fundy.

On May 14, 1749, Lord Cornwallis, in the *Sphinx*, sailed into the inlet which would become Halifax harbour. He had thirteen sail in company, carrying 2,576 souls. Cornwallis was incorruptible, though an aristocrat. It was spring and the winter was over and gone. The lush green matched that of Ireland, open spaces at the water's edge speckled with white petals of wild strawberry, the forest showed its demure ladies' slippers and bluets. The vernal days were warm as the feathers of a nesting bird. The merchants of Halifax and New England started a healthy trade. They built Saint Paul's church and soon there were streets with four hundred lanterns, these, alas, a target for roistering sailors. The port of Halifax was open to trade and a naval dockyard was started.

Captain Cook wintered in the port of Halifax in *Pembroke* before he navigated and led Admiral Saunders's fleet of thirteen ships of the line and the plodding transports carrying General Wolfe's seven thousand soldiers to the assault on the city of Quebec in September 1759.

From 1755 on, the Commander of the North American naval station, Vice-Admiral the Honourable Edward Boscawen, RN, made Halifax his northern base. In 1814, Admiralty House was built as C-in-C's residence, at that time Vice-Admiral J. B. Warren, Bt, KB. (It was sedate enough then, no doubt, but when it was an officers' mess in the thirties, forties, and fifties and my shipmates and I, flushed with wine, took our ease there, it was a rambunctious place. Since 1910, the Canadian Admirals have lived in more modest quarters, as befits our national psyche, British elegance finding little fertile soil in Canada.) By the 1860s, Nova Scotia had a fishing fleet of three thousand vessels, schooners mostly; the fame of one in particular, *Bluenose*, was told from Savannah to Port Said, from Cape Horn to North Cape. In 1910, HMCS *Niobe* steamed sedately into the port of Halifax under a backdrop of gold and red autumn leaves. The first Canadian Senior Naval Officer in Halifax was the ubiquitous Captain Walter Hose in 1919 and from him to Vice-Admiral J. C. Woods, CMM, CD, in 1985, Canada's east-coast naval interests have been well served.

So it was that from the 1700s Canada was open for business from sea to sea – *a mari usque ad mare*. The *Pax Britannica*, enforced by the Royal Navy, ran for a hundred years until the Great War of 1914-18, years during which Canada could develop unmolested. During these years the traditions, the folklore, and the customs of the Royal Navy were handed over to us and many became our own. From 1910 until the eve of the Second World War in 1939 we continued to grow while under the ever-lessening tutelage of the RN. We took it from there.

The Highest Award for Valour

For courage mounteth with occasion.   *King John,* Shakespeare

The salient fact about courage is that all men are capable of it. The man who has never been shot at is in awe of acts of courage that he has read or heard about. The only universal fear that I ever noticed in untried men was that they might not show courage when the time came and they were first under fire. The most universal satisfaction that I have ever seen in men, and I saw it in ship after ship, is exemplified by the look of placidity on their faces when their moment of truth has passed and they, in their innermost hearts, judge that they did indeed acquit themselves as they should have. The faces of men who have not faltered when under fire for the first time look as if they now had a personal knowledge of the God from whom all virtues flow – including the virtue of courage.

Every man I know who has received an award for valour has realized that had one of his shipmates been in *that* position at *that* time, they would have done what he did. Awards are received for being at the right place at the right time. When a Captain is awarded some high commendation for a hazardous battle brilliantly fought and says, "I am proud to accept this award and I do so in the name of my ship's company," he is not mouthing an empty phrase. He means it. "No man is an Island, entire of it self" is particularly true of a ship's company, a platoon, or a gun's crew. All members rely on their mates and are painfully sensible of the fact. Raw courage is admirable; trained courage is awesome. To say any of this takes away not one jot or tittle from those who wear badges of courage. For, in the final analysis, another quote is even more appropriate, "Greater love hath no man than this, that a man lay down his life for his friends." And the Victoria Cross is the most aristocratic of recognitions.

It has always seemed to me entirely appropriate that the ultimate badge of courage, the Victoria Cross, was instituted by a queen who fought a long rearguard battle against a constitutional monarchy that in many ways she had done more than anyone else to create. A constitutional monarchy, to Victoria, implied a democracy, and, as we know the term today, this was against her regal sense of what was right and proper. But the Victoria Cross epitomizes democracy. Admirals with mere CBEs or even DSOs or DSCs are envious of junior ranks with VCs. I do not use "envious" in the pejorative sense; it is only that they would rather have a VC than all the other medals that adorn their uniforms.

The few winners of this highest award for valour have mostly agreed with Queen Victoria's dictum that duty is paramount of all the Christian virtues. From her accession to the throne in 1837 to her death in 1901 she restored public confidence in a tarnished monarchy. A very shaky lot the kings and queens of England had been! The accession of the Hanoverian kings (George I and his successors) made future succession always a matter of doubt even though they had been weaned from the divine-right-of-kings complex over the last hundred years or so. But Victoria's sense of duty as wife, mother, and queen and her simplicity, dignity, and evident honesty in accordance with her code of ethics, endeared her to her subjects in a unique way.

Through my father I met Milton Gregg and Georges P. Vanier, two army VCs of the Great War; the simplicity of the lives of these remarkable men was evident – they had walked with kings and not lost the common touch. Gregg I saw from time to time when he was my father's colonel, when he was a cabinet minister in Ottawa, and when he was Canadian High Commissioner to Guyana. My relationship with the Vaniers was more personal. A son, Jock, was a Sub-Lieutenant in the aircraft carrier *Magnificent* in the fifties when I was the Fleet Gunnery Officer; both Catholics, we had many a quiet chat on most unmilitary subjects. Madame Vanier was the Chancellor of the University of Ottawa when, after I retired from the navy, I taught there. General Vanier in Government House in Ottawa was the same simple man as the shivering evacuee plucked from a sardine boat in a pelting rain off Dunkirk by *Fraser*. (He had stayed at his post in Paris a little beyond the point of safety and had had to hoof it to the coast.)

In the Maritimes, simplicity of life is a centuries-old trait. Peter

Newman has said that the aristocracy in Canada is subject to rapid change and is based not on where you come from but on what you have done. We may infer that, in the financial world he observes, he means what you have done *recently*. This is not so in Nova Scotia. There, money is only part of being an aristocrat, and an incidental part at that, not necessary at all. At the top of this aristocracy of Nova Scotia were the schooner Captains. In fact, any seaman ranked high on the social scale even though they were often not the type of men one would invite to tea on Sundays. They were men in an honourable calling. Rough, yes; profane, often. But many had the simple elegance of the true aristocrat. Such a man was Petty Officer William Hall, VC.

I was not inducted into the folklore of Nova Scotia until in the 1930s when, in my high school years, I first met the girl who would become my wife. Alma's grandfather had been a shipwright who had helped to build the schooner *Bluenose* in Lunenberg at the turn of the century. Other forebears had been merchants in Halifax and her father was a chemist in that city. He was not like the pharmacist of today, but a man who mixed his own medicines with mortar and pestle. He also doctored rumrunners when brawls with foreign seamen or longshoremen along Water Street resulted in many a slash or cut whose stiching-up an MD would have had to bring to the attention of the constabulary. His payment was the apotheosis of simplicity – a two-gallon keg of rum left anonymously at his back door in the dark hours of Christmas morning. Through Alma's father and mother, uncles and aunts – those of English and Lunenburg extraction – and through some of my schoolmates at St. Mary's College whose fathers owned the rumrunning boats which plied their joyous trade between St. Pierre and Miquelon, the West Indies, and the inlets of Nova Scotia, I learned the lurid legends of those seafaring people. Petty Officer William Hall was part of those legends. On a gusty day in November 1947, I attended a ceremony in Hantsport, Nova Scotia, when the Flag Officer, Atlantic Coast, Rear-Admiral Cuth Taylor, unveiled a memorial to this humble hero.

William Hall had been born in Horton's Bluff, Nova Scotia, in 1827. During the War of 1812 his father was being shipped from the west coast of Africa to the United States in a slaver. A British frigate intercepted the slave ship, brought the cargo to Halifax, and freed the slaves. The government of the day helped them to find work and to settle in Nova Scotia. Hall's father, after adopting the name "Hall" from the Nova Scotian benefactor who found him work with a farmer

in Hants County, married a girl who had also escaped slavery by fleeing to one of the ships of the British fleet which captured Washington
in 1812. When William was old enough he joined the Royal Navy as a
seaman in HMS *Rodney*. If his father and mother had felt a debt to the
navy that had set them free, this debt was repaid by their son, William.

Able Seaman William Hall remained in the *Rodney* through the
Crimean War. He was awarded the British and Turkish medals – the
former with the Sebastopol and Inkerman clasps – and then went to
HMS *Victory*. After a short time in *Victory* he was drafted to HMS
Shannon, where he served as Captain of the Foretop. *Shannon* was
escorting troops to China in readiness for insurrections expected to
break out sooner rather than later, but on Sunday, May 10, 1857, the
Indian Mutiny broke out in Meerut. The Indian Mutiny, more properly called the Sepoy Rebellion, spread rapidly. The Sepoys took
Delhi and Cawnpore, where they killed all white women and children
as well as the white soldiers, and Lucknow found itself beseiged with
only a small garrison to hold the walls.

The seige of Lucknow is not often mentioned as an example of the
versatility of seapower, but such it undoubtedly is. From those parts of
the Empire close enough to provide help, expeditionary forces were
sent to swell the ranks of the relief army assembling in India. That is a
soldier's story, but the navy was not absent from the ranks of those
soldiers. In the Great War sixty years later, sailors would serve the
guns and stand to in the trenches in Flanders just as they did in India.
From Hong Kong, two naval brigades sailed in the *Shannon* and the
Pearl. They arrived in Calcutta in August. These 450 men had six
8-inch guns, two 24-pound howitzers, and two field guns. Not a crush-
ing force, considering that Lucknow was beseiged by fifty thousand
Sepoys, but one not to be ignored – as we shall see.

The ships steamed eight hundred miles up the Ganges River to
Allahabad. Sweating sailors manhandled the guns (the unwieldy
8-inch guns had to be left behind) and fought their way to Cawnpore;
there they joined up with the soldiers preparing for the relief of
Lucknow. The remnants of the garrison were still holding out – a
handful of men in the residency now in ruins and supplies running
out. The total relief force to face these fifty thousand mutineers was
five thousand. A walled enclosure, the Sekandarhagh, was the first
bastion, then the Shah Nujiff, a walled mosque. By mid-afternoon of
the day of the attack the 91st Highlanders and the Sikhs had taken the
Sekandarhagh at bayonet point. The mosque was more difficult; its

walls were seven feet thick and it was garrisoned by thirty thousand Sepoys.

The *Shannon*'s brigade dragged their guns to within four hundred yards of the wall and commenced their bombardment. Their shot had no effect on the massive structure. Two hundred yards from the wall and heavy rifle fire from the mosque inflicted dreadful casualties, but still no breach could be effected. The Highlanders attacked but were repulsed with heavy losses. The naval guns moved forward again, this time to within twenty yards. Soon the crew of one gun were all dead. Of the other, only Hall and Lieutenant Young were still alive, and Young was badly wounded. Hall calmly served his gun under murderous fire. Sponge out, reload, fire, sponge out, reload, fire. On and on. He did his duty at the gun as he had been trained to do. Fire, sponge out, reload, fire. Finally one of Hall's rounds opened the walls. The Highlanders poured through the breach thus effected. The Sepoys fled. It was over.

Sir Colin Campbell, who had commanded this action (and who would later become Lieutenant-Governor of Nova Scotia), said of Hall's devotion to his duty:

> Finally, in one of the most supreme moments in all the age-long story of human courage, Hall fired the charge that opened the walls and enabled the British to push through to the relief of the garrison and ultimately to the quelling of the mutiny and the restoration of peace and order in India.

William Hall served in the navy until he retired back to Nova Scotia in 1876. He never married. His last public appearance was in Halifax in 1901 in a parade of veterans during a visit of the Duke of York (later King George V, the Sailor King). Hall was honoured by riding in a carriage in the Royal Procession.

Men of my generation of Canadian sailors have tended to stop for a few minutes at Hall's memorial as they pass through Hantsport in the 38 years since it was unveiled by Admiral Taylor. For the 75 years of the Royal Canadian Navy's existence, Hall has been part of the folklore we inherited from the Royal Navy, and this year, 128 years since Petty Officer William Hall breached the wall at Lucknow, the present generation of Canadian sailors will pay their respects to a man whose sense of duty they have inherited.

Nearly nine decades after Hall's deed of derring-do at the relief of

Lucknow, another Canadian sailor was awarded a Victoria Cross – Lieutenant Robert Hampton "Hammy" Gray, VC, DSC, RCNVR. King George VI awarded the VC to Gray on November 13, 1945. The citation read:

> The King has approved the award of the Victoria Cross posthumously to the late Lieutenant Robert Hampton Gray, DSC, RCNVR, HMS *Formidable*, for valour in a successful attack on a Japanese destroyer in Onagawa Gan on 9th August, 1945, in the face of fierce opposition, an action which cost him his life.

Gray was the only Canadian sailor to be awarded the VC in the Second World War and he was killed just six days before the Japanese surrender.

Since our naval origins started with the Royal Navy, it is to my mind appropriate that the king who elevated Gray to the peerage of gallantry, King George VI, had gone through the training ships and had himself been awarded a Mentioned in Despatches from the Battle of Jutland by his father, King George V, who had gone through the same arduous route of junior officer's training, subsequently commanding the gunboat *Thrush*. Before him Edward VIII went through the naval colleges and served his midshipman's time in HMS *Hindustan*. Edward VII was more of a soldier but not ignorant of life aboard ship; he spent three years aboard HMS *Bacchante* in a world tour. (The name of that ship was not inappropriate, I hear, for the nature of the tour.) The line, regal and naval, has been going for quite some time. Queen Elizabeth II's consort, Prince Philip, served in destroyers on Russian convoys during the Second World War (and I first met him when I was in *Sioux* and he in *Whelp*). After the war he commanded a frigate. Their son, Prince Andrew, fought at the Second Battle of the Falklands in 1982.

So, Hammy Gray's is but one in a series of awards that continued to be bestowed by the monarchy up to the Korean War in the 1950s when Bob Welland won his second DSC. The signifigant point is the *continuity* of our Canadian navy. It does not detract one tiny bit from Gray's deed to say that he did no more than he was trained and expected to do.

Hammy Gray was born on November 2, 1917, in Trail, British Columbia, twenty-four hundred miles west of the birthplace of William Hall and an immeasurable distance above him on what Canadians somewhat diffidently refer to as the social scale. He went to public and high schools in Nelson, British Columbia, and graduated with a Bachelor of Arts degree from the University of British Columbia in 1940. While at UBC he was an editor of the university year book, *Totem*, and he started his military in the Canadian Officers Training Corps.

It was a wonder that he finished his BA at all, he told me, so keen was he to get into "the fun that had started in Europe in September 1939." Hammy was always a man who planned his future even at an age when most university students had the attitude of the Cavalier poets of the sixteenth century, *carpe diem* – enjoy the day. The war might be fun but it would not last forever, and a BA would help him get established in civilian life when the war ended. The week he graduated, he joined the Royal Canadian Naval Volunteer Reserve as an Ordinary Seaman, Officer Candidate, and in July was shipped overseas for training with the RN. After finishing the training common to all naval officers, he went to the naval air station at Gosport for flying training. Following the usual hairy take-offs and bumpy landings he got his wings and was sent back to Canada for further training at Collins Bay, near Kingston, Ontario. He was promoted to Sub-Lieutenant in December 1940. Six months after he left UBC he was qualified to cause alarm and despondency among the enemies of the Crown – and he did.

Gray began with 757 Squadron in Winchester, England, and after other squadrons – 795, 803, and 877 – he joined the aircraft carrier *Ilustrious*. There is a saying in naval aviation, "There are old pilots and there are bold pilots. But there are no old bold pilots," but Hammy seemed destined to prove it wrong. He was cautious in the sense that only a fool would ignore proven tried-and-true precautions in a hazardous occupation, but that being said, he pushed himself and his kite to the limits and sometimes beyond. He was good, certainly; he had to be to put a plane through what he did and live to discuss it with a Commander (Air) who did not always approve. He was destined, in my opinion, having watched thousands of carrier take-offs and landings, to be an old bold pilot. Until, of course, the moment came when the only way to achieve his mission – sinking a Japanese destroyer – was to forget caution and take the consequences. Caution when an enemy *has* to be sunk is *not* a virtue!

In August 1944 he joined HMS *Formidable*, then part of the Home Fleet based at Scapa Flow in the Faeroe Islands. I was in *Sioux* and it was there I met Hammy in many of the ship-to-ship visits which were just about our only form of entertainment in harbour. Our main job in

51

the Home Fleet that year was taking convoys, mostly loaded with war equipment for the Russian army, to Murmansk to enable the Russians to maintain pressure on the German eastern front. It was a three-thousand-mile voyage up an enemy-held coast. In summer, daylight lasted the clock around and air and U-boat attacks were frequent. In winter, a few days after steaming north, darkness and gales were constant. Welcome diversions from these convoys were attacks on enemy convoys hugging the Norwegian coast. Usually a flotilla of destroyers and one cruiser, we would dash in under cover of darkness, annihilate the convoy – a piece of cake, really – and get out under our air cover before daylight brought the threat of being clobbered by the *Luftwaffe*. The *Formidable* seemed to be our constant companion and very glad we were to have her with us.

The main threat to shipping in the area was the German battleship *Tirpitz* – the Lonesome Queen we called her. She sat in Alten fiord for years and, apart from one raid on Spitsbergen, she never fired her guns in anger. Her mere presence forced our Commander-in-Chief, Sir Bruce Fraser, to have each convoy accompanied by a covering force of at least one battleship and several carriers. Heavy and light cruisers and up to forty destroyers screened the heavy ships and the convoys. The only time *Tirpitz* left harbour with apparently serious intent she caused the scattering of convoy PQ 17 off northern Norway which resulted in the loss of most of that convoy from air and submarine attack, and she did nothing, returning to base within thirty-six hours. She didn't really have to do anything. The very fact that she was there made us hold up sending our fleet to the Pacific where the sea battles were reaching a climax. When Sir John Tovey was C-in-C he had sunk the *Bismarck*. Sir Bruce had sunk the *Scharnhorst* the previous Christmas. *Tirpitz* was the only battleship the *Kriegsmarine* had left and we couldn't get at her. To all of us this was infuriating. Five times we went after her, finally attacking her in her anchorage because she would not come out.

It was on one of these forays that Hammy Gray first made his mark. With three battleships, three large and four small carriers, and cruisers and destroyers galore, we steamed to about fifty miles off the coast. Barracuda torpedo bombers and corsair fighters were the striking force. Forty-one years have passed since that day, but the picture is as clear to me as though it was yesterday. In August, first light in those latitudes is just after midnight. About a hundred planes took off, circled the fleet once to get formed up, and headed for Norway, just over the horizon. It was a clear warm morning, the breeze light, the sea smooth. Away they went and we in the fleet waited, mentally flying in with our planes.

Gray led his section of fighters to strafe the shore batteries that ringed the fiord; his job was to divert them from the torpedo bombers who alone could sink such a behemoth as *Tirpitz*. No luck. Smoke generators obscured the target. All the torpedoes were fired but as far as we could determine they either hit rock or perhaps the zariba steel net that protected the great ship. Five days later we went in again. Again Hammy led his flight, this time against three Narvik-class destroyers which were as capable of hitting our bombers as were the shore batteries. The hail of fire against our planes was intense and shattering. Nevertheless, Gray pressed home his strafing attack to point-blank range. That he shot up his Narvik good and proper was certain, but he, in return, had most of his rudder shot away. He bumbled and staggered back to mother. The flight deck of *Formidable* was like Toronto airport at March break. It is a general rule that damaged aircraft come in last so as not to foul up the flight deck with their wreckage, so for about half an hour Hammy waited his turn, circling *Formidable* until his controller called him in. He might as well have come in first. His landing was neat but not gaudy. No sweat. He knew how to handle his kite; the arrestor wire caught his hook, stopped him, was released, and he taxied to the parking area.

For this effort he was Mentioned in Despatches "for undaunted courage, skill, and determination." Whoever writes these awards up certainly caught the essence of Hammy Gray – courage, skill, determination.

Tirpitz was finally sunk by the RAF. I say this with professional regret, but more power to our gallant comrades in light blue. Sir Bruce was now free to take command of the British Pacific Fleet and out he went. In April 1945, *Formidable* joined him. The sea battle was moving northward to the Japanese homeland, and by July installations on the coast of Japan were being attacked. Gray's flight was strafing airfields in the Tokyo area. On July 24 he led a strike on ships in the Inland Sea, damaging one merchant ship and strafing airfields and a seaplane base. On July 28, another attack sank a Japanese destroyer. Here it was that he picked up his DSC "for determination and address in air attacks on targets in Japan." "Address" is one of those arcane

Admiralty terms, faintly perplexing to Canadians. Imagine the question, "What did you get your medal for, Daddy?" And the answer, "For address, my boy, for address."

Strange are the ways of their Lordships of the Admiralty. This fanciful bit of levity on my part assuages some of the grief I still feel. Hammy's death was only twelve days off.

On August 9, Gray led his flight against Onagawa Gan naval base. Five warships were in the harbour and there was, of course, the usual circle of shore anti-aircraft batteries. The combined fire of the guns was murderous. Hammy chose his destroyer and headed for it. He was hit; then a second time; streaks of flame marked his attacking course. Hit twice and on fire, he held to his course and did not release his bombs until he was within fifty yards. They hit. The destroyer sank. And Hammy Gray's plane hit the waters of the bay.

Hammy Gray's war was over. Six days later it was over for everyone. Japan surrendered. Hammy would never use his BA to get established in civilian life.

Vice-Admiral Sir Philip Vian, not a man given to hyperbole, said:

> I have in mind firstly his brilliant fighting spirit and inspired leadership – an unforgettable example of selfless and sustained devotion to duty without regard to safety of life and limb. The award of this highly prized and highly regarded recognition of valour may fittingly be conferred on a native of Canada, which Dominion has played such a great part in the training of our airmen.

There was a side to Hammy Gray which non-flyers like me never saw. It was the cold professionalism of a pilot with five years' experience in fighting in aircraft. The odds would always be weighed, but he would never be in any doubt that when the stakes were high both he and his plane were expendable.

Training Ships

If you ask me what is the good of education, the answer is easy - that educa-
tion makes good men, and that good men act nobly, and conquer their
enemies in battle, because they are good.

The Republic, Plato

The type of training that seamen of Canada's navy undergo today owes much to the training ships of Great Britain – amended up to the 1980s to suit the Canadian ethos and modern technology. But for the first fifty years, officers and men of our navy relied upon the training ships of the British.

After the Napoleonic wars and all through the Pax Britannica, the British were the political and naval masters of the world. The Royal Navy controlled all the seas and the Merchant Navy brought the gold and frankincense and myrrh and ivory and spices and anything else of value to that sceptred isle. James Thompson rhapsodized:

> When Britain first, at Heaven's command,
> Arose from out the azure main,
> This was the charter of the land,
> And guardian angels sung the strain:
> "Rule, Britannia, rule the waves;
> Britons never will be slaves."

Britons were the masters, too true. In India fifty thousand Britons ruled ninety million natives. Garrisons were everywhere in the colonies and the protectorates; and provisioning, ammunitioning, and (later) coaling stations were in every latitude and longitude. By about the 1850s, some million and a quarter Britons, including fifty-six thousand soldiers in the imperial garrisons, were living abroad. Oscar Wilde voiced the thoughts of Victorians:

> Set in this stormy Northern sea,
> Queen of these restless fields of tide,
> England! what shall men say of thee,
> Before whose feet the worlds divide?

During the incessant wars between the reign of King Henry VII and that of Queen Victoria – over three hundred and fifty years – the Merchant Navy suffered in the hands of the Royal Navy by impressment of its men and seizure of its ships. Trained able seamen – ABs – were always at a premium. Now that peace allowed men to enjoy the blessings of the land and the fruits of their labours, the Merchant Navy began to prosper.

In 1850, the Board of Trade drew up an "Act for Improving the Condition of Masters, Mates, and Seamen, and maintaining Discipline in the Merchant Service." In 1851, this became law. In 1857, HMS *Hastings*, an old two-decked ship of sixty guns, jury-rigged and with small steam power, became a training ship for the RN and cruised local waters encouraging volunteers; she, in a sense, was the forerunner of the Canadian Naval College at Halifax and Esquimalt, and, later, HMCS *Royal Roads*. In the late 1800s the Boy Seaman training ship was HMS *Impregnable*; HMS *Powerful*, the youth training ship. Technical training ships became necessary as equipment became more complicated – HMS *Vernon* for the Torpedomen, HMS *Pangborne* for the Engineers when steam entered the navy, and HMS *Excellent* in 1830 for the Gunners as gun ranges increased from one thousand to forty thousand yards.

The sea-going careers of many of the men who tell these tales started in the training ships whose histories are briefly laid before you here: Many started in the Merchant Navy training ship *Conway*.

Conway in 1859 was but a recent step in the history of world trade: first-year cadets were called "new chums" but the ship itself was a new boy in the ancient history of the commerce of the world. John Masefield, himself a *Conway* boy, caught the feeling:

> Quinquireme of Nineveh from distant Ophir,
> Rowing home to haven in sunny Palestine,
> With a cargo of ivory,

And apes and peacocks,
Sandalwood, cedarwood, and sweet white wine.

Stately Spanish galleon coming from the Isthmus,
Dipping through the Tropics by the palm-green shores,
With a cargo of diamonds,
Emeralds, amethysts,
Topazes, and cinnamon, and gold moidores.

The first *Conway* sailed with His Majesty's Fleet in the Napoleonic Wars. It was the second ship of that name in the Navy List that became the training ship. As you can see from her picture she was a frigate, what is called a "jackass frigate," a sixth-rate, 652-ton man-of-war of twenty-six guns, launched at Chatham in 1832, and carrying a complement of 175 men and boys. On her first voyage she sailed to Port Royal in Jamaica; she was in the Pacific in 1837; the Yangtze River in the Chinese war of 1840; the Cape of Good Hope in 1843; a flagship at Portsmouth and Queenstown until 1857; and then a coast guard ship at Devonport until 1858. The *Liverpool Mercury* for May 19, 1859, carried a whole page on her, part of which read:

THE SCHOOL FRIGATE *Conway*

To the attraction of that tempting resort Rock Ferry there has been added the frigate *Conway*, now metamorphosed into a boarding school for intending seamen. . . . The steamer that runs to *Hastings*, south of the slip, also attends upon the *Conway*, north of the pier. There, denuded of her twenty-six guns, and deserted by fighting seamen, the *Conway* rides at anchor, ready for active service in the cause of youthful education and civilizing commerce instead of naval warfare, and yet easily reconvertable, in case of improbable emergency, into her original capacity for attack or defence. . .

During forenoons, half the cadets worked in the schoolrooms on academic subjects – with a strong leaning to mathematics and navigation – and the other half worked on deck and aloft: at noon they changed around. Two years in *Conway* counted as one year to your Mate's Certificate after you got to sea. In 1865, Queen Victoria granted an annual prize of £50 "to encourage the boys to acquire and maintain the qualities which will make the finest sailor. These consist of cheerful submission to superiors, self-respect and independence of character, kindness and protection to the weak, readiness to forgive offence, desire to conciliate the differences of others, and above all, fearless devotion to duty, and unflinching truthfulness."

Alas, in young boys these qualities are not always easy to come by.

One hot afternoon on a half-holiday two boys were in the library, one on duty there and the other under stoppage of leave. How to have a cooling swim? There was no good asking permission. But if one fell out of the after port and the other jumped in to save him, who could condemn them?

Splash.

"Man overboard! I'll get him."

Splash.

The duty cutter's crew were called away to pick them up. As it pulled up to the ship's ladder the boys saw, to their horror, that the Captain stood there.

"What are you doing out of the ship without leave?"

"Please, sir, I fell overboard, sir."

"Not another word. Go below, shift into dry clothing, and fall in on the quarter deck."

The Captain asked the second cadet the same question:

"Why were you out of the ship without leave?"

"Please, sir, I jumped in after him."

"Good boy. I am delighted with you."

The hero received £5 and a gold watch from the "survivor's" parents. The two rascals agreed he would have to keep the watch but they would share the money. The Royal Life Saving Society gave him a certificate, the Liverpool Shipwreck and Humane Society awarded him a first-class silver medal.

There is a story which has been going the rounds since the 1870s about the windsail that is spread between the fore and mainmasts, to send the breeze to the mess decks below, it being sewn into a round funnel as it went below deck. It was the custom of the seniors to lash tight the lower end of the windsail funnel, then, going on deck, to seize new chums and hurl them in. Soon the lower end would be filled with writhing and twisting bulges. The seniors would then go to the hold with marlinspikes and prick the bulges in the bag. When they tired of this, one of them would report to the Officer of the Watch, "Please, sir, I am afraid that some of the new boys are skylarking in the windsail." The Officer of the Watch would go below, release the wretches, and put them on report.

A score of men I served with in the RN and the RCN started their nautical training in *Conway*. Take James Butterfield, for instance. A man born to the sea is our James. I met him first when we served together in HMCS *Micmac*, he as Navigator – "Pilot" – I as Gunnery Officer – "Guns." James cannot remember a time, even as a small boy, when he ever thought of anything else to do with his life. At the Duncan Boarding School on Vancouver Island, he lost his heart to the Canadian Pacific Empresses: *Empress of Russia, Empress of Japan.*

At age twelve he was having tea with his mother at the Cowichan Bay Inn and an elderly gentleman sitting in the corner asked the innkeeper if he could be introduced to James's mother. He was Captain A. E. Aikman, the general manager of the Canadian Pacific Empress Lines (Pacific Service). Now, in many chronicles the expression "a likely lad" is found, meaning a certain type of boy, high-spirited, bursting with health, restless and wanting to get cracking, energetic as blazes and needing a certain amount of firm direction. Captain Aikman thought James "a likely lad." If ever Mrs. Butterfield agreed that her son should go to sea, he said, she should get in touch with him. And so it came to pass that James, later that same year, was taken to see Captain Aikman and signed on as a cadet for the *Empress of Russia* four years later – in August 1939.

James Butterfield joined *Conway* at age fourteen in 1936: his uniform was also his first pair of long pants. In his years there were 150 cadets, mostly from the United Kingdom and the dominions, the colonies, and the protectorates; but also from the continent: there were two German counts, Pfeffer and Winter, and two Russian princes, Tolstoi and Sukulov. The royal families of Europe sent their progeny to train in the schools of His Britannic Majesty's Royal Navy and Merchant Marine. James joined the *Empress of Russia* after graduation, got his Mate's Certificate, sailed in other ships, joined the navy in 1944, and is now master of *Queen of the North*, running between Victoria and Alaska. "To paraphrase what Dr. Johnson said about the city of London, if you're tired of the British Columbia coast you're tired of life itself, for the *Queen of the North* and the B.C. coast hold all that life has to offer. I'll die believing it."

Wilf Pember joined the Royal Navy on October 11, 1918, and credits himself as being the man who stopped the First World War. "You see, when I joined, the Kaiser heard of this secret weapon we had just got in the navy and he called off the war within a month, November 11." He joined *Impregnable*; bow to stern from her were *Inconstant* and

59

Black Prince – all wooden ships of the line. There was also an old hulk, the *Circe*, which, with her upper deck and masts removed, was used for a swimming pool.

The Royal Marines Recruiting Sergeant who signed him up asked, among other things, "You got any identifying marks, scars?"

"Just this one on my thumb, sergeant."

"Is that all you got? What about the one between your legs?"

In his innocence, poor Wilf didn't know this standard joke on Boy Seamen.

When boys joined, the first thing was to feed them. In the galley they were given a big basin – no cups and saucers in those days – containing cocoa with blobs of fat floating on the surface, a hunk of bread, and a slice of bacon. "While drinking this cocoa I had my first introduction to cockroaches. One fell off the deckhead right into my bowl. You suck the stuff between your teeth and strain the darn things off."

The training was mostly in seamanship on board, swimming in the hulk, and parade drill ashore in Devonport. The discipline was strict and unyielding but mostly fair. Stoppage of leave was the usual – not that there was much, usually from noon to 5 P.M. on Saturdays and Sundays. The other punishment was six strokes of the cane. This was rare; generally the boys wanted to do well and conformed to the ship's routine laid down by the Powers That Be. Up to twelve strokes could be awarded but Pember never saw it. He got six, just once. He still thinks that he was set up for this by Petty Officers who thought that no boy should leave the training ship without being caned at least once. Apparently, he said, he had been told to get his hair cut but he can't remember to this day. Disobedience of orders, said the Petty Officer, and he was paraded in front of the Captain. "He," said Pember, "with a great smile, ordered six cuts."

Now the navy can make an impressive ceremony of everything: the parading of the Queen's Colour in the presence of the monarch; the White Ensign when the monarch is not present; the Sunset Ceremony with guard and band and sunset gun (this is impressive in many ways but particularly, I always thought, when the Chief Yeoman of Signals, looking at the ship's clock, reports, to the second, "Sunset, sir," and the Officer of the Watch replies, "Make it so," thereby confirming that the sun may indeed now set); the piping of the side when the Captain comes on board and all hands on the upper deck freeze into immobility; and the caning of a Boy Seaman Second Class. All the other boys are assembled in the recreation space (in *Impregnable*, anyway; a nice touch of irony, this), the culprit is strapped over a box horse, as was Wilf on this occasion, duck pants tight around his stern end, his Divisional Officer and the doctor in attendance, and the Master at Arms standing by with his six-foot cane, giving it occasional flicks to get the whoosh of it. The doctor came over to examine Pember to see that he was fit to take punishment.

"Boy Pember fit for punishment."

"Carry on, Master at Arms."

ssssst-CRACK.

"One."

The doctor came over and took a look. "Carry on, Master at Arms."

ssssst-CRACK.

"Two."

And so on up to six.

"It was damn near six minutes before I got these six cuts. I couldn't sit properly for a week."

Pember left the training ship, joined HMS *Cairo* on the China station in Weihaiwei, was rated Ordinary Seaman, landed with an armed party to settle a difference of opinion between warring provinces ("dead bodies floating down the river; theirs, not ours"), then rated Able Seaman, sent home to qualify Torpedoman, then rated Leading Seaman, another China commission, then patrol craft, destroyers, and battleships, then out to Halifax. While in Canada he transferred to the RCN and went all the way up to Lieutenant Commander. He doesn't regret his time in the training ship or in the navy, "I can't think of anything else I'd rather have done."

When Pat Budge joined the Royal Navy at age sixteen in 1923, he was sent to *Impregnable* as a Boy Seaman Second Class. Like Pember, the first thing he was given was a tepid mug of cocoa with blobs of floating grease and then his class were turned in for the night. He and another boy were given a hard time by the others of his class because they were still wearing their schoolboy shorts. They were backed into a corner and had put up their dukes when the Master at Arms came along with a stonachie in his hand and threatened them with "death or such lesser punishment as may be hereinafter mentioned" and they were piped down.

Next morning they were awakened to the pipe, "Early whirly, boys muster through the spray." They fell in outside a gun casement, stripped naked, cold as charity, and went into the gun casement to live

61

steam mixed with a disinfectant. Twenty screaming boys! The training in 1923 was much the same as in 1918, seamanship and parade ground. Parade training in duck suits in the middle of winter. Budge remembers the Chief Gunner's Mate who drilled them on the parade ground ashore, "Red nose, little, lean, very competent." When first learning the intricacies of marching and squad drill it is easy to get confused and so it came to pass one day that Boy Budge displeased his instructor who came striding over and stood behind him.

"What's the matter with you?" and slashed Budge across the backside with the chain of his whistle.

"You know, I'd never been whipped before and although I was sixteen, tears of humiliation came to my eyes and rolled down my cheeks. Then the Chief came to the front and looked at me and, I realize now, was ashamed." Years later Budge, now a Leading Seaman Torpedoman, met the Chief and had the opportunity to say "Chief, I was a Boy Seaman under you and you did me a lot of good."

The human side often shines through the harsh regimen and gives a luminosity to the navy which those who have not served are prone to miss. One afternoon in the first dog watch the boys were shifting to night clothing and the pipe came through, "Boy Budge, lay aft."

"Oh, what have I done now?" Budge went aft to the brow and there to his amazement, standing on the jetty, were his mother and father and the neighbour next door.

"Is this your mother and father, Boy Budge?"

"Yes, sir."

"You may have them on board."

His parents had never been on a ship before and as far as Budge was concerned civilians never boarded His Majesty's ships. He was terrified of taking them through the Seamen's messes to get to the Boys' mess forward "because I thought they would poke Charlie at me and there might be some hands just finished bathing or something and running around with no clothes on. I didn't realize then how basically chivalrous the sailor is. They'd have respected my parents just as if the Captain had walked by. So I took my mother and father and our neighbour along the upper deck to the forecastle and down the ladder. My mother, a typical English lady, said she would like a cup of tea. But the tea cannister and the sugar were locked up and the Petty Officer had the key. If I'd had any sense I'd have asked the Leading Hand; anyone in the mess would have fallen over themselves to look after these two ladies and my father."

But they all had a nice chin wag and the guests left. When they had gone, the Divisional Petty Officer chewed Budge's ear off, "You give your mum a cup of tea?"

"No, PO, the tea caddy was locked."

"Why didn't you come down the PO's mess and tell me? For that matter, you could have brought them down there and we'd have given them a cup of tea."

The first *Excellent*, a 74-gun ship launched in 1787, fought in the Battle of Cape St. Vincent against a Spanish fleet of twenty-seven ships and was commanded by Captain Horatio Nelson. She fought other actions off the Brittany coast, in the Mediterranean and in the West Indies until she became the gunnery school. The second *Excellent*, a 104-gun ship launched in 1810 to the same design as *Victory*, fought the French at Toulon, took part in the blockade of Genoa, was damaged, and became the second school. The third started her life as *Queen Charlotte* (100 guns) and fought the French fleet off Brest. After further actions she became the final floating gunnery school; the shore establishment was built in 1891 and it was there that I learned the art and the science of naval gunnery. *Excellent* was docked at Whale Island, Portsmouth, and was thus always known affectionately as "Whaley."

As the great gun began to dominate the tactics of these sea battles so did the status of the men who manned the guns increase. A gun carelessly handled is as much a danger to its crew at the breech end as it is to the enemy facing the muzzle. Instant obedience to orders is essential; that those in charge are perfect in their knowledge – not good, not very good, perfect – is essential. Thus, the Master Gunner was supreme. A sober, steady man who had come up through the hawse pipe from Boy Seaman, usually; he had been rated Seaman Gunner, then Captain of the Gun, and after many actions and many years where he proved his ability and dependability, gained the trust of the quarterdeck and was made Master Gunner. It was natural that the Captain should entrust to him the training of the "young gentlemen" when they went to sea.

Until 1869 *Excellent* kept the mizzenmast rigged and trained the boys in seamanship as well as gunnery. Seaman John Burnett wrote to his mum in 1838: "They pipe 'up hammocks' at 6 o'clock in the morning. We then clean ourselves and the mess tables until 7 o'clock. We are then piped to breakfast which consists of cocoa. At half past 7 I go to the rigging loft. . . . At 1 o'clock the drums beat to quarters where we are instructed in great gun exercise; after that sword [he means cutlass] and musket drill. . . ."

Since the 1700s the Royal Naval Academy had been situated in the dockyard in Portsmouth; it was moved in 1873 to what is now the Royal Naval College in Greenwich. (This is King Henry V's old palace started in 1428 and added to by succeeding monarchs – Henry VIII and Queen Elizabeth I were born there.) Here the young gentlemen took their seamanship examinations for Lieutenant and on passing were promoted to Mate – the equivalent of the Sub-Lieutenant today. In the mess there were generally about thirty Mates and a very rumbustious lot they were, much given to practical jokes. These practical jokes became a tradition as the years passed and it behooved each subsequent Sub's course to leave Whaley with one such joke to their credit – on the eve of their departure, of course, to avoid reprisals. One officer told me that his class got one of the barrage balloons that were tethered around the Island to protect against low-level bombing attacks, and fastened it to the door of the Captain's house. But I can't see why they were not carried aloft by it. He said they attached it to a truck to move it, but I still am dubious; you can't believe all you are told.

The 1920s were good years for these expressions of *joie de vivre*. The RCN had four officers qualifying as Gunnery Lieutenants there: Scotty Brodeur, Boomer Hope, Dick Oland, and Jim Roy. Boomer Hope, who was my Commodore later, told me that some of the more unimaginative classes were satisfied with rolling the antique guns now used for decoration down to the parade ground or the football field; after they had enjoyed the initial outrage of Properly Ordained Authority – the Parade Chief Gunner's Mate – they only had to sweat and grunt the guns back up again. More imaginative by far was the class who manhandled an old Chinese cannon to a position outside the wardroom. They gathered scores of onlookers at the improvised gun drill and, finally, with much jibbering of orders barked in Whale Island fashion but in Cantonese tone and with a suitable bang and clouds of smoke, the gun spoke. The Sub-in-Charge then announced that exams had not permitted the calculation of the time of the fall of shot but that all would be informed in plenty of time to observe the "splash" in the area of the parade ground – near the parade training office door above which hung a sign, "As the Tree Is Trained So It Grows."

After sunset the word was passed that splash-down was in a few minutes. Around the parade ground grinning officers and Petty Officers and Seamen gathered in their hundreds.

View of Halifax from Dartmouth, 1759. (Public Archives, Nova Scotia)

From 1837, ships of the Royal Navy's Pacific Station patrolled from Cape Horn to Alaska. HMS Boxer *in Esquimalt shows the transition from sail to steam.* (Maritime Museum of British Columbia)

Above left: From earliest days, sailors got an issue of rum daily – until 1740. Then Admiral Vernon decreed the rum should be cut with water. Because of the grogram boat cloak he wore, Vernon was known as "Old Grog," hence grog. (Department of National Defence)

Left: HMS Shearwater *dressed to welcome* HMCS Rainbow *on her arrival in Esquimalt in 1910.* (DND)

Above: HMCS Niobe, *a heavy cruiser with 6-inch guns, was purchased, together with* HMCS Rainbow, *a light cruiser with 6-inch guns, from the British Admiralty in 1910.* (DND)

Right: Commander Walter Hose, RCN, *Captain of* HMCS Rainbow *in the First World War. He rose to Rear-Admiral and Chief of the Naval Staff.* (DND)

Instructional staff of HMCS Niobe. *Square-rig Petty Officers in sennet hats. Officers and the Chief Petty Officer in fore-and-aft rig,* i.e., *peak caps.* (DND)

Boys' Training Ship (left) HMS Impregnable. (National Maritime Museum, Greenwich)

Boy Seaman Budge, 1923. (DND)

Rear-Admiral Budge, 1963. (DND)

HMS Conway, *1932* (National Maritime Museum)

Above left: Training schooner, HMCS Venture, in the 1930s. (DND)

Left: Training cruiser, HMCS Quebec, in the 1950s. (DND)

Inset: Petty Officer William Hall, VC, RN, of Horton's Bluff, Nova Scotia. Photo taken after retirement, circa *1901.* (Maritime Division, Nova Scotia Museum)

Above: Lieutenant Robert Hampton Gray, VC, DSC, RCN, of Trail, British Columbia. (DND)

Survivors of torpedoed merchant ship. Painted by Harold Beament. (National War Museum, Ottawa)

Left to right: Lieutenant-Commanders H. G. DeWolf (St. Laurent), *H. N. Lay* (Restigouche), *and J. C. Hibbard* (Skeena). (DND)

HMCS St. Laurent. (Public Archives of Canada)

HMCS Restigouche. (PAC)

HMCS Skeena. (PAC)

Left: U-boats passing on patrol. (Bibliothek für Zeitgeschichte, Stuttgart)

Above: Günther Prien, U-47. (Photo Comrad)

Inset: Otto Kretschmer, U-99. (Ullstein Bilderdienst)

Left: Joachim Schepke, U-100
(Ullstein Bilderdienst)

Below: Officers of Assiniboine *after sinking* U-210. *John Stubbs (holding puppy), on his left Ralph Hennessy.* (PAC)

Above right: Depth charges exploding. (DND)

Below right: Survivors of HMCS Clayoquot *being picked up by* HMCS Fennel. Clayoquot*'s Captain, Lieutenant-Commander Craig Campbell, is at lower left.* (DOH, NDHQ)

Hunted to exhaustion, a crippled U-boat surfaces and is boarded. (DND)

HMCS Athabaskan. (PAC)

MTB 726, May 1944. (DND)

Surrender of U-889 in Shelburne, Nova Scotia, after VE day May 17, 1945. The Captain (in white cap) brings her alongside for the last time. (DND)

A deafening explosion, lurid flame, clouds of smoke. The centre of the parade ground erupted. In the middle was a large smoking crater. From the parade training office three Sub-Lieutenants appeared, dressed in smocks, one carrying a tree, one a spade, and the third a watering can. With slow and measured tread they approached the crater, planted the tree, and watered it. Loud cheers from the assembled throng. Whether this was an appropriate skit on this sign is dubious for the tree had to be replanted in a more suitable spot next day. But full marks for effort.

Hugh Pullen did his Lieutenant (G) course in 1933 and was back in the UK in 1935 for the celebration of the Silver Jubilee of King George VI. He attended the formal dinner at *Excellent* which was also the last dinner of the graduating class. Admiral of the Fleet Lord Jellico of Scapa was the senior guest at dinner, probably remembering his Long Course of 1884, and sixty-six other Flag Officers attended. While speaking, a distinguished Admiral was interrupted by a flight of ducks released through the wardroom skylight by the departing class of Sub-Lieutenants. The ducks circled, a few bombed the guests, but when they landed they were forgiven the interruption and the bombing. Each duck was wearing a pair of black gaiters – the badge of office of the gunnery instructor.

Work on Whaley is strict and arduous and on Sunday mornings there is inspection and church.

> Six days shalt thou labour and do more than thou art able,
> And on the seventh, holystone the decks and black the cable.

The naval brigades which fought ashore in the Crimea and in France and Gallipoli started here, learning how to strip to its component parts their 12-pounder 8-hundredweight guns and the 3.7-inch howitzers – the screw guns of the Indian army – then ferry them ashore and assemble them again; the relief of Ladysmith was helped by a naval brigade. But training of this sort seemed remote from naval gunnery.

Because a gun is dangerous at *both* ends and because the Master Gunner and his Mates had devised drills which demanded smart and alert men drilled in exact and instant obedience to orders, it was, I suppose, inevitable that the training of troops in parade drill fell naturally within the orbit of the gunnery staff. We disciples of St. Barbara – the patron saint of gunners – have always felt that this was a secondary role, and with the increasing complexity of weapons the true test of a gunner was ensuring that modern equipment was truly a fatal annoyance to the Queen's enemies. Nonetheless, in parade training, officers and Petty Officers were called to the front to take charge of several hundred men and direct their movements in platoons, companies, and battalions. No relevance to the modern navy, said many. That was not at all the point. The point was that the man in front had to take charge, think before acting, make his commands clear from a distance, and act swiftly to avoid disaster. It didn't matter if disaster struck and the troops went marching off to some undetermined and distant spot. All that happened was that the wretch got a good bollocking. Comments were often humorous, seldom hurtful, never coarse. It was a contest of wits, memory, and improvisation.

The stories come down to us through the years. One Gunner's Mate had his class of Sub-Lieutenants fallen in facing the sun while he gave them rifle drill. After about twenty minutes he shouted, "Three, rear rank, wipe that grin off your face, sir."

Number three of the rear rank wasn't grinning but realized his face was screwed up to avoid the sun's glare:

"I'm not grinning, Chief, it's my natural face."

"Then take your natural face round the island."

"Around Whale Island" is over a mile and a trial in sports rig. With doeskin uniform, heavy boots, and a rifle it is uncomfortable in the extreme.

Yet, the healing balm of consideration for others and a very real interest in their welfare ran like a warm stream through all our lives. Dick James did his Gunner's Mate course in 1950 and his officer-instructor was Lieutenant (G) Henry Leach. James says. "Lt. Leach had a deep interest in our wellbeing, personal as well as professional. A truly considerate man. The Captain of the Island was too, Captain Elkins. I remember our passing-out [graduating] parade. We three Canadians in the class were the top three so I invited all our class and all our instructors to a passing-out party at my place. Captain Elkins wrote a note saying he would like to come and said that since it was a "passing-out" party he supposed I would be serving lots of our strong Canadian rum."

Another Canadian who left his mark on Whale Island, along with the rest of his class, was Sub-Lieutenant Peter Chance. They decided that they would add a refinement to the tree-planting skylark of the previous century. They had been to the torpedo training ship *Vernon* prior to Whaley and had had the mysteries of detonators and explosives unveiled to them. Full of piss and vinegar and this new-found knowledge, they, in the dark of a December night, planted a tree in the middle of the parade ground. On the Island at that time in 1942 were several thousand sailors, Wrens, Subs, Lieutenants, and many more senior officers.

"I can see it to this day. Our Subs' course and all the others milling around in the dark of the morning waiting to fall in for Divisions. First of all, one must imagine the senior Parade Chief Petty Officer who wore around his neck a large whistle and, of course, wore gaiters which marked him as the man of the hour. When he blew his whistle everybody stood stock still, rigid, frozen. As the morning light strengthened, came the first blast of the whistle. 'Ship's Company, fall in. Carry on.'

"Everybody belted like mad; classes never walked, they doubled, and faster. A great deal of shuffling, scuffling, and commands in stentorian voice. As the light strengthened more came another blast of the whistle.

" 'The class responsible for that there tree on the parade ground, *remove it.*'

"WHOOMP.

"Up went the tree. Its top reached a height of about twenty feet. It wasn't a *big* tree."

In 1936, Cadet Bob Welland, RCN, joined the 8,000-ton training cruiser, HMS *Frobisher*. She carried about three hundred cadets; very few seamen, the cadets acted as the seamen would in other than a training ship, besides instruction in seamanship, navigation, and the rest, working part ship in evolutions, cleaning, and maintenance. "I think that about a quarter of the cadets were from Canada, Australia, New Zealand, India, Malaya, Nigeria, and Ghana; cadets from Greece, Turkey, Norway, Denmark, Holland, and the rest of the world were there in lesser numbers – 'the odds-and-sods' the Brits called us. The RN trained everybody else's navy except a few who were *persona non grata* like Americans and Germans and Japanese."

As usual, the Petty Officers were very much to the front in the cadets' training. Welland was in the forecastle division and one day a very heavy anchor cable had to be moved across the deck while mooring ship. The Petty Officer sang out, "Right, two seamen over here and we'll move this."

"But, Petty Officer, there are no seamen."

"Right. Ten cadets, then."

The first training cruise was to the home of the North America and West Indies Squadron based in Bermuda. The second was to Gibraltar and Trondheim and Bergen.

A Warrant Officer Margot dominated the lives of the cadets. "Nobody else much mattered to us. None of the other officers, just Mr. Margot, he was the one who disciplined us. Stoppage of leave, extra work. Everybody liked him, he was so goddamn *tough*," said Welland.

Cadet Ralph Hennessy was a shipmate of Welland on that same cruise. "Mr. Margot, a gentleman I'll never forget! He harried the cadets morning, noon, and night. He would jump on you for the slightest little thing you did wrong. One day during stand-easy I was having a cigarette on the foretop and 'Out Pipes' sounded. I took a final drag on it when the next thing I knew I was quivering in front of Mr. Margot while he instructed me on the meaning of 'Out Pipes.' 'It means out pipes, cadet, and your pipe, if I can so refer to that thing dangling between your fingers, is not yet out. Put it *out*, cadet, *now*.' "

Another time *Frobisher* was at anchor in Bermuda in quarantine, off Ireland Island. The cadets were allowed ashore only for a walk in the dockyard. Hennessy stayed on board the first night but when those who had gone ashore returned half-seas-over, he saw that shore leave here could not be entirely dull. He landed the following day. Cadets were not allowed in any of the buildings; this, of course, included the wet canteen. But the cadets the previous night had established that you could order from outside, throw your money in, and the beer was passed out. So here you have six of them sitting in front of the canteen sipping beer when who should walk by but the Captain, the Commander, and Mr. Margot. "At that time, as cadets," says Hennessy, "We stood up and doffed our hats as they went past. They saluted and walked on. Had we got away with it? No. After a few paces they did a marvellous double take, the Captain looked at the Cadet Gunner, Mr. Margot, and he came storming back. 'You have broken the quarantine regulations.'

" 'No, Mr. Margot, we haven't.'

" 'You have broken the quarantine regulations. Back to the ship,'

" 'Aye aye, sir.'

" 'And leave that beer where it is.'

"We got seven days' extra work and drill. The extra work was nothing but the rifle drill was under Mr. Margot. At the end of it I had two bleeding shoulders from the rifle bouncing as we doubled. We did muscle builds. Bring your rifle to the firing position – with both hands, of course – then take one away still holding the rifle steady. 'You're allowing your rifle to *droop*, cadet. Hold it *up*, cadet.' That is why I remember Mr. Margot."

Yet there was the understanding that always seemed to go together with the apparently unbending code of discipline. Welland says, "One day I was in charge of a parade and my hat blew off, over the side. I went to Mr. Margot, mildly panic-stricken, as cadets get although they are not supposed to, 'Please, sir, my hat blew off.' Mr. Margot whipped his off and jammed in on my head. Saved!"

"His Majesty's Canadian Schooner *Venture* was a three-master built at Meteghan, Nova Scotia, and in 1938 I was appointed to her for her winter cruise." said Charles Dillon. Commander Bully Pressy was Captain – also called Hard-a-starboard Pressy because of the permanent tilt of his head to the right – Lieutenant Jimmy Hibbard was First Lieutenant; they were both RCN. Navigator was Lieutenant George Stanley, RCNR; the Sub-Lieutenant was John Ruttan. We had a Coxswain, a Stoker Petty Officer, four Able-Bodied Seamen, several Ordinary Seamen, a lot of Boy Seamen – *Venture* was their training ship – and me, then a Paymaster Lieutenant, RCNVR.

"We departed Halifax in a gale and off Chebucto Head we got the full force of it, freezing cold. For thirty-six hours we were hove-to and I was so sick I was afraid I was *not* going to die. The third day the wind abated somewhat, so on to Bermuda. A few days to refit the standing and running rigging, service the guns – we had two 3-pounders forward – tiddley up the boats – two whalers and a skiff – then sail.

"In Barbados the Captain had a retired Brigadier and his wife on board for drinks and Pilot George Stanley came back on board half-seas-over after a run ashore. He roared 'I want my blankety-blank dinner and tell the blankety-blank Captain to get his blankety-blank guests off the ship.' The Captain was furious and his guests embarrassed. As Officer of the Day I persuaded the pilot to get below. But he stormed on deck again and when I told him to get below, he charged and I fled. (Being a Paymaster, I was not a seaman in the Pilot's book; 'a little counter-jumper,' he called me.)

"The Captain shouted, 'Don't let him hit you. Don't let him hit you. It'll only make things worse.'

"Now, there are not so many places to go in a 112-foot schooner, so

I ran up the mizzenmast rigging where I sat on the cross-trees clutching my telescope. Stanley started up the port rigging and I down the starboard rigging, while the Captain jumped up and down below shouting, "Get a guard. We'll have to overpower him."

"The guard appeared, armed with rifles. I said, 'Put those bloody things away. It's muscle we want,' so they grabbed him, handcuffed him, put him in leg irons, and slung him in his bunk. He wasn't court-martialed because the least punishment would have been 'dismissed his ship' and then we would have had no sailing master, so he was logged. He took an even dimmer view of me after that.

"One night in the Tortugas I was sleeping on deck; the Coxswain shook me.

"'You'll have to come below, sir. There's been an extraordinary accident.'

"This Ordinary Seaman was standing under his hammock by the mess table, underpants around his ankles, holding a vital part of his anatomy that was covered with blood and yellowish substance with glass glistening through.

"'What happened?'

"'He fell out of his hammock and broke the mustard pot.'

"'What?'

"'He fell out, his thing went into the mustard pot, and broke it – the pot, I mean.'

"I surveyed this 'thing' with distaste and from a distance. 'Bandage it up and we'll see to it in the morning.'

"Next morning it was stitched up by the medical officer ashore. Was all well? No. The next night all hands were awakened by this Seaman's anguished screams. He had been dreaming of his next night in port and his stitches had broken.

"So much for the domestic side. On the international side we met the officers and men of the Royal Navy: HMS *York*, *Leander*, *Ajax* of the Royal New Zealand Navy, and *Exeter*. Commodore Harwood was driving her; he who had cornered Captain Langsdorff in the pocket battleship *Graf Spee*, forcing her into Montevideo in the River Plate. Also, there were lots of millionaires in the West Indies in their expensive yachts . . . and we were being paid to do this – $90 a month. Not quite the same luxury but life was good. During the week we worked hard and on weekends we played hard.

"After about three months we shaped a course for Halifax. The day we were making up to Chebucto Head a near gale was blowing from abaft the beam. She was under full sail: topsails, lowers, jibs, everything. She liked that; she was better off the wind than on it. With the wind on the starboard quarter she logged fourteen knots for three hours, then we had to shorten her sail to enter harbour. She was really boiling along, it was a real thrill.

"The saga of His Majesty's Canadian Schooner *Venture* really starts with the London disarmament conferences of the 1930s," said Frank Caldwell. "Very strange this, and perhaps a harbinger of what a strange life she was to lead. How did a schooner not yet even on the drawing board and whose armament would be two 3-pounder guns, come to be on the agenda of a disarmament conference where world powers were discussing battleships, heavy cruisers, and the like? Because Viscount Maunsell was First Lord of the Admiralty. Maunsell was a retired naval officer and was interested in bringing back training in sail for young sailors and young officers, but the Sea Lords wouldn't have it. Captain Percy Nelles, RCN, was at this conference and he too was very keen on this kind of training. They talked. Nelles said that it was obvious that he was going to rise to the top of the Canadian naval hierarchy and when he did he would pursue the idea of training in sail for the RCN.

"And he did. In the mid-thirties he succeeded Admiral Walter Hose as Chief of Naval Staff and he set up a competition for the design of such a vessel. It had to be sail-powered and have lots of room for pulley-hauley trainees.

"The designs submitted were not what we wanted. One was a rather Jerome Kern, *Showboat* affair – a houseboat really, with three decks above the waterline and three stubby masts on top. No good for the North Atlantic. The design contract finally went to the man who designed *Bluenose*, Bill Roué. He had at first refused because our fee was risibly small – perhaps a thousand dollars – but he finally agreed, though his attitude was, 'Well, if that's all the money you've got, that's all the design you'll get.' So he took a Grand Banks schooner design, cut her in half, added thirty feet, and gave her three masts instead of two.

"We had lots of between-deck accommodation. The difficulty was that everything was handraulic, pulley-hauley, and the mainsail was too much to handle, so the mainmast, which carries the big driver, was shortened. She was, therefore, never really balanced for sail; she did not have the driving power a Grand Banks schooner normally had; she was better off the wind than on it.

"The builder chosen was a man called Theriault in Meteghan, Nova Scotia. Like most people in the thirties, he was short of cash, so he badly under-bid his costs because he needed some money coming in. He got a payment on the signing of the contract; he would get more money on the laying of the keel; again on the decking, planking, launching, and so on. What he did with the first payment we cannot know but can guess – paid off some bills. He asked for a second payment and we made it, but there had been little work done. Some wood had been laid down for the keel but the shipwrights were cutting trees and using green wood as ribs and planking. I served in *Venture* two years later as a Sub-Lieutenant, and when she was working in a hot climate the sap would still run out of the wood.

"The great day for launching finally arrived – many months late. No grand sliding down the ways and landing in the water with a great splash for *Venture*. No. She was pulled down the slip by a series of ropes and pulleys connected to a capstan driven by a horse and an ox walking around it. She was hauled over to a jetty on a high tide, tied up, and rum was broken out for all hands. The tide went out, *Venture* wasn't properly secured, she fell on her side, and the next tide flooded her.

"The next thing was the masts. Following an old custom down east Theriault went around to derelict schooners to lift the spars, which often had a longer life than the hull. The builder managed to use one of these as foremast but you lose perhaps four feet in unshipping these masts so the taller main and aftermast had to be shipped in from British Columbia – more expense. Then there were the sails. Subcontracted to a Lunenburg sail-loft, these were delivered as the vessel neared completion. Plus one deputy sheriff. He nailed a lien to the mast saying that he was in charge of the builder's assets until the sails had been paid for.

"This put the RCN in the position of having a vessel ready for sea but impounded. We got around this by drafting a crew to her, and appointing Lieutenant-Commander Ken Adams as Captain; and he, prior to joining, was sworn in as a Deputy Sheriff. Now we had two Deputies, each with equal authority. Our Deputy, as Captain, sailed *Venture* to Lunenberg to get the auxiliary power installed – the small diesel engine. Then, on to Halifax. The Deputy Sheriff/Captain explained to the Deputy Sheriff that when *Venture* was alongside in Halifax the heads on board would be shut down for alterations and additions. The heads ashore were just across the jetty and up the way a piece. The next morning the Deputy trotted over for his morning devotions, Ken promptly hauled down the Red Ensign, hoisted the White Ensign, put an armed sentry on the brow, and that's how *Venture* became HMCS *Venture*.

"I joined her for her second winter cruise in October 1938. Lieutenant Jimmy Hibbard was Captain; Lieutenant O. C. S. Robertson, RCNR, was First Lieutenant; I was the Sub, the Navigator, Training Officer, and everything else; the crew numbered forty-two, twenty-four of whom were trainees.

"We departed Halifax in stiff winds and cold. At Chebucto Head we set a southeasterly course and the rigging promptly froze. We held this course until we hit the Gulf Stream and it thawed again so we could tack. Ten days later we made Bermuda. To get to Barbados took twelve days; it's only a short hop but we had no wind at all to speak of. Through the Leeward and Windward islands to Port of Spain, then from Trinidad north again to rendezvous with our destroyers, transfer our Ordinary Seamen marked TR – trained – and take on a new class.

"Besides standing middle and afternoon watch, fixing the ship's position, and training the Ordinary Seamen I had plenty of paper work. There had not been a fair-log submitted for the first cruise, not for a year and a half. I had to rewrite history. Sometimes the Officer of the Watch hadn't entered the wind and I had to invent one; that and add a few appropriate comments to keep a reader's attention; you can't have days going by with no entries. One cryptic comment in the log was, 'The Sailing Master was placed in irons.' Apparently he had come back on board slightly under the weather and told everybody off. I changed that to 'was placed under close arrest.' I became expert at forging the initials of those who preceded me.

We got back to Halifax in April 1939 and I returned to *Saguenay*. The war caught up with us in September.

"Early in the war, *Venture* was accommodation ship for Admiral Sir Stuart Bonham-Carter's headquarters ship HMS *Seaborn*. Then she became communications link at the Narrows for convoy ships coming out of Bedford Basin. She was sold out of the service at the end of the war and went sealing in the Gulf of St. Lawrence.

"And that's my time with wooden ships and iron men."

"I was appointed First Lieutenant of *Venture* when I came back to Canada after serving my time in the Mediterranean Fleet – about 1937," Rear-Admiral Jimmy Hibbard told me. "Probably the biggest fleet in the world then. Several battleships and battle cruisers, twenty or more heavy and light cruisers, perhaps fifty or more destroyers, fleet auxiliaries, fleet tankers, a fighting fleet preparing for a war which we all knew would break out sooner rather than later. Day firing exercises, night exercises, anti-aircraft firings, torpedo firings, armed landings, action-information exercises, full-speed manoeuvres of the whole fleet. Radar was being talked of and I knew that that would be what won battles. Asdic (our submarine detection device) was coming into the fleet. I knew that the German U-boats had done well enough in World War One and would probably do better in World War Two. Asdic would sink U-Boats and I wanted to learn about it and sink some. I had been First Lieutenant of two modern destroyers in the Med Fleet and back in Canada I was sent to be First Lieutenant of the *Venture*, a sail-powered training ship for ordinary seamen.

"Now I agree that training in sail is good, nothing better to teach the rudiments of seamanship and living at sea. It teaches dependence on your shipmates, instant obedience to orders, how to overcome fear, how dangerous the sea can be, reliance on your Petty Officers and officers and, most important, upon *yourself*. Self-reliance is essential to a seaman.

"But here I was, after preparing for war as second-in-command of fighting destroyers, as second-in-command of a schooner where the most modern equipment was the sextant. I hate to sound critical of my superiors but that is no way to prepare seamen for modern war. All right if we had the time but I knew we didn't. Still, we did what we could and turned out some pretty good hands who did well in destroyers I commanded later."

Lieutenant O. C. S. Robertson, Big Robbie, came by his sea-going career honestly. His father was a master mariner, a grandfather served in the tea clippers, and one great-great-grandfather had been Admiral Nelson's Signal Lieutenant at the battle of Copenhagen. Big Robbie first went to sea as a deck boy at age nine, during the summer holidays, and did this until age twelve; his pay was twenty-five cents a month. At sixteen he ran away from home and went to sea for good. His father couldn't say much; he had done the same thing. Then came Chamberlain's Munich Agreement with Hitler, "Peace in our Time." Big Robbie was sent to *Venture* as First Lieutenant and Sailing Master.

"I joined her in September 1938," said Robertson. "Godfrey Hibbard was Captain. An elder cousin of Jimmy Hibbard, Godfrey ended up as a commodore. Godfrey was a gentleman of the old school. A very even-tempered man. Any time he lost his temper, he did it by design. It was well calculated. You know, I learned that from him. There are times to lose your temper and times not to lose your temper. When you want to reinforce something, you fly into a temper. I got to know Godfrey very well. He was a very religious man, capable, a good seaman; he was one of my heroes.

"We had forty-two Boy Seamen. Most of them had never seen salt water. They didn't even know how to wash their clothes. We took them away to the West Indies for five months. The best job in the navy. Go yachting and get paid for it. We went from St. Kitts to Nevis, then to Antigua, a hundred and ten miles. We went everywhere. Frank Caldwell was the Sub-Lieutenant. Fred Bingham was our Gunner's Mate. Not that the two 3-pounders were much to a man like him. I never liked guns much, they frighten me. Anyway, they fouled the jib sheets. We weren't entitled to a Gunner's Mate but we bribed the officer-in-charge of the gunnery school. A bottle of rum for him and a bottle of perfume for his wife. Fred was Training Officer and he stood a watch by himself. God, he was a strong right arm! I don't know what we would have done without him. We took our forty-two Ordinary Seamen back marked TR and took on another lot.

"Those in destroyers rather looked down on this sailing training ship. But I knew destroyers; I had done lots of time in several. One time in harbour we were alongside *Skeena*. I always turned out my hands a half-hour earlier than the destroyers did – it was good for them. One day I had most hands aloft to strike the topmast. Herbie Rayner was First Lieutenant of *Skeena*; later he became a Vice-Admiral and Chief of Naval Staff. His hands were falling in at eight o'clock and watching us with interest. He called across, 'Hey, Robbie, what's the object of that exercise?'

"I was up in the cross-trees and all his hands were grinning. 'That's to show you destroyer men what seamanship is.' Herbie was not amused.

"Another time we were towing a target for *Skeena* and *Saguenay* to do a surface shoot. We crowded on everything – three lowers, jumbo jib, inner jib, outer jib, flying jib, three gaff topsails, and two fisherman's staysails. We had a good breeze, making about eleven knots. They had 1-pounder sub-calibre guns fitted inside the 4.7-inch guns, but the guns weren't properly lined up. I had three kids on every cross-tree in case a gaff topsail let go. I was on the mizzen and could see everything.

"They opened fire. Blazed away. Suddenly a little round hole appeared in the mizzen gaff topsail. I bellowed, 'Haul down the clear-to-fire flag.' Bingham brought it down in a flash with one huge jerk. Then I made a signal by light to *Skeena* from First Lieutenant to First Lieutenant: 'Thank you for giving me the opportunity of exercising my hands aloft under fire.' It got into the hands of Herbie's Captain and again, Herbie was not amused.

"I was terribly proud of Fred Bingham and the young seamen we trained. When we left Halifax on a training cruise we had to go out on engine; nobody knew how to handle the sails. But when we returned to Halifax five months later, with all sails set, we *sailed* her alongside. 'Down all sail,' and down they came in a few seconds. We nudged alongside with bare poles. Kids we had at seventeen were all Chief Petty Officers before the end of the war. So we felt a certain satisfaction. We had done our job. We had turned them into seamen. Because they were permanant navy – not reserves – they all went to destroyers, naturally. The reserves were mostly in corvettes and frigates; the more complicated destroyers needed pre-war-trained RCN. And they nearly all did well – those that lived. And they still talk of the good times and the good training they had in His Majesty's Training Schooner *Venture*.

"Godfrey Hibbard left and I took over command but war was upon us and I went in command of the Halifax mine-sweeping flotilla, the old coal-burners, *Fundy, Gaspe, Bras d'Or*, and the rest. I commanded destroyers later and, after the war, our Arctic patrol ship, *Labrador*. But she is one of my loves, is the old *Venture*. She *lived* under your feet the way a power-driven ship cannot do – for me, anyway."

Venture turned out sixty Ordinary Seamen a year, sufficient to our pre-war needs. It was not until the war years that we got the training establishment, HMCS *Cornwallis*, a shore base in the heart of the lush Annapolis Valley in Nova Scotia, a few hours' drive from Halifax. Most of the senior staff were products of the training ships of the RN: *Impregnable* and *Frobisher* for the Boy Seamen and the cadets, *Excellent* and *Vernon* for the Gunners and Torpedomen, and, for Junior Ratings or Midshipmen, the cruisers and battleships of the RN's Home Fleet, Med Fleet, Far Eastern Fleet, West Indies Squadron, and, towards the end of the war against Japan, the Pacific Fleet. Thus it was that the centuries-old training experience of the RN which had started the RCN on its way in 1910 continued into the post-war years – but with a difference.

Since our coming of age from 1939 to 1945 we had discarded those methods and traditions which were not in accord with the Canadian temperament, kept many which were, and added some unique to our country. As a small and irreverent example, we had, in our wartime fleet, shown a fine disregard for Britain's College of Heraldry in the matter of ships' crests and armorial bearings. Not for us were the figures engrailed, embattled, indented, invected, nebuly, dancetty, raguly: nor the field azure, the lion couchant, the unicorn d'or, the wolf rampant. Our corvette *Wetaskiwin* was Canadian built and Canadian manned and her ship's badge showed a shapely queen fallen into a puddle of water – crown askew, slim legs kicking, breasts heaving – HMCS *Wetaskiwin*, the Wet Ass Queen. I always noticed that we had a lot of fun mixed up with the rather grim training of teaching men how to kill effectively.

To *Cornwallis* was sent a Chief Petty Officer Gunner's Mate, a Whale Island product; Dick James had just arrived back from Shanghai where *Crescent* had replaced an RN destroyer sunk in the war between the Red Chinese and the forces of Chiang Kai Shek. He got a pier-head jump to *Cornwallis*. He said, "I just got back from China. What about my leave?"

"You go to *Cornwallis* now. Commander Budge is there and he has pre-selected his instructors. You're one. Get cracking."

James went to the parade ground staff. He and the Parade Gunner and the rest of the Gunner's Mates had known one another since they were killicks or Petty Officers at Whale Island. As it has been since the Turkish janizaries or the Roman legionaries, new entries were rattled and shaken and drilled and drilled and roared at and pleaded with ("not *that* right turn, Bloggins, the *other* right, the one the rest of the world uses"). One day James got particularly fed up with one such man and put him in the trash bin at the edge of the parade ground, "Now you are where you properly belong, with the trash. Promise me you'll buck up and you can come out. Put down the lid now and I'll call you later." But down came the Parade Gunner. "Chief, you're supposed to have a squad of sixteen. I see only fifteen. Where's the other?" James pointed, the Gunner lifted the lid, the culprit promised he would buck up and was released from his durance vile.

As in any training establishment, the instructor was supreme. Extra work, drill in the dog watches doubling with rifle extended or held over your head, was a routine punishment. But, all of those instructors of the *Cornwallis* of those years have told me, it was extremely hard to catch a man out as the days lengthened into weeks and the weeks into months. And James told me, "I've had a lot of ODs under training and we were pretty hard on them but none resented it. They knew what it was all about and took it in good faith."

And what about the Commander? "In my estimation and in that of most of the instructors I knew, Budge was excellent. One thing we didn't agree with was that he had us on one duty-watch each four days. We didn't like it but he insisted and that was *that*! He was always on the ball and you knew where you stood. He told you your terms of reference and that's what you did, that was *it*! A man of great vitality, on the base at six-thirty every morning. He'd go through one of the living blocks or the galley and God help the Petty Officer who wasn't doing his job; certainly no one else could. He'd have regular meetings with the staff and he'd air his beefs and we'd air ours. If we could persuade him something needed changing, he'd change it, not tomorrow, today. A strict man and a fair man."

Was he strict? Very. Was he fair? Very. And he pushed you. But you could push back, and sometimes get away with it. I have known Pat Budge for forty-five years – since I was a Midshipman and he was a Torpedo Gunner instructing us. As a killick he had always trained the reserve sailors and officers when they came to the coast for their summer training; the RMC cadets were always assigned to him; in the early days of the war he and Boatswain Pett worked up corvettes and frigates in Halifax to make them competent to try their hand in the Battle of the Atlantic; through the command of the corvette *Sorel* and the destroyers *Ottawa* and *Gatineau* he continued a training as well as an operational role. When I was Staff Officer for Reserve Cadets in Hamilton he was Chief of Staff to Admiral Ken Adams and in our trips to the reserve divisions across Canada I was told many a yarn. And he shook up the reserve navy more than somewhat.

He shook up everyone he met, at least to start with. Start tough was his motto; you can always give a little slack later. You can't do it the other way around. It's ass about face, that. He carried on this philosophy when he was appointed Executive Officer of *Cornwallis* – the Commander: "This was a job I thoroughly enjoyed. I don't think I ever worked harder in my life and my wife, Myrtle, put in a good stint, too, because she entertained the staff and the visitors a great deal. It was a good, good job. My Captain was Pip Musgrave.

"I intended to start a taut ship and we had a new staff of Chief and Petty officers, who, at that time, were in excess of the complement of Seamen in the navy. For some time past they had been in *Stadacona* or *Naden* and they had been standing duty watches about one day in nine, one day in ten. I decided the whole staff would be in four watches, one day on each four. They didn't like it. And the Paymasters and the Schoolmaster Officers, all the officers, and the Cooks and every one of the odds and sods. The Captain and I were practically watch on and stay on. I got up to the main gate at 6:30 every morning and if the Duty Chief and the Duty Officer weren't properly turned out, shaved, new shirt, glossy collar, uniform whisked, *boy*! Then I'd inspect the galley or a living block and then it would be 0800 and time for the morning parade, Divisions."

Divisions is the formal start of the naval day. All the ship's company fallen in and inspected first by their Divisional Petty Officer, then their Divisional Officer. These are then reported to the Commander, "So-and-So Division correct, sir, all accounted for, one on leave, one in sick bay."

"Thank you. Stand them at ease, please."

When all divisions have been reported to the Commander the parade stands motionless, silent. The Commander then reports the ship's company to the Captain.

In stentorian voice, "Paraaaade. Shun!"

"Ship's company correct, sir."

"Thank you, Commander. Stand them at ease please."

Silence again. The hands relaxed, alert, motionless – disciplined men.

To the second, the Chief Yeoman of Signals reports, "Eight o'clock, sir."

"Make it so."

Eight bells is sounded.

The ship's company is called to attention again and the Officer of the Guard calls "Guard, present arms."

You can see strained faces of ODs, lips forming the drill – "up, two, three; up, two, three, *smack*!" As fifty ODs smack their rifles on the third movement of the Present Arms the band hits the opening notes of *O Canada*.

The naval ensign rises slowly up the mast and is two-blocked on the last note of the anthem. The Captain inspects the Guard, then the parade is ordered "Off Caps," and stood easy for morning prayers and a hymn to suit the needs of that day, usually the Naval Hymn that goes back a hundred years and more:

Eternal Father, strong to save,
Whose arm doth bind the restless wave, . . .

And another day in His Majesty's Training Ship *Cornwallis* has begun.

Now you should know that this decorum is not inviolable. Oh, no. You should also know that HMCS *Cornwallis* had a pet, not the ship's mascot but popular with the hands. This was a crow, "Joe" by name. "Crow Joe." There wasn't a single muster of the hands that Joe didn't attend. A real sailor's crow. He would walk at their feet and try to undo their boot laces. Joe enjoyed Divisions very much. What intelligent crow wouldn't? All his friends gathered in one spot. Joe favoured the dais to observe the peculiar actions of mankind. With other dignitaries such as the Captain, the Commander, the Chaplain during prayers, and visiting Admirals, he particularly liked the dais and would walk around the rope and brass stanchions with which it was fitted. This might have been eminently satisfactory for Joe but was unsettling for whatever man was holding forth at the time. One day when Off Caps had been ordered and heads were bowed in prayer, Joe sailed off from the dais and settled on the head of one unfortunate OD. The newly acquired imperturbable air suitable for disciplined troops was severely strained and there were shaking shoulders and a hesitation in the clerical tone of the Padre. On another occasion it was shattered.

In calling the parade to attention Budge bellowed, "Paraaaade. . ."
"AWAAARK," ordered Joe.
All hands collapsed into mirth.

One day the Captain said to Budge, "Commander, form a choir."
And Budge replied, "Aye, aye, sir."
I heard that choir in Halifax and in *Cornwallis* and on the radio many times and very good it was. And now I give you the legend which came out of the *Cornwallis* drill hall of nearly forty years ago about the formation of the *Cornwallis* choir:
The Commander announced at Divisions one morning that all

hands would be required on board for supper the following night and to muster in the drill hall at one bell in the last dog watch – 6:30. All hands. No exceptions except those on watch. Rumour ran wild. What was this? What *could* this be? What was Budgie up to now? Who had committed a naval sin of such magnitude that all hands had to be mustered to witness. . .what? Witness punishment? Each searched his conscience. Not me. Then who? What? As four bells of the last dog watch sounded the hands started trickling towards the drill hall. At 6:10 it became a stream, at 6:20 a torrent. There were chairs for all. Not a parade, then. At 6:27 Captain Musgrave appeared. Him too? The hands rose as one. The Captain waved them to their chairs again. An uneasy murmur ceased as the ship's bell sounded. The silence was complete. Ten, perhaps fifteen seconds passed. Then, the Commander strode onto the stage, brass hat jammed over his eyes, telescope under his arm. At the centre of the stage he faced them. Several more seconds went by. Then, in a firm, soft voice which carried to the back of the shed, he spoke:

"You have been called here tonight for the purpose of learning how to sing. . . ."

Shocked incredulity.

"You may think that you do not *want* to learn how to sing but I, your Commander, assure you that you *do* want to learn how to sing."

He can't mean it.

"Now, we musicians use terms that are foreign to the common seaman. For instance, you may think I am standing on a dais. But I am not standing on a dais. We musicians refer to this as a podium. What am I standing on?"

A few uncertain voices, "a podium."

"Not loud enough. *What am I standing on?*"

"A *podium.*" (Getting the hang of it now; the magic starts to work.)

"*No.* Reply in a loud and seamanlike manner, *What am I standing on?*"

"*A podium.*" (The relief from tension complete.)

"Better." (He threw his telescope to the Commander's messenger and received back a swagger stick of some officer's RMC days.)

"Now, you may think that what I am holding in my hand is a stick. It is not a stick. We musicians call this a baton. *What am I holding in my hand?*"

"*A baton.*" (Eager faces of ODs, Chief and Petty officers grinning – even the Captain. Old Budge was at it again.)

"Very good. Now, how do we start? Well, as you have been taught, when we want to start a squad on its merry way we give the order, 'Move to the right in file, right turn, quick march.'" (He turned right smartly, and marched off the stage. Loud crashes from behind the wing curtains. A sense of theatre had Budge. He reappeared.) "But this is not for us. We musicians start a different way. The conductor – that's me – mounts the. . .?"

"*Podium.*"

"That's correct. And raises his. . .?"

"*Baton.*"

"Very good. Now, one more thing. Male voices are of two categories. There are the tenors who sing on the ascending scale, 'Doh, ray, me, fah, so, la, te, doh.' (A falsetto squeak on the top "doh.") And the basses who can sing on a descending scale 'Doh, te, la, so, fa, me, ray, doh.'" His baton shot out down the centre aisle. "From here to the right, tenors; from here to the left, basses." With the speed of light, pre-briefed messengers handed out song sheets; a piano was pushed onto the stage, and the schoolmaster appeared and played "Shenandoah" over and over until the rustling had ceased.

"Ready? Tenors only." Baton poised. Down it came:

> Oh Shenandoah, I love your daughter,
> Away you roving river,
> Oh, Shenandoah, I love your daughter,
> Away I'm bound to roam,
> 'cross the wide Missouri.

"Good. And again." Louder and more certain this time.

"Now, you basses sing harmony; a different tune, as it were. Play it, Schoolie. And again. Right, you basses, all together."

> Oh, Shenandoah, I love your daughter,
> Away, you roving river,
> Oh Shenandoah, I love your daughter,
> Away I'm bound to roam,
> 'cross the wide Missouri.

The Budge plot unfolded as several hitherto unidentified civilians placed in strategic chairs among the "tenors" and the "basses" sang lustily the tenor and the bass parts – members of the local Anglican choir in the village. Two clarinet players from the band appeared at the back of the hall, on opposite sides, and sweetly intoned the tenor and the bass tune on each side of the choir.

Do it again. And again.

The hands looked at each other in wonder as the sweetness of the music they were making became a living thing. Outside the hall the band had quietly mustered, out of sight, the bandmaster at the door of the hall keeping his eye on the conductor, coat and hat thrown now away.

And again. And again.

The voices swelled. The bellwether clarinets played forte. The band rose to fortissimo. It was over.

"That is all for tonight. Upon the first notes of the next march you are to double out of here and join your loved ones – you married men to your wives and children, you ODs to your Divisional Petty Officers."

The hands streamed out, it is sad to relate, in a disorderly fashion, chattering excitedly, faces alight, the Chief and Petty officers and officers more sedately. And from that night, the ship's company of His Majesty's Canadian Training Establishment *Cornwallis*, wanted to learn how to sing.

Upon leaving *Impregnable* and being rated Ordinary Seaman at age seventeen-and-a-half, Pat Budge joined a cruiser, HMS *Despatch*, bound for the China station – Weihaiwei. Training of young seamen never stops, be they Midshipmen or ODs and in this ship was a man who was to affect Budge profoundly. This was Leading Seaman Sam Gilby, the ODs' instructor for their rate of Seaman Torpedoman, and the Leading Hand of their mess. "He taught me so very much and was a man of high principles, a good sound Christian. He had a quiet dignity about him that commanded respect." Budge was rated AB two years after leaving the training ship – exceptionally fast promotion, this – and continued his inexorable way up the promotion ladder through the twenties, the thirties, the forties; the fifties found him as Captain Budge in command of our training cruiser, HMCS *Quebec* (training Ordinary Seamen – how suitable!). A training cruise took him to the city of Quebec and then Montreal with the Flag Officer, Atlantic Coast, Rear-Admiral Roger Bidwell, wearing his flag in *Quebec*. A friend told Budge that Sam Gilby lived there. Sam had left the Royal Navy in 1928 and come to Canada. Work was hard to get and he took a job as maintenance man in the generator and battery room of the Montreal Telephone Company.

"Well," said Budge, "there was one thing that Sam knew inside and out, backwards and forwards, and that was generators and batteries. Twelve hours on watch looking after the battery backup – a low-voltage system. Not that much actual work in his twelve hours on – he just had to be there for routine maintenance and in case of emergency. Now Sam was never a man to sit on his backside and so he uncovered all the brass tally plates, scraped the paint off them, and polished them till they gleamed. It didn't take long before he came to the attention of the higher-ups in the company and Sam progressed from maintenance man to manager of the whole Montreal area."

Budge telephoned Sam and invited him on board his cruiser for a reception to be held the next evening. He hadn't seen him since Wei-haiwei.

Picture the messdecks of HMS *Despatch* on the China station thirty-odd years before: at sea with the scuttles dogged down, hot air foetid with the sweat of twenty men eating, sleeping, playing cards, writing letters, or yarning in their time off in a space no larger than a small room in the house where you read this account – claustrophobic, no privacy, ever! Ordinary Seamen scuttling to obey the barked commands of Leading Seaman, Petty Officers, Chief Petty Officers, everyone; the ever-present dread of being found remiss in adhering to the mass of custom, tradition, ship's orders, station orders, Admiralty orders which directed their every waking hour; the hope of promotion and the certainty that a slip would not only lead to punishment, certainly, but would also delay being rated Able-Bodied Seaman; Leading Seaman seemed too high to dream of – yet; the skylarks that irrepressible boys everywhere will spontaneously, hilariously indulge in, to them always within the shadow of ship's orders. And amidst this, their guide, their mentor, the strict yet indulgent killick of their mess, the Gibraltar in their youthful uncertainties, Sam Gilby.

Now picture the quarterdeck of her Majesty's Canadian Training Cruiser *Quebec* as the sun sank behind Mount Royal. The ship spotless, paintwork nearly as bright as Sam's brass tallies in his generator room of decades before, the brasswork certainly as bright, the hands clad in pristine white uniforms, white awnings spread over the forecastle and over the quarterdeck where the side party and the Officer of the Watch were fallen in to greet the guests. And below, the Captain's cabin, thirty feet from side to side, large scuttles to port and starboard, French-polished mahogany dining table to seat eighteen, a settee and armchairs with white covers and blue piping, mahogany desk for the paper work, carpets, a sleeping cabin to starboard and a Captain's pantry to port. All his. A world apart from the Boys' mess of *Impregnable* or the ODs' mess of *Despatch*.

Commander Ralph Hennessy, Captain Budge, and Admiral Bidwell also there opposite the side party awaiting the guests, telescopes under their arms. Captain Patrick D. Budge, DSC, CD, Royal Canadian Navy, on his own quarterdeck, not that much different to the quarterdeck of HMS *Despatch* which, thirty years before, had never, never seemed attainable. The Montreal guests started to arrive.

"I looked up the jetty and there, sure enough, were Sam and his lady. Aged a bit but still Sam Gilby. I was very proud to be able to introduce old Sam to my Admiral. 'Sir, I would like you to meet Leading Seaman Gilby, the killick of my mess.'"

Combined Operations

The army should be a projectile to be fired by the navy.

Admiral of the Fleet, Lord Fisher,
Captain of HMS *Excellent*, 1883.

Amphibious attacks, with sailors and soldiers acting in concert, have been known since before the Peloponnesian Wars. Admiral Roger Keyes attack at Zebrugge is a dashing example of such an attack from the First World War and the allied landing at Normandy in June 1944 is the most perfect example of the art of the navy (in five hundred ships) projecting several armies (to a total of about one million soldiers). Perhaps the best known Canadian example was the 1759 assault on Quebec City. Admiral Saunders's fleet, navigated up the little-known waters of the St. Lawrence River by Lieutenant James Cook, RN, landed General James Wolfe's soldiers to defeat the French under the Marquis de Montcalm. The battle on the Plains of Abraham has had two interpretations ever since – the English and the French (*chacun à son goût*).

Less well known to Canadians but worthy of scholarly interest here is the October 1939 Battle of St. Jean d'Orleans – about fifteen miles downriver from Quebec City. Paymaster Lieutenant (later Rear-Admiral) Charles Dillon was part of the staff of the Naval Control Base at Quebec during this first combined operation between the Royal Canadian Navy of Admiral Percy Nelles with the men of the Royal 22nd Regiment – the Van Doos – and the *Kriegsmarine* U-Boats of Admiral Karl Dönitz.

Dillon had joined the Sea Scouts in 1926, the RCNVR as a Midshipman in 1931, and, on the Glorious First of June had set off to Halifax to learn his profession in HMCS *Saguenay*. More summer training followed in 1932, and in 1933 he had his first experience in combined operations near Quebec when *Saguenay* landed soldiers at Les Emboulements, "a real ragtag and bobtail affair and a bit of a Chinese fire drill." In 1934, Dillon, in *Skeena*, went from Esquimalt through the Panama Canal over to the Azores to exercise with the Home Fleet – the battleships *Rodney, Nelson, Malaya,* and *Barham,* the aircraft carrier *Furious,* and assorted cruisers and destroyers. Nineteen thirty-five found him in *Champlain,* 1936 in HMS *Dragon,* 1937 in *Skeena* again, and 1938 in *Venture.* In September 1939 he was appointed to the Naval Control Service Office in Quebec.

Quebec's NCSO was charged with keeping track of all shipping in the St. Lawrence River and approaches as far as the Atlantic where NCSO Halifax took over. The Extended Defence Station at St. Jean d'Orleans had two 18-pounder guns manned by a militia artillery unit from Quebec, but no searchlights. Upriver was Fort la Martiniére, also manned by militia, which boasted two 7.5-inch guns of ancient vintage. These hadn't been fired since 1908 for fear of breaking windows and upsetting livestock and residents. Afloat were HMCS *Chaleur* and *Madawaska,* 73-foot ex-RCMP cutters, each with a crew of ten and armed with a machine gun, a few rifles, and a pistol for the Captain. From these two vessels, incoming ships were boarded and their log books and credentials checked. A civilian motor boat called *Fernand Rinfret* was used for boarding ships in port and for harbour patrol. The port of Quebec harboured many ships worthy of attack by the enemy, among them the 80,000-ton *Empress of Britain.*

"The eyes of the Naval Control," says Dillon, "were the members of the Department of Transport Signal Service. These worthy gentlemen were stationed at intervals along the St. Lawrence River and the Gulf as far as Pointe Amour, and all were connected to Quebec by party telephone line or by telegraph. Their duty was to report all in- and out-bound shipping."

At 6:25 P.M., October 14, at NCSO Quebec, the Duty Officer's telephone rang. It was the Signal Service. They had a report from their agent at Cape Salmon (downstream from Murray Bay). He had seen two submarines on the surface steaming toward Quebec. Yes, two. Yes, on the surface. When? About two and a half hours ago, but you know what the telephones are like. Yes, the agent knew what submarines looked like; he had seen them in the last war.

Captain R. L. Jermain, RCN, retired in 1923, now back in "for the duration," was the Naval Officer in Charge. He was told the electrifying news. Could they be ours? No. He therefore closed the port of Quebec to shipping, ordered *Chaleur* and *Madawaska* to patrol the north and south channels at St. Jean, and called the army District Officer Commanding, who responded enthusiastically by alerting the Royal 22nd Regiment, the Van Doos, and, with Gallic panache, decreeing that Quebec City must be blacked out – pull the main switch! He was persuaded not to do this as it would eliminate both lights and telephones. Then he would stand-to all other units in his command. Yes, he would recall all his men from leave to repulse this invasion. Patrols would go out now.

Captain Jermain wanted more ships at St. Jean. The Department of Marine offered the buoy-tender *Druid* and the fire tug *Lanoraie*. The latter need not be fitted with a gun since she already had one – a water gun. Both ships would ram if given a chance, coming in in the time-honoured tradition of bows pointed and guns blazing – in *Lanoraie's* case with gun spouting, presumably reducing the U-boat's crew to drenched shivering wrecks ready to shout "Kamarad." But could the army provide a gun for *Druid*? Well, the armouries had some 18-pounders but the recoil cylinders had been emptied and they could not be ready for forty-eight hours, but there were two at the proofing range at Val Cartier and they'd get those in. One could be put on *Druid's* forecastle and the other sent downriver. The only ammunition they had was shrapnel but that was better than nothing.

Druid and *Lanoraie* appeared alongside the embarkation jetty quickly. The Van Doos lived up to their fine reputation and produced a platoon promptly. "They also lived up to their regimental motto, *Ils ne passeront pas*," said Dillon. "Armed in full field equipment, including entrenching tools, two Vickers machine guns, and sandbags, they built a zariba on the boat deck with the sandbags, mounted the Vickers, and took up battle stations." *Druid* was ready to sail, hands standing by. But there was no 18-pounder.

The panic button having been well and truly pressed, tension mounted. Where was the gun? Well, it had come unhitched from the truck and careened into a ditch. It would arrive presently. At midnight it did and was hoisted aboard and secured with blocks of timber and great spikes. The militia field battery surveyed their work and found it did not at all conform to their soldierly sense of what was right and proper. They said that with the first round fired the gun would recoil, probably kill some of the gun's crew, and fall back into the well-deck. They led a signal lanyard from the trigger to the bridge so that, after the gun had been pointed at the enemy, its crew could jump clear, and it could be fired from the bridge without maiming the crew, though still, presumably, killing Germans.

Captain Jermain had contributed one Lieutenant-Commander and one naval Signalman to *Druid,* but the civilian sailors of the buoy-tender didn't at all like this bellicose dedication to the war-god Mars. Their confidence didn't increase when they saw the man in charge, Captain Jermain, arrested by a couple of National Harbour Board gendarmes. Was not the dock area sealed off and were not unauthorized civilians forbidden? The Captain certainly *looked* unauthorized in his natty tweeds (his 1923 uniform didn't fit; his new one had not arrived); certainly *sounded* unauthorized with his very British accent, and (most suspicious) he spoke no French. Dillon rushed over and explained in fluent and idiomatic French that this was *le Commandant* and Jermain was released. Dillon then rushed back to the office, grabbed a White Ensign, hurried back and threw it on board saying, "Here, you'd better have that." So, properly commissioned as one of His Majesty's buoy-tenders, *Druid* (being in all respects ready for sea and equipped to do battle with enemy) sailed. *Lanoraie* had sailed four hours previously to join *Chaleur* and *Madawaska* off St. Jean.

Meanwhile, the army, vigorous and versatile as always, had found a "submarine-diviner" who had confirmed the presence of two submarines. The navy had heard of this man and viewed him with skepticism. He could tell them exactly where the submarines were with his plumb-bob. Charts were obtained and laid on the floor. The diviner went into a trance, stiffened, sweat poured off his face, and the plumb-bob started going round and round. "I see a submarine. There are sixty-two men on board. It has six torpedoes." The plumb-bob stopped circling and quivered. "That's where it is."

With slightly more science, the navy had plotted the U-boats from their first reported position at 3:55 P.M., estimated a course and speed, and concluded that their ETA would be midnight.

Shortly before zero hour preparations had reached a fever pitch. The army was marshalling its troops, patrols were searching for those on night leave – restaurants, theatres, taverns, brothels, dancehalls, even homes. The St. Jean and Fort la Martiniére batteries were standing by, guns loaded with shrapnel. *Chaleur* and *Madawaska* patrolled, guns at the ready. *Druid*, with her 18-pounder, fifteen artillerymen, and twenty Van Doos manning their .303 machine-guns, rifles, bayonets, and entrenching tools, approached at a high rate of knots.

Zero hour passed.

Suddenly a red flare was seen. "Enemy in Sight." *Chaleur* and *Madawaska*, at opposite ends of the patrol, turned to close the enemy at maximum speed. Each thought the other had fired the flare. *Druid* was still some way off. The battery at Fort la Martinière opened fire. Lacking anything to sight on they used the buoy in the middle of the channel. Shrapnel whizzed and plopped and sizzled. This is great stuff, thought the Gunners ashore. Round followed round. Through the snow squalls, *Chaleur* and *Madawaska* steamed towards each other at top speed – head to head, machine guns cocked, rifles ready, Captains with their hands on their revolver butts. Both ships looked, what with the dark and the snow, like U-boats – low flush decks, low bridge where a conning tower would be, mast where a periscope would be. They sighted each other. *Druid* was puffing up closer and closer.

Both the converging patrol vessels were about to open fire when one officer said, "Wait. That looks like our opposite number. Flash the challenge."

The reply was correct. It *was* their oppo.

Both ships altered away, followed by *Druid*. The shore battery ceased fire. Quiet descended.

The enemy submarines never showed up. There never had been any submarines. The red Very light must have been a shooting star.

And that was the Battle of St. Jean on the night of October 14 and the morning of October 15 in that second month of the Second World War.

The U-boats of Admiral Karl Dönitz did not penetrate the St. Lawrence River, actually, until about three years later, but then they came in goodly numbers and sank many a merchantman and several of His Majesty's Canadian ships within a few miles of Quebec City. Dillon's may not be much of a tale of derring-do, but there is a moral to this story somewhere, for on that same night, the German submarine, U-47, made her way past the north coast of Scotland into the Pentland Firth and to the Orkney Islands where, in Scapa Flow, the Royal Navy's Home Fleet made its base – *Nelson, Rodney, Royal Oak, Furious*, and the rest. The U-boat approached the northern channel of the small island of Lamb Holm in clear weather (unlike that at Isle d'Orlean). Under the coast defence guns and through the boom defences, blockships, and anti-boat nets she made her way into the Flow.

U-47 torpedoed and sank the battleship *Royal Oak* with a loss of nine hundred and thirty-three men blown up or drowned. She escaped before daylight.

Perhaps because of the confluence of these events in time, the *Montreal Gazette* carried this editorial:

On this page appears a reminiscence by an officer identified only as "C. J. D." in the Royal Canadian Navy's Monthly Review. It relates the effects, perhaps comic now, of the first reports of Nazi submarines in the St. Lawrence. The report came to RCN headquarters in Quebec City on October 14, 1939.

The efforts that were made to battle the two U-Boats said to be coming up the river are only comic when it is recalled that the two U-Boats were not there. The efforts to float some kind of defensive shipping, the contingent of Royal 22nd men who made themselves the first Canadian marines, the 18-pounder field gun which was mounted on the fire tug "Lanoraie" [sic] – it all seems comic opera until it is recalled that the subs might have been real.

And what of the men involved? Is it a battle for which they won decorations? Probably it is one they recall with laughter now.

But it was not funny then. Those infantrymen on board their tug, with their machine guns up behind sandbags; the civilian sailors who manned the ship and took her, without protest, down the river to meet a well-armed enemy, it was not funny to them.

We must never be so unready, so alone and helpless, again.

Perhaps that is the moral of the story.

Pomp and Circumstance
and Other Sexual Activities

In 1937, USS *Dunlap* paid a ceremonial visit to Montreal, and, as is the custom, her Captain – rigged out, of course, in cocked hat, frock coat, medals, and sword – was to call upon the senior naval officer in HMCS *Donnacona*. Since the Canadian navy had no staff cars to send for him he set off in a taxi.

"Where to, M'sieu?" said the cabby.

"Ten sixty-two Mountain Street, please."

"You dress kinda funny to go dere, no?"

The Captain, with a seaman's lofty condescension to a landsman's inappropriate remark, ignored this.

When the cab pulled up at 1062 Mountain, the Captain noticed that all the blinds were drawn. Strange. He got out. Were there people peeking out from upstairs? Funny. Never mind.

"Cap'n," said his cabby, "you take your time. Enjoy yourself. They call me and I come for you when you finish."

"Very friendly, these Canadians," thought the Captain, and then, with a dignity befitting a Commanding Officer of the United States Navy, he strode forward, medals jingling, the gold on his sword glinting in the sun.

Next door, Commander Reginald Brock, RCNVR, similarly attired, bosun's mates ready to pipe the side, stood waiting to greet the distinguished visitor. He watched in horror the purposeful course the USN officer had set out on.

"Head him off. Head him off," he barked to the Officer of the Day.

The OOD darted out, shouting, "Not there, sir. Not there. Over here. It's 1060, not 1062. Over here."

It is safe to assume that the girls next door were disappointed. Not that they weren't used to guests from exalted circles, oh no – they had many, both regular and transient. But in broad daylight? And so gloriously attired?

On a more elevated and perhaps more virtuous note, is the following signal sent by a keen, if somewhat careless, Flag Lieutenant anxious to see to the dhobying of his Admiral's white uniforms when the fleet entered harbour.

From Flag Lieutenant to Senior Officer, dockyard: WHO DO YOU RECOMMEND FOR ADMIRAL'S WOMAN?

The senior officer was understandably perplexed, and perhaps indignant, at the implied appetites of the Admiral. He asked for a repeat and got: REFERENCE MY SIGNAL. PLEASE INSERT WASHER BETWEEN ADMIRAL AND WOMAN.

You will have noticed that these stories are far from bawdy and certainly not vulgar. It must always be thus when we are speaking of Personages, People of Consequence. This story has gone around the world many times in naval circles during the last forty years, and variations of it are now firmly entrenched in the folklores of many navies.

In the early 1940s, the Commander-in-Chief of the Mediterranean Fleet was Sir Andrew Browne Cunningham. A simple and direct man, he was known to his sailors as ABC. He was a fighting man who combined audacity with craft and was the scourge of the German and the Italian fleets. A vigorous man, Sir Andrew! He became "Sir Andrew" rather than simple "Andrew" when the king made him a Knight Commander of the Bath – KCB. Then, because of his successes in the Med, he was awarded the Knighthood of the Thistle. Had he not already been "Sir Andrew," had he been plain "Andrew," this Order of the Thistle would have given him the title.

This thought occurred to the Admiral based in Gibraltar. He and Sir Andrew had moved up the promotion ladder more or less together since they had both been cadets and this emboldened him to send the following signal when Sir Andrew's new distinction appeared on the King's Honour List:

From Flag Officer, Gib. to C-in-C, Med.: TWICE A NIGHT AT YOUR AGE. NOT BAD.

In the Home Fleet, in 1944, we had four or five battleships. The Commander-in-Chief, then Admiral Sir Bruce Fraser, rode in one on such operations as the sinking of the *Scharnhorst*. The Second-in-Command, Vice-Admiral Sir Henry More, usually rode in another. Rear-Admiral Sir Roderick McGrigor drove one cruiser squadron, Rear-Admiral Sir Dalrymple Hamilton another. There was a Rear-Admiral (Fleet Carriers) and a Rear-Admiral (Escort Carriers) each leading perhaps as many as three carriers on a particular operation. There was a Commodore (Destroyers) on the operation I am thinking of, a third attempt to sink the *Tirpitz*. And there were perhaps four Captains (Destroyers) leading four flotillas, a total of thirty-two destroyers. There were also other convoy-screening destroyers. But the carriers had become the main weapon and the whole fleet had to manoeuvre at high speed to alter into the wind when the aircraft took off or landed from them. Also the screening destroyers had to change formation rapidly from anti-submarine defence to anti-aircraft defence to anti-surface defence. I was in the Canadian destroyer *Sioux* and creaming through the fleet to take up a new station was exciting for me. It could also be dangerous, for we had to go at full speed, thirty-two knots, by the most direct route through the massive capital ships.

On that day, with white cumulus clouds against a pale blue sky, with a fresh twenty-knot breeze ruffling the Arctic Ocean and causing the sun to dance on the waves, Sir Bruce Fraser faced a dual problem. Enemy aircraft were approaching; the ships had to alter into the wind to allow aircraft to fly off and, at the same time, the destroyers had to swing out to form the anti-aircraft circle around the fleet. When I think of it now, Sir Bruce didn't have that much of a problem. He just had to order it done. It was the destroyers who had the problem.

It was a mêlée. An organized mêlée with each of the fifty-odd ships knowing where to go, but a mêlée nonetheless. The capital ships wheeled ponderously to their ordained course, the cruisers moved further out, the destroyers further yet, all at thirty-two knots, speeding this way and that, a white bone in the teeth of each, some passing ahead and some astern of other ships with only a few yards to spare. One wretched destroyer Commander found a large fleet carrier steaming directly in his path. He would have to alter to pass her and take up his new station. This would delay him and Sir Bruce wouldn't like that. Should he pass ahead or astern? Astern! So he steered right for her midship section, right for 23,000 tons, 760 feet long. She would pull ahead, her bearing would draw right as he approached. He would pass under her stern. Close, but he had no time to spare. A thousand eyes watched. The destroyer's bow was pointed now at the carrier's island, now abaft it, now still further aft, and within only a couple of ship's lengths. Nerves of steel had that destroyer Captain. He trusted his judgement and held his course.

His judgement was true. His forecastle – eighteen feet above the water – passed under the rear of the carrier. You could have thrown a biscuit from the destroyer to the carrier's quarterdeck. Then his bridge – thirty feet above the water – flashed up to the receding carrier's arse end. Would it pass, too. Yes!

Suddenly a rogue wave rolled the destroyer to starboard. The carrier's stern sank and wallowed in a trough. The top of the destroyer's bridge dinged, just barely dinged, the carrier's stern. He had collided with a fleet carrier, the one in which an Admiral wore his flag.

The destroyer boiled away to her allotted station. The carrier steamed furiously on, her deck alive with planes waiting to fly off. There was a breathless hush on the Admiral's bridge as the great man grabbed a signal pad and scribbled his feelings on this most unseemly affair.

The Admiral thrust the message to his Yeoman of Signals.

From Admiral Commanding, Carriers, to Destroyer: IF YOU TOUCH ME THERE AGAIN, I'LL SCREAM.

Dunkirk

It takes only three years to build a ship. It takes three hundred to build a tradition.

Admiral Sir Andrew Browne Cunningham
C-in-C, Mediterranean Fleet,
on the evacuation of our troops from Crete

When the German *Wehrmacht* broke through into France in 1940 and drove back the French and British armies until their backs were to the sea, there sailed from English ports a fleet such as the maritime world had never seen before, a fleet comparable to that of Drake when he had sailed against the Spanish Armada three hundred years before, or that of Admirals Lord Jellico and Beatty at Jutland some twenty years before. In fire power, no; in the size of the ships, no; in numbers, yes; and in audacity, flare, courage, and eagerness to come to grips with the enemy, definitely yes. Our troops were in trouble and the odds were all in favour of the enemy. Never mind. We would lose many ships. Never mind. Not to do our best was unthinkable. Muster all ships. Find crews for them. *All* ships! The pongos have got themselves into a bind, let's get them out. So we sent over to the coast of France the destroyers and small sleek luxury yachts, the large ungainly cross-channel ferries, the transports and fishing smacks and motor boats and anything else that might be able to pick up a few soldiers. For eleven days from May 24 to June 4, 388,226 soldiers suffered stoically, strafed and bombed on the beaches, before gratefully hoisting themselves inboard and sailing home. The bedraggled British Expeditionary Force sailed home with its tail between its legs, not to return for four years, this time to the beaches of Normandy, to drive the Germans back to Berlin.

This withdrawal brought up the spectre of an invasion of England by the Germanic tribes, an indignity which had not threatened since the Roman garrisons were recalled to Rome in the 400s. What cheek! Over *our* waters! The threat was real; Hitler had mounted an operation, Sea Lion, to invade southern England.

On April 9, 1940, German forces had smashed into Norway and Denmark; six weeks later, with Holland and Belgium under their heel, they plunged through France toward the Atlantic Ocean, to a stretch of coast from Dunkirk to the southern port of St. Jean de Luz where two Polish divisions were fighting with the French. The French surrendered but the Poles refused to and withdrew in good order to the sea. In May, British destroyers were fighting at point-blank range with German tanks entering Boulogne. The invasion of Great Britain was probable. The Admiralty signalled Halifax for help.

On the afternoon of the twenty-fourth of May, the ship's companies of *Restigouche, Skeena,* and *St. Laurent* were recalled from leave in Halifax. A disgruntled lot of matelots they were – three days in between convoys for the last nine months. In the dog watches as dusk settled over Halifax came the familiar pipe, "Cable party muster on the forecastle, special sea-dutymen close up, hands to stations for leaving harbour."

Another bloody convoy! Keeeerist! What a frigging navy!

But the hands fell in, the ships slipped, shaped course for Plymouth, and didn't return for well over a year. *Fraser* was also on her way direct from Bermuda where she had been prowling the southern seas looking for German raiders or intercepting German merchant ships running for home.

Lieutenant-Commander Nelson Lay in *Restigouche* was senior and led the way. Lieutenant-Commander Harry DeWolf followed in *St. Laurent* and Lieutenant-Commander Jimmy Hibbard was Tail-end Charlie in *Skeena.* Commander Wallace Creery was driving *Fraser.* Lay thought a little drill on the way across would be good so night-encounter exercises were practised. He would order the others to a slower speed (they had to steam at economical speed to get across which was only sixteen knots anyway), he would increase speed, pull ahead, and reverse course after dark; ships blacked out, of course. This didn't suit DeWolf; he wanted to get to the action as quickly as possible. "You know," he grumbled to the bridge watchkeepers at large, "Lay and I will be known in the RN as those two Canadians, DeWolf and DeLay." But on arrival in Plymouth the First Lord of the Admiralty seemed not to notice and a message from him awaited them.

> The presence of units of the Royal Canadian Navy in our midst inspires us to a still harder effort. Confident both of your skill and of your valour we wish you good luck in the fierce and exacting toil which lies before you.

On June 9, *Restigouche* was patrolling off Le Havre. Our retreating troops had destroyed all they could to deny oil and machinery to the Germans. The flames mounted and a pall of smoke hung over all. So close in did Lay get that he fouled one of his screws in the anti-submarine net across the harbour. When fast ahead and astern engine movements did not clear the wire, Lay, with customary impatience, went full ahead and broke it. He was ordered to pick up troops of the 51st Highland Division at St. Valery en Caux. Arriving at first light on the eleventh – about 5:30 A.M. – he found another destroyer, a liner, half a dozen transports, railway ferries, and many small boats evacuating French and British wounded – but no Highlanders in sight. DeWolf said later it looked like Dunkirk in miniature. Nobody seemed to be in charge. What to do? Lay told his First Lieutenant, Debby Piers, to send someone ashore to get in touch with the Highlanders' General Fortune.

Piers hared it for his cabin, looked at himself in the mirror, and said: "Piers, you're the one who's going ashore."

And replied to himself, "Aye aye, sir."

Packing binoculars, a signal lamp, chocolate bars, a bottle of whiskey, and sundry other appropriate items in his golf bag he reported to the Captain, "any other orders, sir? I'm off ashore."

"You going yourself, you bloody fool?"

"Yes, I am."

"Okay, find out what's going on and signal it back."

St. Valery is a village of perhaps a thousand souls with a stone pier where the river joins the sea, high tides and higher cliffs. The French overall Commander had not given the orders to retreat although some French troops were doing so. The General of the 51st Highlanders had been out of touch with his headquarters for several days and decided not to go: if he held the perimeter of the Dunkirk evacuation, more of our soldiers would get safely off to fight again another day. Neither he nor Lay realized that the Dunkirk evacuation had finished; his troops were surrounded by General Rommel's Panzer Divisions! So the sixty thousand troops of the 51st stayed. Nothing Piers could say would persuade the General. "But we've got five, six, seven ships here. We can take off thousands." But no; they all went into the bag – four years in P.O.W. camps.

Meanwhile, back in *Restigouche*, lying about two miles off, Piers's information was received by signal light. By this time *Restigouche* had been joined by *St. Laurent*, which had been a little further up the coast embarking French troops. Piers's boat had damaged its propeller and could only make a half knot so Lay ordered *Restigouche* inshore to get him. The boat was hooked on and hoisted. Panzer tanks appeared at the top of the cliff and opened fire. Shells came soughing and rushing overhead. *Whooosh. Whooosh.*

Harry DeWolf in *St. Laurent* opened up with his 4.7-inch guns – the first Canadian ship to fire on the enemy in the Second World War.

Restigouche then opened up. Both banged away at the Germans on top of the cliff. German shells banged back perhaps three or four feet above the bridge. Everyone flung themselves flat. Lay remained in his chair, erect. The Germans guns straddled *Restigouche* – over and short – again and again. Shell splinters cut through the rigging and ting-ting-tinged the upper deck. Piers went to the bridge to report. By this time *Restigouche* was doing thirty-two knots and zig-zagging.

"Well, Number One, what's it all about? No excitement?" So Piers told him as the shrapnel whizzed overhead. Later Piers said, "I was ducking and there was the Captain with his steel helmet on, just sitting there as if nothing was happening at all, just an afternoon picnic. That can really inspire confidence in a crew, it was really wonderful." Thirty-eight years later, Nelson Lay told me at his farm in Balderson, Ontario, "I noticed the Officer of the Watch and the Yeoman of Signals and the rest were ducking down behind the canvas wind dodgers. This struck me as absurd and I started to laugh. Canvas is no protection against a 3-inch shell and, in any case, when you heard the shell it was well past."

To few sailors has God given this gift of coolness.

St. Laurent went up the coast to engage shore batteries while *Restigouche* made for Plymouth at thirty-two knots. Out of the sun a fighter aircraft dived. "Open fire," said the Captain. But against such a sudden attack, none of the 4.7-inch guns could be brought on. After the aircraft was away astern a few rounds from a Lewis gun were managed. The fighter circled and flashed by Aldis light, "Damn poor shooting." They found out later it was a Canadian pilot with time on his hands who beat them up just for the hell of it. "I hope he had plenty to do in the Battle of Britain later," Lay observed with some asperity.

In Plymouth, *Restigouche* topped up with fuel and stores and set off again. Steaming out they saw German fighters attacking the barrage balloons which were exploding and dropping their red-hot mooring wires. They picked up the liner *Arandora Star* and crossed the Bay of Biscay, sighted HMS *Galitea* and *Fraser* – which had picked up, among many others, Colonel Georges Vanier, the Military Attache in Paris, who had made the coast and escaped in a small fishing boat. They arrived in St. Jean de Luz, near the Spanish border. They were to take off two Polish divisions who had been fighting with the French. The French had surrendered and tried to persuade the Poles to do likewise. No bloody fear, not us mate, said the Polish Commander – or some equivalent of this. As well as the Poles, Lay took on board a Basque priest, several women, a Captain, RN, and two Polish Generals. One of these, overcome by the occasion, kissed the rescuing Captain on both cheeks: the other pinned on Lay's breast a Polish Eagle from his shoulder badge. About sixty were brought in the "Rustyguts," thousands in *Arandora Star*. Later the Polish Government in Exile awarded Lay and three of the crew the Polish Cross of Valour to augment the General's Polish Eagle.

Course was shaped to join up with HMS *Calcutta* and *Fraser*. They were to go up the Gironde River and blow up all they could to deny it to the advancing Germans. This never came to pass for, that night, *Calcutta* rammed *Fraser*, cut her in two, steamed on, and told *Restigouche* to pick up survivors.

Back in Plymouth to land survivors and repair damage, *Restigouche* was drawn in to the world-wide fracas resulting from the abject surrender of the French to the Germans, and the formation of what many Frenchmen thought was a traitorous government under Marshal Pétain. Admiral Darlan was Minister of Marine. What would the French navy do? If their warships were taken by Germany it would be a disaster for us. The First Lord of the Admiralty, A. V. Alexander, and the First Sea Lord, Admiral Sir Dudley Pound, made contact with Admiral Darlan and received solemn assurances that the French Fleet would not be allowed to fall into German hands. But could these assurances be trusted? In Plymouth and Portsmouth there were two French battleships, four light cruisers, some submarines including the 3,000-ton *Surcouf,* eight destroyers, and about two hundred mine-sweepers and anti-submarine craft. At Alexandria, after long negotiations between our Admiral Cunningham and the French Admiral Godfroy, the French immobilized their ships and landed most of their crews. At Dakar the *Richelieu* was attacked by one of Cunningham's aircraft carriers, HMS *Hermes.* At Martinique a French aircraft carrier and two cruisers were immobilized. But at Oran, Admiral Sommerville's emissary, Captain Holland, was refused an interview by the French Admiral when he went ashore by motor boat to arrange a settlement. From about ten in the morning until about six in the evening exhortations were tried – in vain. At 6:26 P.M. Churchill sent this signal to Sommerville: "French ships must comply with our terms or sink themselves or be sunk by you before dark." But Sommerville had opened fire at 5:54. A ten-minute bombardment followed by an attack by aircraft from *Ark Royal* blew up the battleship *Bretagne,* the *Dunkerque* ran aground, the battleship *Provence* was beached, and *Strasbourg* escaped and reached Toulon.

Back in Plymouth, Nelson Lay had been put in charge of ten small French vessels lying moored in the harbour. He had ten officers and fifty-two men. They boarded the ships at 4:00 A.M., daybreak. Nobody was on watch as Lay's men boarded. The ten Captains were brought to him and shown Winnie's billet doux. The alternatives they were offered were: to turn their ships over to the British: to put them out of action; or to sail them to America where they would be interned for the duration of the war. Ninety-nine per cent opted to return to France and were allowed to pack their gear. Leaving a prize crew on board, Lay returned to his ship. An hour later he got a signal telling him that there appeared to be a mutiny aboard the ten ships. Quickly gathering some officers and men he returned to his prizes of war to find not a mutiny, just a lot of French sailors who had got into the wine – along with their British guards. Two days later, four hundred and sixty French sailors from the ten ships were put on board one French ship, which then sailed for Le Havre. Most perished when the ship was sunk by a U-boat on the way across.

In England at the time were many young Canadians who had finished their cadet time in *Conway* or other training ships, done their midshipmen's two years in RN cruisers or battleships, passed their seamanship examinations, and were now, at age twenty, Acting Sub-Lieutenants about to start their technical courses on the more specialized training ships. At the gunnery school HMS *Excellent*, in Portsmouth, air raids were frequent and study was difficult. Acting Sub-Lieutenant John Charles – who would later rise to Rear-Admiral, RCN, told me about the part he played in repelling Hitler's expected invasion, Operation Sea Lion.

About the twenty-sixth of May Charles's group was turned to, fallen in, and detailed off. He was the senior Sub-Lieutenant. He and one other were assigned to a party consisting of one Gunnery Lieutenant, one Sub-Lieutenant, a Chief Gunner's Mate, and about forty-eight sailors which was detailed to mount 6-inch naval guns around the coast of England. At this time, the fall of France was imminent; Dunkirk was just beginning. Charles and his Lieutenant, a fellow called Beckwith, were given a little car, two double-decker London buses, one ten-ton truck with a big concrete-mixer, and a two-ton estate truck, and were sent to Margate sea-front, where they were to find some yellow crosses on the pavement in front of the hotel, on which they were to mount two 6-inch naval guns. They were equipped with a piece of paper from the Admiralty authorizing them to requisition accommodation both for the troops to site the guns and the crews to man them afterwards. On the yellow crosses, they were first to build a form twelve feet by twelve feet and fill it with concrete. They were then to plant in the centre of the concrete an iron ring about two feet high with twenty-four bolts. The gun would be mounted on this ring. The guns – 1906 vintage – and their pedestals were to be waiting for them at the railway station. "We got rather clever at this," says Charles, "We built a little ramp and put the gun on the back of the truck and then we would back the truck up and get the gun into the hole in the pedestal and just run it in with the truck. It took us a while to get onto this. We were working from sunrise to sunset.

"We had the sea-front hotel. It was good fun at night. The Chief could sing like a bird and we'd go down to the pub and he'd get on the piano. I thoroughly enjoyed it. We worked hard all day and then sang until eleven or twelve at night, until the pubs closed. Then a good night's sleep and up at dawn."

They were at Margate five days to do five guns then on to Newhaven to repeat the exercise. They then did Seaford, Littlehampton, Worthing, and Brighton. At Seaford, where Charles was the advance party, there weren't hotels but summer homes. This young Canadian

Sub-Lieutenant had to go into this house behind the crosses and say, "I'm sorry but you will have to leave your house. We need it." It's hard to believe, but the residents accepted that and went without animosity. At Portished, in the Bristol Channel, the troops were in a hotel just along the front, but Charles lived in a house right behind the gun-sites. The owner, a woman in her thirties whose husband was a Major in the Eighth Army in Africa, had rigged up a bed for him in the living room. On the second night, after a sing-song with the troops in the pub, Charles turned in and heard, *varooom, varooom*. He'd heard Heinkels before but he thought, "Gee this is crazy – way out here in the west country?" Then, *swoooosh, swoooosh*, and he was under the table. *Rumpety, rumpety, rump* – out flew the windows in the living room with a hell of a tinkle of glass. The Major's wife rushed downstairs crying, "Save me, save me." She was in a light nightdress, he in pyjamas. I don't know what the Major would have said if he had walked in at two o'clock on that morning.

The next town on the list was Cardiff when Beckwith said, "You're pretty good at this now. You go on to Cardiff and put up the guns and I'll take a couple of days' leave." In Cardiff the crosses weren't on the pavement; they were out on a sand spit facing down the Bristol Channel and there was no road. There was a railway spur which had obviously once run to a jetty where either coal or sand was loaded. Charles clearly couldn't get the trucks out on the spit, so he went down to the railway station to see if the Great Western Railway would move the material there on a flat car. The station master said, "Oh yes, we'll move them out there, but we don't have a crane with enough strength and swing to reach out over the pedestal." Charles found out that the nearest crane that would do was in Birmingham, so he approached the Rear-Admiral in command of the Cardiff area. I guess the Admiral was a bit puzzled to have a young Canadian Sub-Lieutenant asking for a crane from Birmingham, however, Charles had his invaluable little chit of paper from the Admiralty, and, lo and behold, the crane was shifted down from Birmingham. After the next one, in Penarth on the other side of the Bristol Channel, all the sailors and equipment were sent back to *Excellent* – Whale Island – and the gun crews left behind to man the guns settled down in the local pubs with quiet satisfaction to await the arrival of the vanguard of Hitler's Sea Lion invasion fleet.

"We got back to Whaley somewhere during the first week in July," says Charles, "before the French Fleet contretemps, which I think was the seventh of July. What had happened was that the French had surrendered so there were quite a number of French ships in British ports. In Portsmouth, at *Excellent*, we were at dinner, dressed in bow ties and wing collars, when, at about eleven o'clock, they fell the class in and divided us up into parties. I ended up with a party of about fifty husky sailors detailed to take over a French destroyer in Portsmouth harbour. It was raining like hell and H-hour for this boarding and take-over of the French warships was four o'clock in the morning. I had a little chit of paper which I was to hand to the French telling them they could either leave their ships and be returned to France or stay and fight the enemy with us.

"It was four o'clock in the morning. There were two gangways out on this French destroyer. Another Canadian Sub-Lieutenant, Freddie Frewer, went over the after brow to go aft and deal with the officers and I went over the forward brow to deal with the sailors and NCOs. Both of us had .45s strapped on, gas masks, tin hats, wing collars and bow ties, and it was still raining like hell."

"We went down to the various mess decks, turned the hands out, and separated the NCOs from the sailors. They had big tubs, rather like rum tubs except they had red wine in them, *vin ordinaire*. They practically brushed their teeth in wine. They all turned out and had a slug, and another, then more. Freddie and I got them ashore by nine or ten o'clock in the morning.

"The idea was that when they were ashore on the jetty, somebody would ask again whether they wanted to go back to France or stay in England. About 90 per cent went back to France, but, in this vast and frantically ad hoc administrative arrangement, nobody had thought to provide food. They hadn't had any breakfast, just dinner the previous evening and that *vin ordinaire* was surely tempting. By eleven o'clock in the morning we had a bunch of pretty happy French sailors around.

"Yes, it was a funny summer."

Acting Sub-Lieutenant Bob Timbrell, RCN, was in the same class as John Charles doing his gunnery course at *Excellent*. He too was summoned to help stave off the attack of the Hun hordes. Behind him lay the training ship *Conway*, the RN Naval College, the training cruiser *Vindictive*, and two years as a Midshipman in the battleship *Barham* and the battlecruiser *Hood*. He felt about ready to take command. And, at age twenty, that was what he did.

The evacuation from Dunkirk was starting. He appeared before an ancient and harried Captain:

"Name?"

"Timbrell."

The Captain scribbled on a piece of paper. "Join the *Llanthony*."

A puzzled Sub-Lieutenant marched out and found a Petty Officer (usually the fount of all knowledge, he had learned). "Petty Officer, I've been told to join *Llanthony*. Do you know where she is?"

"King Stairs, sir."

So there Timbrell went and found a beautiful white yacht with a yellow funnel and about eight people standing about. What now? Finding the omnipresent and usually omniscient Petty Officer, Timbrell asked, "Do you know where the Captain is?"

"No sir, we've just been told to report here."

Further perusal of his piece of paper disclosed that *he* had been appointed by Their Lordships, Commissioners of the Admiralty, "in command of His Majesty's Ship *Llanthony*." His crew? What he saw around him: two civilian diesel engineers from the London Transport Company and six ordinary seaman in what were obviously brand new uniforms, these hands evidently snatched from new-entry training. All from Newfoundland, though, so probably fishermen, they must know something about the sea. Wood cutters or lumberjacks all. Ah well, we must sail. But to his dismay Timbrell found that *Llanthony*, just completed for a Maltese millionaire, had no charts and the compass was not adjusted. He must sail anyway. So they buoy-hopped around to Ramsgate, adjusting the compass on the way. The boat was heavily armed – Timbrell had one .45 revolver (1914 vintage) with a leather belt and a holster that kept slipping between his legs. Up the English Channel to Ramsgate, fuel, embark victuals, get charts, and sail for Dunkirk. The jetties were to be used only by destroyers and ferries; get your troops from the beach.

Llanthony navigated safely through the minefields, slipped her two boats at Dunkirk, and took off as many soldiers as she could carry – about one hundred and twenty; no mean feat this, there's a healthy tide runs through the Channel. About 300,000 soldiers were left waiting on the beach. Shells arriving from the German guns, now within range. The RAF was overhead but the odd German plane got through. The town in flames; a pall of smoke over all. Assembled there were every conceivable type of craft including scores of Thames pleasure boats. One of Timbrell's *Conway* term was in command of a car ferry, another had a mud hopper used to dredge silt from the rivers. On the way back they came across a Thames tour-boat, loaded with troops, that had broken down. "Pass her a line and we'll tow her."

"She's got no towing bollards, sir."

"Then put a line completely around her and we'll use that."

On May 22 it was hoped that 10,000 men a day could be taken off. But by May 26 Operation Dynamo (as it had been named) had 129 ferries, coasters, yachts, dredges, and skoots (Dutch *schuitjes*) and the proposed number of men to be taken off was upped to 22,000 a day. Other Canadian Sub-Lieutenants besides Timbrell were there. Peter Bennett was driving the *Prince of Wales* – not the battleship, the Thames River pleasure boat. He too had an unreliable compass and didn't know what part of the French coast he had approached. A destroyer, mistaking him for a German, nearly rammed him before he got off the correct recognition signal. He then asked an anchored French ship, *"Ou est l'armée Britannique?"* and was answered by a revolver shot. Strangers were suspect. Sub-Lieutenant Ronald Williams was also wondering where exactly he was and landed to find out. About a quarter of a mile inland he hailed two soldiers. *"Lieber Gott!"* they replied and fired on him. He fired back and felled these two but others came running. Bennett hastily fled to seek a more friendly beach.

Timbrell arrived back in England with his first load. He disembarked his troops and returned to Dunkirk. Another hundred-odd troops were embarked. Sail a third time, and a fourth time. Then *Llanthony*'s luck ran out. A German bomb hit the forecastle. Five of the crew were killed, the anchors were lost as their cables parted. The fuel lines to the engines were chopped; the ship stopped. She drifted back on the beach and landed the troops whence they had plucked them such a short time before, they, understandably, reluctant to go. Then Timbrell put his crew over the side to dig a trough underneath the propellors and rudder so that *Llanthony* would not be damaged when the tide left her high and dry. The tide receded to waist level around the yacht, and soldiers waded out to ask if they could come on board. Timbrell said they could when the tide came in.

It occurred to Timbrell that embarkation would be easier if he made his own jetty. He got these soldiers to get trucks off the beach and drive them out as far as possible as the tide fell, to form a long line of them out and out until the water started to rise again. The remainder of the dispirited troops on the beach squatted and waited. Then, into this gloomy scene wafted tones similar to those heard on *Excellent*'s parade ground – so long ago now it seemed. "Left, right, left, right. Pick up your dressing. Squad halt."

It was the remains of a regiment of the Brigade of Guards which had been fighting the rear-guard action. Not as smart in appearance as when they were on duty at Buckingham Palace, but a lot better than the rest of the soldiers on the beach. Eight of them. The Sergeant waded out. "Sir, we want to get out of this. Is there anything we can do for you?"

"Yes, go and get a bren gun carrier [like a small tank] and run it to seaward of me so I can use it as a sea anchor."

"Very good, sir. Squad, about turn. Quick march."

The Sergeant provided the sea anchor and more. He brought back some machine guns and anti-tank rifles. *Llanthony* was now truly an armed yacht, which was just as well, for by now the German E-boats were harrying the evacuation fleet. The water rose, the fuel line had been repaired, they hauled the *Llanthony* off, embarked troops, and returned to England to land them.

But in England the Sergeant of the Guards thought he could do more. The Sergeant allowed as how the Captain might have further use for him and his men, and, with respect, would the Captain like them to stay and make further trips?

The Captain most certainly would, and thank you, Sergeant.

Timbrell was by now considered an old and experienced hand by the authorities ashore and so, for the next trip, was given a flotilla of four trawlers. He called a Commanding Officer's conference of these four skippers (with a combined experience at sea of about a hundred years, he with two) and issued his orders. "We'll sail from Ramsgate, you stay close to me as I have a chart of the minefields, we go to the beach, anchor, load up, and return. We sail across at night and load at dawn."

They stayed close, all right, their bows practically rubbing the stern of the next ahead. But one strayed too far to port and blew up on a mine.

Then the E-boats came in to attack. With considerable glee, Timbrell's marines, the Guardsmen, opened up with everything they had brought off the beach, Timbrell joining in with his .45. Under this withering volume of fire, the damaged and startled E-boats sheered off and disappeared into the dark.

This last day was the hottest of them all. To the shelling and bombing and strafing of the past days was added mortar fire as the Germans closed in. The troops who were left were nearly at the end of their ability to function at all – except one. He came zig-zagging down the beach in such a way that no sniper could ever have hit him. Drunk, royally drunk, but ambulatory. He must have spent most of the night and probably the day before in a wine shop. "I want to go back to England, sir. Please don't leave without me. I'll just go back and get my ticket. Just a few minutes." Off he weaved and disappeared into the lethargic mass of waiting soldiers. He reappeared some ten minutes later – with a case of brandy. "Here's my ticket, sir." He was hauled aboard, staggered below, and fell asleep.

Llanthony sailed back for the last time, not the trim and immaculate yacht Timbrell had started with; both masts were smashed from the E-boat shells, there were holes in the superstructure, she was dirty, the signs of the sea were showing plain. All hands stank to high heaven, none having washed in twelve days. The troops were landed: the remaining sailors returned whence they had come, and Timbrell and his "marines" marched out the dockyard gate into the stream of Portsmouth traffic hauling their gun carriage, bren guns, two anti-tank guns, and case of brandy covered with canvas.

"Where can I get a bus to *Excellent*?" asked Timbrell of a bus conductor.

"You back from Dunkirk, sir?"

"Just got in."

The conductor went to the front and spoke to the driver, told the passengers the bus was going to Whale Island first, helped them load their gear, and deposited them at the entrance.

The Guardsmen returned to their regiment the following day. The Sergeant was later awarded the Distinguished Service Medal. Timbrell had recommended him for this, a naval decoration; soldiers usually get the Military Medal.

On May 24, there had seemed little chance of escape for the allied soldiers pinned against the coast of Flanders. It seemed as if the words of John McCrae's poem, "In Flanders fields the poppies blow/Between the crosses, row on row, . . ." would refer to soldiers of the Second World War as well as the First. By June 4, 338,000 had escaped – 600 of them in Bob Timbrell's *Llanthony*.

Evacuations are not much talked of in army circles. They don't add that much glamour to regimental history. But there were others besides Dunkirk. At the time that the German forces were rampaging through Europe after the fall of France, the Chief of the Imperial General Staff decided that British soldiers had best occupy Norway. Could the navy land them there? Of course. And they did. But a day later the Germans arrived in Norway and after a week or so it was apparent that our troops had best get out. So the navy took them out again, with considerable losses. It was the same in Crete a few years later. The German forces were just too much to handle and the navy took the troops out of there.

We in the navy often pull the legs of our comrades-in-arms, the soldiers, affectionately known to us as "pongos." Also it seems a characteristic of our troops to tell of these defeats (for that is what they are) with a mordant humour. I doubt if the following conversation ever took place but I have heard versions of it all over the world – in naval messes of course, usually when a soldier is present. But I give it to you as showing another facet of the fighting man.

Two friends who had been in school together, one now a sailor, one a soldier, met in London in about the fourth year of the war. They settled down over a beer to fill in the interval since their school days.

"Well, and where have you been?" asked the sailor.

"First our outfit was in Norway. But we had to get out."

"Then what?"

"Then we went to France but we had to get out of there, too, at Dunkirk."

"Bad luck. Then what?"

"After a while we were sent to Crete but. . ."

"Well, where are you now?"

"My regiment is with Monty in the desert."

"And how do you like that?"

"Not much. Too far from the navy."

Battles in the English Channel

And the sun went down, and the stars came out far over the summer sea,
But never a moment ceased the fight of the one and the fifty-three.
Ship after ship, the whole night long, their high-built galleons came,
Ship after ship, the whole night long, with her battle-thunder and flame;
Ship after ship, the whole night long, drew back with her dead and her shame.
For some were sunk and many were shatter'd, and so could fight no more -
God of battles, was ever a battle like this in the world before?

The Revenge, Alfred Lord Tennyson

Perhaps not before but certainly after. In the autumn of 1943 and throughout 1944 His Majesty's Canadian Tribal Class Destroyers *Haida, Huron, Athabaskan,* and *Iroquois* had a busy time of it.

The year 1943 had seen a decrease in U-boat sinkings of our merchant ships in the North Atlantic – down to 309 from 1,091 in 1942: and 1944 was to be better – only 100 lost. After four long years of dreadful losses, we were winning the war. Our soldiers were in Africa and about to cross to Sicily, then Italy: a million men were massing in England to attack Fortress Europe, on the beaches of Normandy as it turned out. Operation Neptune was the name of the seaborne assault by the navy across the English Channel, Operation Overlord the landing of our soldiers in Europe.

It was Hitler's 1940 Operation Sea Lion in reverse. After the retreat of our soldiers from Dunkirk Hitler had gathered men, arms, matériel, and landing craft along the coast from Ostend south to Calais, Boulogne, Dieppe, and Le Havre to cross the English Channel and invade a confused and disorganized England. That the ships of the Royal navies would have used their policy of "sink, burn, and destroy – at any cost" was never in doubt either in London or Berlin. A hundred and thirty-four years earlier Napoleon had looked out across the Channel, contemplating the invasion of England. Command of the sea was essential for his conquest of England and the mastery of the world, but between him and his ambition stood the Royal Navy and the ships of Nelson. Britain's world-wide merchant navy supplied the British Isles and her Empire. Alfred Thayer Mahan later wrote:

> Those far distant, storm-beaten ships, upon which the Grand Army never looked, stood between it and the dominion of the world.

After much backing and filling Hitler cancelled Sea Lion for the same reason as Napoleon had to cancel his invasion. What neither of these had dared to do we now had to do in Operation Neptune, taking our soldiers to France against a defended coastline.

And along that coast the *Kriegsmarine* had formidable forces to disrupt our landings: there were perhaps ten Narvik- and Settier-class destroyers with four 5.5-inch guns (our Tribals had six 4.7-inch guns), with a speed of thirty-six to thirty-nine knots (we could crank up thirty-two), 2,400 tons (we were 2,000), eight 21-inch torpedoes (we had four). Our Tribals treated the Narviks with a great deal of respect: so indeed did the light cruiser that often went along and she had 6-inch guns as opposed to the Narvik's 5.5-inch; but, although she had more guns she was four knots slower. There were also perhaps fifteen Elbing-class destroyers in the German Channel Fleet: smaller, lighter gunned, but just as fast as us and with more torpedoes. Then there were twenty or so Möewe-class and T-class torpedo boats – bristling with 4- and 1.1-inch guns, rapid-fire machine guns, and six torpedoes. Add to these a large number of *sperrbrechers*, minesweepers, armed trawlers, and up to thirty E-boats and you can see that getting our dear old pongos across the Channel was not going to be easy. Not with these German surface ships afloat.

So sink them, burn them, run them on shoals, blow them up. Clear the Channel of the enemy!

It did not start very well. In the Autumn of 1943, German troops and cargoes were moving at will along the French coast and several sweeps failed to intercept them. But on the night of October 22 the cruiser *Charybdis* led six destroyers to intercept a convoy of about six German merchant ships escorted by six Elbing destroyers. She illuminated with starshell at 4,000 yards, sighted torpedo tracks approaching, swung her helm over to comb the spread (allow the torpedoes to glide harmlessly past on either side), but was hit – first in a boiler room and then further aft. *Charybdis* listed to fifty degrees, then slid to a vertical position, stern under and bow sticking up for nearly two-thirds of her length. Her Commander, who was in a carley float, said, "She remained in this position nearly half an hour, then sank." The destroyer *Limbourne*, second-in-command, was also hit, in the foward magazine in her case, and the resultant explosion blew off her forecastle. The forward bulkhead of the forward boiler room held, however, and she limped toward home stern-first. But this left both the first- and second-in-command out of action. Heavy rain squalls started. A mêlée ensued: nobody sure who was in command. Who was where? Friend or foe? The fog of battle! The enemy convoy and escorts escaped. *Limbourne* could not be towed so her sea cocks were opened, but she refused to sink. Daylight was approaching and with it the certainty of air attack. A torpedo was put into her by *Talybont*. She *still* floated. It was now 6:40 in the morning. *Rocket* put another tin fish in her and at last she sank. All her survivors had been transferred and all that were left in the water from *Charybdis* had been picked up – 107 in all. Her Senior Officer, Captain Voelcker, was not among them.

Not a good operation. The seas would not be kept safe this way.

From January 1944 the Tenth Destroyer Flotilla was based at Plymouth as a striking force but no enemy could be found until the night of April 26. The cruiser *Black Prince* was leading the Tribals, the senior of which was HMCS *Haida* under Commander Harry DeWolf. Following him were HMCS *Athabaskan* under Lieutenant-Commander Johnny Stubbs, HMCS *Huron* under Lieutenant-Commander Herbie Rayner, and HMS *Ashanti*.

Besides fighting together, *Huron* and *Ashanti* were what is known as "chummy ships." That is, the ships' companies mingled a lot during their brief days in harbour and the two First Lieutenants, Pat Budge and Terry Lewin, were particular friends. To this day, Terry Lewin (now Admiral of the Fleet Lord Lewin) is proud to be an honorary member of the "*Huron* Association." But to get on with the war:

Enemy convoys ran from Brest to the Channel Islands. It was a "tramline" route, travelled consistently by the enemy because they had a friendly coast to flee to with mounted protective guns and radar sets to direct them against the maurauding British, Canadians, and Poles. It was hard to know where we would meet them along this

112

tramline – head on or from astern – we certainly had to go along this route but further to seaward to keep out of the range of the coastal guns whose radar-directed fire could be devastating. Eighteen miles off the French coast we knew the enemy radar was tracking us.

One early night patrol was typical. There was no moon, visibility was about two miles, there was a light northerly wind, short choppy waves. At two in the morning *Black Prince* got radar contact at 21,000 yards – Four Elbing destroyers as it turned out. Nine minutes later the enemy detected us and altered course 180 degrees to the same course as ourselves. A stern chase; we cranked on thirty knots. At 2:20 the range was down to 13,100 yards and *Black Prince* illuminated with starshell and released the destroyers to attack. They bore in. *Huron* and *Ashanti* chose a target and pounded her as she fled to the east. Hit after hit was seen on her after end: another had a fire burning briskly aft. One turned toward the beach and was lost to sight among the rocks. The fourth continued east at, we may be sure, her maximum speed. In passing it would be well to explain that this is not the maximum speed shown on her official trials; oh no! This is the maximum delivered by any ship's engineer, in any navy, who wants to live to fight another day. This one did live but she had one gun and all her radio communications out of action, and fourteen casualties.

See the picture. Four light German destroyers fleeing from a cruiser and four heavy destroyers. The enemy have made smoke but can still be seen from time to time by the starshells bursting over their heads. Three 6-inch guns and eight 4.7-inch guns are hurling high-explosive shells at them at the rate of about ten rounds a minute. That's about forty bricks in the air at any one moment and all heading toward them.

Haida and *Athabaskan* opened fire at 10,000 yards and the red flashes of hits were seen. By 2:36 two enemy were on fire. *Black Prince* altered course to avoid a torpedo which ran 200 yards down her starboard side. The chase was now to the eastward. By 3:15 *Haida* had the range down to 5,000 yards. At 3:25 she saw an Elbing breaking back to the westward. *Black Prince*'s starshell gun had jammed and *Ashanti* had taken over. Now she ran out of ammunition and before *Huron* could take over the Elbing made good use of this blessed period of darkness. *Haida* and *Athabaskan* found their Elbing again and pounded her at 4,000 yards, then in to 1,000. Would you believe it? The Elbing fired back with what she had still working. For *twenty minutes*!

Admiral DeWolf told me about it many years later. "The trouble was that the cruiser [*Black Prince*] opened fire too early so the Germans turned and ran. It was long-range and we weren't doing too well at hitting anything but we were firing thousands of rounds. In the light of the starshell we caught sight of one who had turned back. He was either coming back to fire torpedoes at the cruiser or us or he was trying to escape. He appeared in the starshell only 5,000 yards on our starboard bow – it was the T29. We switched target right away, hit him with the first salvo and that was that. He was on fire and we hit him time and time again after that. I led *Athabaskan* over to this Elbing and we went past him firing at his waterline hoping just to sink him so we could go away. We went back a second and perhaps a third time. It was murder, really."

And as long as she could, the German fired back. Gallantry is not the exclusive province of our side. Two Elbings were sunk that night. A German survivor said, "The British ships in complete comfort were hacking us to bits. No matter how we twisted and turned the salvos always straddled us. It was an eerie feeling."

And still T29 would not sink. Now all four Tribals pounded her with twenty-four guns at a range of one mile. Then she sank.

Thus was executed the Commander-in-Chief's order, "Sink, burn, destroy."

The next foray was the night of April 28. Our fast mine-layer *Manxman* – she could do an incredible forty knots – was to lay mines off Ile de Bas and photo reconnaissance had shown two Elbings at St. Malo. *Haida* and *Athabaskan* were to be a covering force to seaward to prevent interference. And interference there was.

Clear sky, only a light chop, wind NNW Force 3, gentle breeze, ten knots, visibility two miles, and at 3:00 A.M. everyone going quietly about their appointed tasks. The radar plot in Plymouth detected vessels proceeding west at twenty knots between St. Malo and Roches Douvres. The Commander-in-Chief ordered our Tribals to intercept east of Ile de Vierge; they cranked up thirty-two knots. At 4:02, they made radar contact and sent an enemy-sighted report. The enemy were steaming west at twenty-four knots. Our Tribals were steering south; a right-angle head-on approach. Enemy bearing steady on the port bow. This means a collision course and is ideal, much better than a long stern chase, for instance: the opposing forces were converging at about fifty knots. At 4:02 the range had been 26,000 yards: at 4:12 it was 7,300 and *Haida* opened fire with starshell. At 4:14 two Elbings were sighted and *Haida* and *Athabaskan* opened fire in rapid broadsides. The enemy turned away, making smoke and firing twelve torpedoes. DeWolf knew this tactic of firing torpedoes as they turned away and ordered "turn 90 degrees to port together" to comb the tracks of the torpedoes and then, in the middle of the turn, stopped it to keep his after guns bearing, for both Tribals were scoring hits.

Athabaskan signaled, "I've been hit and am stopped." Her guns kept on firing. DeWolf got a signal off reporting this. *Athabaskan* had been hit aft. *Haida* raced on and at 4:18 was hitting her target. She also made a smoke screen for *Athabaskan* and continued firing until 4:22. Then the enemy split. The one which had been hit several times continued to the eastward and DeWolf let her go and followed the one which broke to the southward – towards the coast. *Haida*'s shells rained down on that Elbing for five minutes – that's about 200 bricks – and at 4:35 she was aground on the rocks and burning. "The whole crew was shouting, 'hit, hit,' of course," said DeWolf, "but the bloody things were exploding on the rocks. I got tired of that and said she's beached and on fire. I'm going back to *Athabaskan*." The other Elbing was now seven miles away and could not be caught. In a lull in the firing DeWolf had spoken severely to several hands about not wearing their steel helmets; had he noticed, neither was he. At least, he was wearing only the leather headband; the helmet had been blown off by gun blast.

First radar contact – 4:02. First sighting – 4:14. End of battle – 4:35. One Elbing damaged, one Elbing destroyed, one Tribal sunk.

For *Athabaskan* had blown up. Her crew had manned the pumps, shored bulkheads, and fought the fires for ten minutes; then the after magazine exploded. *Haida* steamed back at full speed and stopped amid the survivors now in the water, nearly two hundred, and started to pick them up. Time 4:57. DeWolf said, "I can stay for only fifteen minutes." Until 5:12. Twilight commenced at 6:16. They were only four miles off the French coast. *Haida* had to be clear of the coast by daybreak. While stopped he too could have been torpedoed by any U-boat or E-boat in the vicinity. He had lost one ship: he couldn't risk losing two. Many survivors were hauled up the scramble nets. All *Haida*'s boats and floats were lowered.

The fifteen minutes was up. It is poignant to imagine the turmoil of conflicting emotions in the mind of Harry DeWolf. His main duty was to his ship and his men. Yet there were drowning friends in the water. If he waited longer some of them would live; just as certain was the fact that if he left many would die. He had been told that other ships would come to succor them. But when? Already there was a faint light showing in the east.

"I'll wait five minutes longer," he said to the hands on the upper deck hauling the survivors inboard. "I'll count down each minute to you."

Those survivors on the lee side of *Haida* had it easier; the ship drifted toward them. For those on the windward side she drifted out of reach. They clung to what rafts or cork floats or whatever flotsam they could. They tried to cheer each other up with ribald remarks, pleading, cursing, comforting. Despite this, some hands, even those who appeared uninjured, said, "To hell with it," and just slid under. On the lee side, Johnny Stubbs was seen in the water by Leading Cook Laurin who noticed that Stubbs's hands and face were burned. He had been blown off the bridge. He moved from float to float encouraging his men to sing, to move their arms and legs to keep the circulation going, exhorting them in the firm voice they knew so well.

The five minutes passed, four, three, two, one. . . .

"Time, sir. Shall I go ahead?"

"We'll wait a few minutes longer."

The daylight strengthened. DeWolf could wait no longer. "Slow ahead."

Men on the scramble net, including two *Haida* hands who were at the bottom helping survivors, were swept back.

A signal had been sent that MTBs would arrive to pick up those who would have to be left. Until 5:30 small explosions were seen from the grounded Elbing. It was now getting red to the east – nautical twilight. With a heavy heart Commander DeWolf steamed away. Johnny Stubbs, the Captain of *Athabaskan*, was last seen in the water with his men. He had given his final order.

"Get out of it, *Haida*. Get out, sir. We'll be all right."

The Commander-in-Chief remarked in his analysis of this action, "I consider that Commander de Wolf (sic) acted rightly in returning to *Athabaskan*'s wreck to pick up as many survivors as time allowed. The signal which he made saying he was returning arrived just as one was about to be made to him to return. His decision, hard as it must have been made for him to make, and leave so many of his countrymen in the water, was correct."

A sequel to the tragedy relieves some of the gloom. *Haida*'s motor cutter had her day in the sun. The cutter's crew had been ordered to drop it unmanned; this didn't seem proper to her Coxswain, Leading Seaman Bill McClure, so he, an Able Seaman, and a Stoker manned it. McClure decided that the best thing for him to do was to pick up those who could not reach *Haida*. He picked up four, including Petty Officer Murray, a particular chum. What luck! He was one of *Haida's* hands who had been swept from the scramble net as she left. Then, wonder of wonders, they picked up the other *Haida* hand, Telegraphist Turner. McClure took note of the course *Haida* was steering. That was where he would head when he had loaded up. He got the Torpedo Gunner's Mate, then two others, then one more. He got a total of six; *Haida* had got forty-two; that left two hundred still in the water. But no, not two hundred; many had been killed and gone down with the ship. The First Lieutenant, Ralph Lawrence, was certainly one who had been killed by the explosion. Then the cutter's engine stopped on a fouled intake. The bloody thing would *not* start. Applying the remedy known around the world for recalcitrant machinery, the Stoker gave the intake a good thump with a wrench, at the same time pressing the starter. Recognizing the touch of a master mechanic, the engine coughed into life. McClure headed for home.

Four German minesweepers hove into view and nuzzled into the sailors still in the water. Then the Elbing T24; their enemy who a few hours ago had energetically tried to kill them, now saved them. Kapitänleutnant Wilhelm Meentzen, who could have stayed in the harbour where Canadian guns had forced him to take refuge, came out and rescued 87; these plus the 42 in *Haida* and the 6 in *Haida's* cutter. A total of 135 saved. The remaining 126 lie in forty fathoms off St. Poi, Finisterre, in the English Channel.

Leading Seaman McClure saw with a touch of alarm one of the minesweepers heading towards his boat. Hell, he didn't need help. Crank on all speed; maybe nine knots. The sweeper rapidly overtook them. Their head start of a mile was now reduced to half that. Then, for whatever reason, the German Captain changed his mind. The sweeper turned away. The cutter chugged stalwartly on. Seven miles off the coast of England the engine failed again. But by this time the sun was warm, their clothes had dried, and so had their cigarettes. They lit up. Two fighters came in sight, flying low. The men in the cutter stood and waved and fired a Very flare. The fighters altered toward. My Lord, they were Messerschmitts! They roared overhead and kept on. Thank God! Now the engine responded to the starter. RAF planes were sighted but went their way on whatever mission they had. The unconscious Torpedo Gunner's Mate worried them. They had no medical supplies; nothing could be done; anyway they didn't know what to do except keep him warm. There was a long way to go but they knew *Haida* would have made their plight known and *somebody* would be looking for them. And thirty miles south of the Lizard in Cornwall, the RAF found them and flashed back the good news. Then a Lancaster showed up. An air-sea rescue launch creamed out and brought them safely into Penzance harbour – six survivors from *Athabaskan* and two survivors and the boat's crew from *Haida*.

The news was telephoned to *Haida* on Sunday morning, April 13, 1944. Plymouth had been under air attack and *Haida*'s guns were part of the anti-aircraft defence. The Captain had just come down from the bridge and gone to his cabin. Fires were burning ashore. The officer who took the call wondered if he should tell the Old Man now. He had been without much sleep for three days and perhaps now was dozing off. God knew he needed rest. The Duty Officer looked at the phone in the signal office marked "Captain." No. Not that. When rung it made a strident "*rower, rower, rower.*" He went aft, stood outside the curtain of the Captain's door, and whispered, "Captain, sir."

"Yes, what is it?"

"The hands in the motor cutter are safe in hospital."

"Good. Get someone down there. They will have news of the others. They must be looked after. We may be able to bring them back. Thank you."

In the West Cornwall Hospital the Matron said they were in fine shape. Wanted to leave, in fact. But the doctor would put a stop to that! *Athabaskan*'s Torpedo Gunner's Mate, Charles Burgess, as the senior survivor, made a careful report and then relaxed. He had to stay but the others left the next day.

Thus ends the voyage of *Haida*'s motor cutter with her crew – Leading Seaman Bill McClure, Able Seaman Jack Hannam, and Stoker Bill Cummings – from France to England.

It is perhaps time to introduce Captain (D) of the Tenth Destroyer Flotilla. He was Basil Jones, DSO and Bar, DSC, RN, known, for a reason I cannot determine, as "Baffle" Jones. He drove *Tartar*: the other Brits were *Nubian, Eskimo, Ashanti,* and *Javelin. Haida* was Divisional Leader of *Huron, Athabaskan,* and *Iroquois.* The Poles were *Blyskawica* (called "Bottle of Whisky" – no linguists, us) and *Piorun.* On taking over command of the flotilla and after a period of settling in and taking the measure of what he had fallen heir to, Jones summed it up in these words:

> He [his predecessor] had certainly turned over to me the most magnificent combination of officers and ship's company I had ever to serve with. I soon realized that the standard of efficiency in the remaining ships of the Flotilla was high, and the commanding officers competent to deal with anything that came their way. The English ships and their COs – *Tartar, Nubian, Ashanti, Eskimo,* and *Javelin* had all had war experience in many situations. The Canadian ships and their COs – *Haida, Huron, Iroquois,* and *Athabaskan* were highly efficient and full of aggressive spirit. The Polish ships *Blyskawica* and *Piorun,* and their COs, were, like all Poles, desperate to get at the enemy.

"Desperate to get at the enemy" is the operative phrase. It sounds laudable and was, I suppose; but, with their country ruled by Germans and little news or bad news about their mothers and fathers and wives and children, they hated the Germans with an intensity we did not know. I heard the stories from Trinidad to Halifax to St. John's to Reykjavik to Scapa Flow to Murmansk to Gibraltar about how the Poles refused to pick up German survivors: how, when ordered to do so, they complied and picked them up – then threw them over the other side: how one of them came into St. John's harbour with hanged Germans swinging from the yardarm. (But nobody who told me these stories said, "I saw it.") I drank with the Poles in their ships in Scapa and they drank with me in mine. They seemed no different from the Norwegians or the Danes or the British or us. But it was sometimes a matter of gentle ragging that they seemed inordinately fond of firing their guns: a measure of the real *significance* of this was that sometimes this was said by Specialist Gunnery Officers who, one would have thought, would never say that guns could be fired too much.

It was from Jack McClelland that I heard of the Canadian MTB actions in the Channel during this period when the Canadian destroyers in the Tenth Destroyer Flotilla were banging away. He had commanded a Fairmile in the Newfoundland patrol and flushed a U-boat or two, then had graduated to MTBs. His flotilla operated out of Brixham to around the Channel Islands and had a lively enough time shooting up and being shot up by E-boats and flakships – they had had perhaps a dozen injured and killed.

As the cruiser would sort of mother the destroyers – she with her superior radar – so the MTBs had a destroyer or a frigate which would patrol within the area they were to cover that night and direct them onto likely targets. It was important to keep to your area so that, if you were picked up on a friend's screen, he knew it was you. Outside our own areas one was presumed enemy and both Germans and ourselves favoured the approach of shooting first and asking questions after. The more moderate Captains open fire and asked for identification at the same time. On any one night there could be up to forty ships – them and us – moving about the Channel. The destroyers were usually along their "tramline," so were the Hun. The MTBs in *this* area and *that* area. The C-in-C's radar kept a benevolent eye on the whole. Radio voice messages crackled through the night: course to steer to close enemy; ships engaging the enemy; ships sinking; ships blowing up; illuminate; open fire; my God, get out of it there are too many of them; the German excited chatter when they made contact and fired torpedoes – they were worse than the Yanks for chatter; if tracer was flying and ships burning outside your area, leave it alone: it's not your problem; your patrol ended at dawn, by that time you had to be out of range of the German shore batteries and under your own air-cover of Spitfires.

One night McClelland's flotilla lay quiet, engines stopped, drifting in their area. They were to leave at four in the morning and there was about twenty minutes to go. They had drifted a little outside their area but the MTB Senior Officer decided it wasn't worth starting up engines since they were leaving in a few minutes anyway.

"Suddenly, out of nowhere came these two Polish Tribals," said McClelland, "they opened fire with their goddamn guns and I will tell you that was an *experience*. Our Senior Officer was saying, '*Blyskawica, Piorun*, for Christ's sake, we're Canadian MTBs!' But they chose to ignore it, which they were entitled to. I have never before had 4.7-inch shells going over my head, it was like a bloody railroad train going by. It was like a great film to see these two Tribals going by running full speed and firing broadsides. We couldn't fire at them; all we could do was make smoke and shoot Very flares. Fortunately they were missing above us, firing high. They could have sunk us if they had been firing well. This always made us think that they knew and were just having fun trying to scare us. We deserved it, too. Finally a British flotilla called the Poles and said, 'I believe you are shooting at Canadians,' and they stopped firing, but it had gone on for five minutes and was a very scary incident. You had a lot of fun experiences.

"One of our hands was killed and another wounded. The Senior Officer of the Canadian MTBs took a piece of Polish shrapnel off his deck and delivered it to the Captain of *Blyskawica* next morning."

One of the "fun experiences" was the desire of the Flotilla Leader have his ships be the first Allied ships to enter St. Malo, and McClelland remembers it as "one that particularly amused me." After D-Day they heard that our troops had captured St. Malo so the Flotilla Leader took six boats, two groups, and went down to have a look. It was about 6:30 A.M., light, and when they got off St. Malo the Leader left three boats out at about ten miles and led three boats in to the harbour – his, McClelland's, and another. They could see these large shore batteries training around to point at them. Their first reaction was, well, they are sort of having fun, and then they began to wonder if maybe St. Malo hadn't been captured by our soldiers and they started to turn back to seaward. They hadn't turned more than ten degrees when the enemy batteries opened fire.

"Boy, we zig-zagged and made smoke, shell splashes landing all around, we all got soaking wet," said McClelland, "shots dropping everywhere; we were bloody lucky to get out without being hit. The other boats of the flotilla, from ten miles out, were calling us on the radio and cheering us on. Quite a dicey experience; there would have been a great Court of Enquiry and courts martial all around if any of us had actually suffered any damage. There was always an amusing side to the navy."

Leaving these rather harum-scarum MTB men and returning to the more decorous battles run by Captain (D) of the Tenth Destroyer Flotilla we still find, amongst the bangs and the glare and the killing, the amusing side of the navy. On the night before the D-Day assault of our soldiers on the Normandy beaches – the third and fourth of June 1944 – the whole flotilla was strung out in a line along the route swept clear of mines by the intrepid minesweepers which led the vast armada across the Channel from England to France. The Tenth was both (A) a screen to protect the thousand-odd ships that carried the troops, and (B) a sea-rescue unit to pick up any downed troops from the Horsa gliders. (These were towed across to land behind the enemy's front line of defence and create alarm, confusion, and despondency to the Hun; also to provide allied-dominated areas for the troops landing on the beaches at dawn to head towards after a beach-head had been established.) Unfortunately, these glider-borne troops were prey to the danger of prematurely parted tow-lines. And so it happened that one of them came down into the sea far short of where she had been headed, but not far from *Tartar*.

Captain Jones said, "They were a picturesque lot, with blackened faces, and, as we arrived along side them, their leader shouted, 'And whose bloody navy are you?'

"We rescued them, and a tot of rum answered the question."

Commander Jimmy Hibbard, the Captain of *Iroquois* remembers his First Lieutenant's advice to him in the heat of action during one of these Channel battles of 1944 with complete clarity. Action had been joined with a formidable force of Elbings and Narviks and both sides were blazing away at each other with enthusiasm; enemy torpedoes had been fired and avoided; tracer was flying both ways. There was the acrid stink of cordite, gunsmoke drifting to leeward, the enemy fall-of-shot splashes getting closer, and erupting geysers of water somewhere out there in the dark. A heavy rain was driving into the faces of all on the bridge and dripping off their chins. Tony Coughlin, Hibbard's First Lieutenant, stepped over to the Captain, who was conning the ship, and, licking his lips, said,

"Sir, I don't know if you've noticed, but this water on our faces is now salty. We are running through the bugger's shell splashes."

Three days after D-Day, on the night of the eighth and ninth of June, air reconnaissance had shown four enemy ships steering northeastwards from Brest, across the Gulf of St. Malo, between the Channel Islands of Guernsey and Jersey, to Cherbourg. Their purpose was to get to the southern flank of the Normandy invasion and to supply the Le Havre E-boat flotillas with more torpedoes – a load of these was carried on deck. There were two large destroyers of the Narvik- or Settier-class, an ex-Dutch destroyer with 4.7-inch guns and the old friend of the Tenth, T24 – the one that got away the night the Elbing T29 was sunk by *Haida*. *Tartar*, *Ashanti*, *Haida*, and *Huron* went along the "tramline" on a colliding southwesterly course. *Blyskawica*, *Eskimo*, *Piorun*, and *Javelin* were two miles to seaward on the leader's starboard quarter. At 1:17 A.M. radar contact was made and the flotilla altered formation from line ahead to line abreast, thus barring the enemy from slipping past. Range, 20,000 yards. When the enemy fired his torpedoes every one of our ships was already on a course to comb the spread. At 5,000 yards torpedoes passed through the Tenth. None hit. The guns opened up. The enemy replied.

T24 and Z24 turned to the southwest: *Haida* and *Huron* went after them at full speed with guns in full voice. Z32 turned to the north and was opened up on by the Poles; she was hit, turned away and was lost to sight. ZH1 turned to the west and was engaged by *Tartar* and *Ashanti*. She slowed and disappeared into smoke so fire was shifted to T24 – already being fired upon by *Haida*. Z32, in turning away from the Poles, now ran close to *Tartar*: as Captain (D) put it, "She was speedily silenced but not before *Tartar* was damaged." Z32 might have been silenced but she slipped off into the dark nevertheless. Where did she go?

Four of her shells had burst about *Tartar*'s bridge, cutting communication to the guns and to the torpedo tubes aft. A fire started abaft the bridge, the mast came down carrying all the radar and wireless aerials with it. Several men were killed and more wounded. A buzzer jammed on and howled away. Splinters pierced the boilers and speed dropped to four knots.

Ashanti and *Tartar* had now shifted fire to ZH1 which had altered away to the west and been lost but now reappeared. *Tartar*, although damaged, kept her guns firing in local control: *Ashanti*, undamaged and so with all her guns in director control, followed suit and added two torpedo hits for good measure. Range was down to 500 yards. ZH1 blew up with a spectacular explosion.

Z24 and T24 had altered away with *Haida* and *Huron* still in hot pursuit. A stern chase; nearly always the enemy outpaced us in a stern chase, as they did this time but not before the Narvik Z24 had been hit in the bridge and the after mounting put out of action. T24 got away again.

In returning, *Haida* and *Huron* ran across the missing Z32 and chased her to the eastward, pounding away. Z32 twisted to the southward and then to the westward. She grounded aflame on a rock and that bit of the action was over.

We must picture all this happening on a dark night with a visibility of about two miles. Twelve warships manoeuvring in tight turns at thirty-two (us) to thirty-six knots (them); the white glare of starshell; the amber flash of the 4.1-, 4.7-, and 5.5-inch guns firing their high-explosive shells; the red glow of hits and fires burning – all within an area of twenty square miles just off shoals and a rock-bound coast – the ever-present threat of mine fields, both our own and German – the arching trajectory of the tracer from the close-range weapons, 20 and 40mm; the white track of passing torpedoes; the air filled with the crackle of voice radios rapping out orders in English and German; the Leader without radar or voice communication for some of the time; dead and wounded in many ships: all this going on for four early-morning hours of darkness. The action information plots chanting out their assessment of the confused picture to keep their Captains in the picture as best they can: the taut Navigators watching their turning and twisting courses to keep their Captains off the rocks and out of the mine fields – and always mindful that they must be clear of the shells of the coastal batteries and the Heinkels and Stukkas that dawn will bring: about 190 men in each ship trying to go quietly and efficiently about their alotted tasks – each vital to the success of the whole: the whole, indeed, is much more than the sum of its constituent parts:

On the strength of one link of the cable,
Dependeth the might of the chain.

In twelve ships, over two thousand men.

If we can see this lurid picture in the mind's eye and hear the cacophony of battle in the mind's ear and sense the strain on these two thousand men in the mind and in the heart, then those who have not experienced it may understand the phrase, "the fog of battle." And those who know it will remember.

The fog of battle was ameliorated somewhat by the action information centre – the operations room two decks below the bridge. Here all the incoming and outgoing voice and radio signals were monitored. Radar sets showed the position of our own and enemy forces. An automatic plot kept a record of the tracks of all ships in the battle area. Radar-triggered IFF (identification friend or foe) generally kept us from firing at friends. I say "generally" because a consort's aerials could be shot away. Voice signals could be garbled. Radar sets could develop "gremlins," those eerie creatures – and nobody ever saw one – who sporadically fed false information into even the most well-mannered and scrupulously maintained technical equipment. Picture a dozen men hunched over their radar and radio, earphones and microphones, murmuring their data to others who need it, flashing screens, shaded lights showing intent disembodied faces, their plots, their telephone lines, each, upon a word from the Operations Officer, giving his bit of

124

information to be assessed and made into a cohesive whole and relayed to the Captain. In *Huron* this was the First Lieutenant, Pat Budge. He paid particular attention to his "headache" operator. This hand, fluent in German, monitored the voice transmissions of the enemy. In the battles told of here, it was known that the enemy would, under different circumstances, alter course to fire torpedoes. *Huron* and consorts creaming along in the dark at thirty-two knots, ship blacked out, only the white bow wave showing: Budge glances at the headache operator more frequently as the crucial range approaches. Overhead the constant blast of the guns, the shudder of each broadside felt below. The headache operator listening intently to his earphones keeps his eyes on the Ops Officer. He raises a warning hand.

"Enemy altering course to fire torpedoes. . .altering to fire. . .NOW."

The Plot Officer lays off his parallel rulers and runs it to the compass rose. "The torpedoes will come from 081 degrees."

Budge glances at the future track of the thirty-knot torpedoes just fired.

"Captain, sir. Torpedoes approaching from green three oh."

On the bridge the Captain orders, "Coxswain, starboard twenty. Midships. Meet her. Steady."

"Steady on 081, sir," says the Coxswain.

By "combing the spread," presenting his 36-foot beam to the torpedoes instead of his 355-foot length, the chances of being hit are lessened. All eyes on the bridge peer intently ahead.

"Torpedoes should arrive in twenty seconds," says the Plot.

And they do. One white wake streaming down the port side and one down the starboard.

On with the battle.

The day-in, day-out, week-in, week-out pace was exhausting. Sailing in the late afternoon to be off the French coast by dark, closed up at action stations all night fighting, get under your air cover by dawn, back to Plymouth by eight or nine, land the dead and wounded, dockyard mateys swarming on board to make good the night's damage so the ship could sail again by evening. And take on ammunition. If the previous night had been particularly busy, thousands of rounds of 4.7-inch, 40mm, and 20mm. On the morning of *Haida*'s return after the sinking of *Athabaskan*, the hands were like zombies, the walking dead. Her mess decks were a frightful mess from oil, blood, the debris of battle, but she had to be made ship-shape and Bristol-fashion by afternoon so that she could sail again. *Huron*'s crew were rested from a short boiler clean. Without any request for assistance being made, fifty *Huron* ratings and two officers came over and, without explanation, shouldered the exhausted ammunitioning party aside and did the chore for them. Were they not chummy ships?

On another return to harbour, *Huron* had been shot up in the night's mêlée; the gun director damaged, holes in the funnel, whaler and cutter useless, several wounded to be taken to hospital, one dead. Also, she had been brushed by *Eskimo* in the pell-mell battle and suffered quite a bit of damage. Budge was chivvying the hands so they could be finished by noon. They needed a stand down so they could sail again. "Any time we were out for action, we used to leave at six in the evening and get back at eight in the morning – at action stations the whole damn time," he said. Besides getting the ship ready again, he had to make up the plot of the night action for the Captain to take to the daily analysis with the other Captains and the shore staff officers. "Lessons learned" were put into orders for future battles. He got only a few hours' sleep a day for weeks.

He sensed someone behind him and, turning, saw a Rear-Admiral observing the bustle with the interest any sailor would have. "What happened, Number One?" asked the Admiral. Budge recognized him as Arthur Minion Dowding and described the night's action. Dowding listened with interest and asked many questions. He was obviously a sea-going man wishing he could get back to sea, absorbed in the story. Then Dowding said, "I'm sorry. I'm taking your time and I see you're busy."

"If you'll excuse me, sir, I was in an old ship of yours. *Despatch*. I was a Boy Seaman in her when she joined the China Squadron."

"And what is a Boy Seaman, RN, doing as First Lieutenant of a Canadian destroyer?"

"When I came back from China my family had moved to Ontario so I requested a transfer to the RCN."

Dowding left and *Huron* resumed her nightly patrols. At last came that blessed time when she was due for a boiler clean. Budge and the Gunnery Officer, Alan Watson, were set to go to Torquay, "which was *the* place to go. All the hotels were open, all the Americans were there, dance bands, palm trees, meals in a spacious dining room, sleep in a wide bed, *all night!* . . . But the quartermaster came up and said I was wanted on the telephone. It was the Admiral's secretary. Would I dine with the Admiral on Sunday night? I said I'd ask my Captain and telephone back. So I knocked on Herbie Rayner's door."

"Sir, the Admiral has asked me to dinner Sunday night but I want to go to Torquay. What should I do?"

"You dine with the Admiral, of course."

Budgie is the most extraordinary man I know for the amount of work he gets done, the amount of work he gets others to do, and the fun everyone has doing it.

All in *Huron*, as in every other ship in the fleet, loved the boating Wrens. These young girls, in fair weather or foul, delivered the ship's stores, the mail, ran liberty boats when the ship was at a buoy, and returned the (to put it mildly) hilarious sailors after their evening in the pubs ashore. Bowman, sternsheetsman, engineer, and, in charge of all, the Coxswain. Admiral's daughters from the exclusive private schools and shop girls from the county council schools, it made no difference. They were devoted to the ships they served. On claggy, gusty nights with the wind howling and the spray coming white over the canopy, they made their appointed rounds without fail. And they knew how to deal with drunken sailors. Was not the Coxswain a Leading Wren, accustomed to taking charge? One night in Scapa Flow when returning with a particularly noisy lot I heard, "Keep silence in the effing boat or I'll have the lot of you in front of the effing Officer of the Watch." Her father, I happened to know, was the Captain of a battleship. Her mother would have been shocked that her gently nurtured orchid spoke thus.

And on a fine sunny day the Wrens were a sight to gladden the eye as they swept up to the gangway. White caps square on the pretty heads, chin stays down, seamens' jerseys and bell-bottom pants, spotless white plimsolls on little feet. Their boathook drill was perfection. Bowman and sternsheetsman with boathooks perpendicularly in front of them. The bow Wren raps the butt of her boathook twice. Then, with precision and as one, both boathooks are swung horizontally overhead to the full extent of the raised arms; then (one and *two*) to shoulder height; then (one and *two*) to the full extent of the lowered arms. All hands watch, breathless. Then the boathooks are thrust outboard to hook on to the ladder. *Never* were seamens' jerseys filled so beautifully.

Budge ran a taut wardroom. No oilskins or caps allowed – "this is our *home*." When possible, the officers dressed for dinner. Before

Huron returned to Canada it was decided that the wardroom would entertain their Wrens at dinner. Wing collar and bow tie was the rig of the day for dining in harbour. The Wrens arrived, demure in their best shore-going uniforms, and, on their white shirts – bow ties. Marvellous!

When *Huron* sailed for Halifax the next day their Wren boat crew were lying off in the stream. They piped *Huron* as she passed, then waved goodbye.

Morning after morning the Tenth Destroyer Flotilla arrived home, the damage from the enemy showing plain. Anxious eyes sought them out when they hove into view.

About 5:30 one morning after a particularly harrowing night the Tenth shaped course for Plymouth. Plymouth, whence Vice-Admiral Drake had sailed in 1588 to help decimate the Spanish Armada, a naval town since 1311. The shipyard artisans had been tending the wounds of our ships, therefore, over six hundred years, and had been particularly busy since 1939. They took pride in *their* ships. The citizens loved *their* sailors.

As Captain Jones put it, "As we slowed down to enter harbour, and steamed up the Hamoaze from Plymouth Sound, crowds of cheering people could be seen on the roads and in the dockyard, and the Wrens of Longroom Signal Station were out in force to welcome us. . . . Somehow the word had got around [that our night had been difficult] and Plymouth did us proud. The Commander-in-Chief and his Chief of Staff were awaiting us at our quay and everything was laid on to put us straight again, including ham and eggs on the quay for the ship's company whose galley had been put out of action by a shell burst."

The next day a signal was received, "The Board of Admiralty convey their congratulations to officers and ships' companies on the spirited action which has caused a potential menace to the main operation [landing the soldiers] to be removed." This formal recognition by Their Lordships was appreciated. But not quite as much as that composed and sent to them by the Wrens of the Signal Station who had waved goodbye and hello to them so many times:

The Fighting Tenth

There are specks on the horizon
As familiar as can be,
D10 with his flotilla
Proceeding in from sea.

Battle ensigns at all mastheads,
An impressive sight to see,
The Tartar and the Tenth D.F.
Come in triumphantly.

The pendants now come visible,
Four-three, Five-one, Two-four,
Tartar, Ashanti, Huron,
Astern there loom five more.

Blyskawica, Haida, Javelin,
Piorun, Eskimo,
Buntings on the Signal Bridge,
Stokers down below.

Passing through the gate at last
They move more cautiously,
The same old signal flying,
"Act Independently."

We hope we'll always see you thus
With ensigns flying free
For the Fighting Tenth's a lovely sight
When coming in from sea.

The dead and the wounded were landed. Although Captain (D) was among the wounded he did not land. Some wounds are painful, some serious, some fatal. But his was mainly embarrassing. He had a small piece of brass from the binnacle cover in his chin and another in his behind.

It is perhaps better to end on a more decorous note. Speaking later on a U-boat kill by *Haida*, Captain Jones said, "There is no doubt that her Commanding Officer, H. de Wolff (Captain (D) showed the fine disregard of a fighting man to such mundane trivia as spelling) or 'Hard Over Harry' as he was known to his friends, was an outstanding officer, not only in skill but in aggressive spirit. Furthermore, he had that priceless gift of fortune. . .of there always being a target [for him to fight] in whatever area he was told to operate."

The bitter fighting that went on from dusk to dawn, night after night, from the fifteenth of April to the fifteenth of September of 1944 – only a few months of the year that these battles lasted – was described by Captain (D) in the lean, factual prose of the operational commander which the Royal Navy has taught us. Not for him the poet's art,

> Ship after ship, the whole night long,
> with her battle thunder and flame. . .

Oh no. He wrote this Report of Proceedings:

SECRET

H.M.S. TARTAR
15 September 1944

TO: The Commodore (D), Home Fleet.
FROM: Captain (D),
        10th DESTROYER FLOTILLA.
COPY: Commander-in-Chief, Home Fleet.

Sir,

I have the honour to submit for your information a revised list of results obtained by the 10th Destroyer Flotilla in the Channel and Bay of Biscay during the five-month period from 15 April to 15 September 1944.

2. All actions were at night with the exception of the sinking of U-971 and the A.M.C. [Armed Merchant Cruiser] on August 12th.

3.

Date	Ships Engaged	Enemy Losses	
		Sunk	Damaged
25-26 April	Black Prince (Senior Officer), Haida, Huron, Athabaskan	1 Elbing	1 Elbing
27-28 April	Haida & Athabaskan (Athabaskan sunk)	1 Elbing	
8-9 June	Tartar (D 10) & all ships of 10th D.F.	2 Narviks	1 Narvik 1 Elbing
13-14 June	Piorun & Ashanti	2 M Class Minesweepers	2 M Class Minesweepers
24 June	Haida & Eskimo	U-971	
27-28 June	Huron & Eskimo	2 Trawlers	1 Trawler
5 July	Tartar (D 10) & Ashanti		4 Armed L.C.T.s (Retired over shoal water to Lanion River.)

9 July	Tartar (D 10) & Huron		4 Trawlers (Retired to St. Malo)
15 July	Tartar (D 10), Haida & Blyskawica	2 Merchant ships 1 Trawler	2 Minesweepers
5-6 Aug.	Bellona (S.O.), Tartar (D 10) Haida Iroquois & Ashanti	4 Merchant ships 2 Minesweepers 1 Trawler	2 Minesweepers
12 Aug.	Diadem (S.O.) Piorun & Onslow	1 Armed Merchantman	
15 Aug.	Mauritius (S.O.), Iroquois & Ursa	2 Minesweepers 1 Flak Ship 2 Medium M.V.s 1 Small M.V. 1 Small Tanker	1 Narvik 1 Elbing
23 Aug.	Mauritius (S.O.) Iroquois & Ursa	5 Armed Trawlers 1 Sperrbrecker 1 Coaster 1 Flak Ship	

4. This makes a total of thirty-five surface ships and one submarine sunk and fourteen damaged.

I have the honour to be,
Sir,
Your obedient servant,

Basil Jones

CAPTAIN (D)
10th DESTROYER FLOTILLA

Battles with U-Boats

Battles might be won or lost, enterprises might succeed or miscarry, territories might be gained or quitted, but dominating all our power to carry on the war, or even keep ourselves alive, lay our mastery of the ocean routes and the free approach and entry to our ports. . . .The only thing that ever really frightened me during the war was the U-boat peril.

Churchill

In the navy we never felt any abiding hatred of the U-boat crews. Of course we cursed them when they sank our ships and we saw our men in the water or came across a lifeboat filled with those who had managed to get off their torpedoed ship but who were now dead from exposure. Of course we yelled oaths at them in the heat of battle. But, in the five and a half years I spent at sea during the Battle of the Atlantic, I neither saw nor heard a first-hand story of the "atrocities" that from time to time appeared in the newspapers. There was scuttlebutt enough but it was never verified. Indeed, we felt a professional admiration for the skill and tenacity of the German sailors in submarines. What else could we feel for a U-boat Captain who would steam down the centre lane of a convoy, fired at by every ship he passed, chased by one of our destroyers, and yet firing his torpedoes left and right, scoring hits, and getting away? This is what Otto Kretschmer did in U-99.

Kretschmer was called "The Tonnage King"; in the first eighteen months of the Battle of the Atlantic in U-23 and U-99 he had sunk more of our ships than any other U-boat Commander – forty-four ships, 266,629 tons. Before the war he had been taught that the way to sink ships was to lie off at about 3,000 yards and fire a spread of four or six torpedoes to make sure of a hit. "Nonsense!" said he, "Get in close; get within the convoy screen, on the surface if you can, within 1,000 yards. One merchant ship: one torpedo." And he did it!

He was sunk, finally, by Donald Macintyre in HMS *Walker*. On the same night and within the same patch of ocean, and, if you can believe it, within the same hour as Schepke in U-100. Convoy HX112 had been attacked on the night of March 15, 1941, and the 10,000-ton tanker, *Erodona*, had been hit and had set the sea afire. *Walker* and HMS *Vanoc* had been hunting a U-boat, had depth-charged it many times, and had considered it destroyed. *Walker* took the opportunity to pick up survivors in life boats from the SS *J.B. White*: the Master, the Mate, and thirty-seven of the crew. *Vanoc* steamed protectively around her as she did so. Then she and *Vanoc* went quietly back to where their previous quarry had been to see if they could get more definite evidence of a kill. This they certainly did for *Vanoc* pulled ahead at full speed shaking and shuddering under the thrust of her 30,000-horsepower engines, disappeared into the gloom, and then signalled back, "Have rammed and sunk U-boat."

Then *Walker* got a submarine echo. Two within a mile of each other? No, impossible; they were getting echoes from the water previously disturbed by their charges. But the asdic operator was insistant that it was a sub. *Walker* ran over the echo, dropped a pattern, and ran out again for another attack. *Vanoc* flashed, "U-boat surfaced astern of me." The glare of her searchlight showed U-99 (for such it was) stopped in the water. The guns' crews of both ships sprang into action with their 4-inch and various machine guns. The night was bright with gun flashes and tracer, "Although," said Macintyre, "I fear their accuracy was not remarkable. Destroyer night gunnery in such a mêlée is apt to be pretty wild." In *Walker*, confusion reigned supreme, for the survivors of the *J.B. White*, with understandable enthusiasm, had nominated themselves as extra ammunition parties. At such a phenomenal rate did the ammunition accumulate that the guns' crews had no room to work their guns. This could have been more serious but at that moment the U-99 signalled, "We are sunking" (sic).

U-99 was then abandoned and she plunged to the bottom. *Walker* manoeuvred to windward of the swimming Germans, drifted down on them, and hauled them inboard. Many were half dead from the cold water and it was hard to bring them around. One was so apparently dead that he was nearly chucked back into the sea again until someone suggested he be put in the warm galley, and he came to life. The last swimmer to approach *Walker* was the U-boat Captain, who could be identified as such as he approached the ship, by the brass hat he still wore. He swam up and climbed over the side. Around his neck he still had his Zeiss binoculars, a very special pair which Dönitz had ordered to be made for certain U-boat aces. This was Otto Kretschmer, Knight's Cross with Oak Leaves, who had always sworn that no enemy would board his ship and no enemy would wear these binoculars. He now tried to throw them over the side but they were grabbed, and, later, appropriated by Macintyre.

But Kretschmer lived to organize an intelligence system in our prisoner-of-war camp at Bowmanville, Ontario, which sent information back to Germany despite our censorship. An indominable man! In Ottawa in the 1950s I heard him speak of those days and I got a letter from him a couple of years ago. Grossadmiral Dönitz said that he was "a man of rare imperturbability. . .quick in sizing up a situation and in realizing how best he could exploit it; and having made his plan, he delivered his attack with calm determination and great skill." The entries in Kretschmer's war diary for two days in October 1940 support this judgement:

18.10

2330. Now attacking right wing of the last line but one. Bow shot at large freighter. The vessel zig-zagged, with the result that the torpedo passed in front of her and hit instead her even bigger neighbour after a run of 1,740 yards. The ship, about 7,000 tons, was hit below the foremast and sank quickly by the bows with, I presume, two holds flooded.

2358. Bow shot at large freighter approx. 6,000 tons. Range 750 yards. Hit below foremast. The explosion of the torpedo was immediately followed by a high sheet of flame and an explosion which ripped the ship open as far as the bridge and left a cloud of smoke 600 feet high. Ship's forepart apparently shattered. Ship still burning, with green flames.

19.10

0015. Three destroyers, line abreast, approach the ship, searching the vicinity. I went off at full speed on a southwesterly course and very soon regained contact with the convoy. Torpedoes from other boats exploding all the time. The destroyers are at their wits' end, shooting off starshells the whole time to comfort themselves and each other. Not that that makes much odds in the bright moonlight. I am now beginning to pick them off from astern of the convoy.

0138. Bow shot on large, heavily laden freighter of some 6,000 tons. Range 945 yards. Hit below foremast. Ship sank at once.

0155. Bow shot on next ship, a large vessel of approx. 7,000 tons. Range 975 yards. Hit below foremast. Ship sank in forty seconds.

In this three-day convoy battle from October fifteenth to the seventeenth, Kretschmer sank five ships and damaged another. With his torpedoes expended he was on his way home. All he wanted was a quiet passage; he had no idea he was so close to U-100 or, indeed, to a convoy under attack. Then his Officer of the Watch spotted *Walker* and *Vanoc* and dived. This was against Kretschmer's Standing Orders. It must be supposed that his Officer of the Watch panicked. Had U-99 stayed on the surface she might well have slipped away.

Walker's officers, merchant service officers, and German officers all used the wardroom together and it was very crowded. After a day or so, conversation was not as strained as you might think. A daily bridge game started up in Macintyre's harbour cabin: *Walker*'s Engineer Officer, the Master and Mate of the *J.B. White*, and Kretschmer.

And there was Günther Prien in U-47 who sank *Royal Oak* in Scapa Flow and racked up a score of twenty-eight merchant ships – 164,953 tons. Dönitz said of him that he "was all that a man should be, a great personality, full of zest and energy and the joy of life, wholly dedicated to his service and an example to all who served under him. Typical of the man and his outlook is a remark he made before the war, when he said: 'I get more fun out of a really good convoy exercise than out of any leave!' In war, notwithstanding his sudden leap to fame and popularity after the Scapa Flow exploit, he remained a simple, frank and courageous fighting man, intent only on doing his job and adding to his exploits. I held him in great affection and esteem." On March 10, 1941, Prien approached a U.K.-bound convoy about two hundred miles south of Iceland. He drove in at dusk hidden by the gathering gloom and the frequent rain squalls. The great seas helped hide his tiny silhouette. But momentarily the squalls cleared, U-47 was thrust up as a huge sea passed under her, and she was spotted by *Wolverine*. Commander Jim Rowland and Lieutenant-Commander Günther Prien looked at each other in astonishment. Prien altered away.

Rowland increased to maximum speed and gave chase. Then Prien made his mistake. He dived and lost speed and manoeuvrability. *Wolverine* raced in and dropped a pattern set to shallow. Down below, U-47 shuddered and shook and heeled and tilted. Her engines and propellors were knocked out of alignment. Prien had to surface and try to make off in the dark. He surfaced. *Wolverine* gave chase again. Prien was forced to dive again. Again he was depth-charged. There was a large underwater explosion, a red glare below the surface, wreckage bobbed up. Prien and Kretschmer would never again drink their traditional two bottles of champagne in Lorient. We in the allied navies certainly held these two in great respect.

The third of Germany's great U-boat commanders was Joachim Schepke who had commanded U-3, U-19, and U-100 and who sank in all thirty-nine ships totalling 159,130 tons. Seven of these he sank within four hours on September 21, 1940, when, in company with a wolf pack, he attacked convoy HX72. Schepke's cap was the despair of the very proper and regulation-conscious Dönitz – always Schepke wore it at the rakish angle suitable to his breezy air and smart uniforms. On March 15, 1941, he and three other U-boats (including Kretschmer's) attacked the forty-one ships in convoy HX112. Four ships were sunk and two damaged but when U-100 was coming in at full speed to attack she was picked up at 1,000 yards by the radar of HMS *Vanoc*. *Vanoc* and *Walker* ran in to the attack as I have described. U-100 dived, was hunted, depth-charged and left for dead. Schepke had thought the hunt abandoned while *Vanoc* and *Walker* were picking up the survivors of the *J.B. White* and tried to make off on the surface, but he was spotted by *Vanoc* who bore in to ram. Schepke had called down the conning tower to his men, "It's all right, he will miss us astern," but he was wrong. He was crushed between *Vanoc*'s bow and his own periscope standard.

This year, 1941, was not kind to the U-boats. Schepke, Prien, and Kretschmer all were finished that year: two dead, one a prisoner. Captain S. W. Roskill, DSC, RN, wrote the three volumes of *The War at Sea*, published by the Queen's Printer in the 1950s. He says about March 1941:

> In one month the enemy not only lost one-fifth of his operational U-boat fleet, but three of the boats destroyed were commanded by celebrated "aces." The death of Prien in U-47, of Schepke in U-100 and the capture of Kretschmer from U-99 not only de-

prived the enemy of the services of three of his most successful U-boat commanders but marked the end of the period of ascendancy of the individual exponent of this type of warfare.

"This type of warfare" refers to the lone attack of the early days as opposed to the massed attack, sometimes as many as eighteen boats, of the wolf-pack days. What can we feel for such men besides grudging admiration? And what about all the other gallant U-boat Captains who continued the war at sea when hope was gone? Over a thousand U-boats were built and over eight hundred of these were sunk. Our clashes always ended in death, sometimes to some of them and some of us, sometimes to all of either one of us. But the individual man and the well-trained team of men doing their duty as they saw it with skill and disregard for their personal safety is always to be admired. Some U-boat battles were short and deadly, others were long and indecisive, some indeed were funny in a macabre sort of way, and some smacked of the lugubrious.

One such was the sinking of the Canadian SS *Jasper Park*, which sailed from Halifax in January 1943. Her final port of discharge was to be Calcutta. But on July 6, she was torpedoed six hundred miles southeast of Madagascar.

Her Master was an irascible old Scotsman who had spent most of his sea-going life on the China coast; the Mate was a retread from the Great War, a first-class seaman who had been Mate of the largest wool clipper out of the port of Liverpool and was now back to "do his bit"; the Second Mate was James Butterfield, a *Conway* boy from age fourteen to seventeen, then merchant navy all over the world until the last couple of years of the war when he joined the Canadian navy.

On the day he met his first U-boat James had the middle watch – 12:00 A.M. to 4:00 A.M. At ten to twelve he was called for his watch by one of the ABs. Scuttlebutt had it that this particular seaman had had eleven ships sunk under him to date, and, as a result, was a little strange, strange enough that the Royal Navy had let him out. He used to go around sometimes with a bucket over his head banging it with a spoon.

"Mr. Mate," he said, "Time to go on watch and bring your life jacket. Twenty minutes ago two torpedoes crossed our bow. They went on their way and both exploded way off the starboard bow."

"And what did the First Mate think of this?" asked James.

"Well, sir, he didn't see them but I told him."

"Now everyone thought this seaman a few bricks short of a full load, perhaps understandably, when in fact he was in full possession of his faculties," James claims. And events were to prove him right.

At ten to eleven the following morning a torpedo hit. James was standing by the deep-sea sounding machine and thinking he should change out of tropical rig to something warmer after he finished this job. He was to be sorry he hadn't because he lost fillings in his teeth from their chattering "like trip hammers" in the cold when he was in the lifeboat later. The torpedo hit somewhere under him and he sailed into the air from the starboard rail, hit a derrick on the way across, and landed at the port rail. Except for four who were killed, the crew abandoned ship. James was in charge of a boat and he was ready for this kind of thing. Had he not been trained for it? He collected all cigarettes, lighters, matches, and chewing gum from his boat's crew. From now on all these goodies would be shared, there would be no hoarding; he would have problem enough getting to Capetown without dissension among his crew.

The ship sank. The full cargo was tea, chests of tea, "Canada's supply of tea for a year, a ten-thousand-ton ship full of tea. A fine day, gentle swell, a slight sea running. The ship sank, the hatches burst, and now, spreading from horizon to horizon, were thousands of chests of tea."

The U-boat surfaced. James was beckoned by the submarine Captain to come alongside, to scramble up on the casing, while a movie camera from the conning tower recorded all this. The Captain didn't speak English very well.

"What ship?"

"*Jasper Park.*"

"What ship?"

"*Jasper Park.*"

"Do not lie. Oh, I know. Like Hyde Park?"

"Yes."

In every merchant ship the name board, about one foot high and ten feet long, is displayed on either side of the bridge in steel brackets; you can slip it out to polish the brightwork. Just then one of the name boards floated slowly by as if in proof of the veracity of Canadian officers. The U-boat Captain continued his questions:

"What cargo?"

"Tea."

"What else?"

"Just tea."

"You must tell truth."

"Tea only," James swept his arm from horizon to horizon. "Just tea."

The truth of the matter was evident. The U-boat captain was satisfied. James jumped back into his boat. The U-boat submerged. James set out for Capetown in his first command. Three days later they were picked up by two Australian destroyers, and, James told me, "I can honestly say that I was disappointed with this turn of events as I was looking forward to a splendid odyssey in sailing the boat at least as far as the African coast, or just possibly, Brazil."

Thus do we remember our youth.

There was always the U-boat threat, but the German surface raiders could not be ignored. This story shows the effervescent character of James as well as the spirit of our times and the sort of youths we were.

After leaving *Conway* James had joined *Empress of Russia*, a CPR ship, in Vancouver. Now, in December 1940, she was a troop ship. She was many times in Yokohama harbour and there were several German ships interned there, about eight. Our sailors kept their weather eye lifted to see if these ships had changed their paint scheme to what might be camouflage, whether they had altered their silhouette, if they had steam up and showed signs of getting under way. They met German merchant seamen in bars ashore. "It was the Brotherhood-of-the-Sea business. We, incidentally, could drink them under the table any time," said James.

On one trip they were on their way to New Zealand to pick up troops, and were south of New Britain and New Ireland, east of New Guinea, and coming down outside the Philippines. Over the horizon hove another ship. All ships had to be treated with caution because there were perhaps twelve or so German merchant raiders on the oceans of the world as well as the German warships: *Scharnhorst*, *Gneisenau*, *Scheer*, and *Lützow*. These warships were easily recognised, but the merchant raiders – *Komet*, *Orion*, *Widder*, *Pinguin*, *Michel*, *Kormoran*, *Stier*, *Thor* – were another matter. Oh yes, there was good reason for caution; they had sunk dozens of our merchant ships and a few of our armed merchant cruisers who were supposed to be their equal but were not. The *Atlantis* was another of the merchant raiders and a very successful time she had had. Could this be her? Subsequent intelligence showed that it probably was.

Now followed a stately minuet. Bow on, *Empress of Russia* had a silhouette not unlike our county-class 8-inch cruisers: high freeboard, three funnels, forward derricks that at a distance could be mistaken for forward gun turrets. The trick was to keep bows on and still pass the stranger. She, for her part, wanted to get a definite recognition but not get too close to what might be 8-inch guns. She had a small aircraft aft which was suspicious enough, said James, who was "cadet dog's body of the watch" on the bridge. He didn't take his binoculars off her for four hours. They passed, certainly to the relief of *Empress of Russia* and perhaps of *Atlantis* as well.

I suppose it was at this point that I asked James what he thought of the Germans as fighting men. He looked at me with some exasperation. "Really, Hal, I've told you of my half hour chatting to the U-boat Captain on the casing of his submarine, of our four-hour dance with *Atlantis*, of our evenings ashore drinking with German merchant seaman. How can I tell you what they were like as fighting men? If you've been listening at all you will see that, up to this point, all my contacts with the Germans were social."

Once, James was returning to Halifax in the SS *Cavina*. She had a 4-inch gun mounted aft manned by naval gunners. It was a big convoy and many ships were sunk by the U-boats which by this time were using the wolf-pack attack. At about nine o'clock every night the torpedoes would start running and the depth charges exploding. "One morning at about one o'clock, guns, depth charges, and flares were going all around. *St Croix* had just been sunk. All at once one whole ship just blew apart about two miles off our starboard bow. It was truly spectacular. The whole thing just blew apart in mid-air. I have never been able to verify the truth of the matter but I believe it must have been *Itchen* after she picked up the *St Croix* hands. It was a really exciting passage. We had a submarine scrape along our side and we couldn't depress the gun enough to fire at her. We were all going a bit mental as the darn thing disappeared astern into the night."

Some got away.

In 1940-41 Lieutenant Bob Welland was serving as Asdic Officer in HMCS *St. Laurent* ("Sally") first to Harry DeWolf as Captain then to Herbie Rayner. As I remember it, the RCN had no Specialist Anti-Submarine Officers at that time. Welland studied it in private as best he could. The Anti-Submarine Detection Investigation Committee

(ASDIC) had made such a secret out of this underwater detection device (later called Sonar to have a common nomenclature with the USN) that very few did know anything about it. Welland got quite good at it and was rewarded when "Sally" got a U-boat contact about three hundred and fifty miles off the west coast of Ireland. She was escorting a convoy when she was ordered to hasten to a position about fifty miles further west where two convoys, one outward bound, one inward, were being heavily attacked. High winds, heavy seas, snow squalls: this on the night of December 1. She arrived to find ten ships sunk and the armed merchant cruiser *Forfar* floundering along with a torpedo in her vitals. "Sally" was ordered to escort her in but was called away again to help another ship under attack further astern. On the way she came across the sinking motor vessel *Conch* and took on board fifty-three of her survivors. A signal told her that *Forfar* had had another spread of five torpedoes fired at her and had sunk. Go back and get the survivors. But on the way when Welland was on watch he sighted a U-boat on the starboard bow. The guns' crews saw it too.

"Permission to open fire, sir."

"No," said Welland. The submarine was steaming slowly and with any luck had not seen "Sally." He might be able to get a couple of hundreds of yards closer which would make a kill easier. "Suddenly, she blew tanks, spray flying and slid under, diving." Then "Sally" bore down and Welland got a firm contact. Herbie Rayner did not try a "pounce" attack. He was the only ship there and might lose the echo in the turbulence of his exploding depth charges. Welland held the echo. Rayner waited until *Viscount* came up and also held the echo. Then began the *danse macabre*. With *Viscount* standing off and holding the echo, "Sally" began a deliberate attack. Welland's asdic set gave him the decreasing range, the Doppler effect – echo higher or lower on the sound scale than the transmitted sound wave from "Sally" – told him if the U-boat was steering away or towards; whether to the left or right was evident from the changing compass bearing. The Captain steered a collision course, and, when over the U-boat, fired a full pattern of depth charges. *Viscount* now went in with "Sally" holding. The diamond-shaped pattern of charges were set both to deep and shallow. Another pattern of charges, always with the disengaged ship "pinging" away on the asdic. Another pattern. The attacking destroyers bucked and reared as the charges exploded. Always one stalker and one waiting her turn. This relentless pounding continued for three hours; over eighty charges, twelve tons of explosive. Welland and Leading Seaman Ray Babich held the echo. Then the contact faded. Oil came to the surface.

With becoming modesty that is typical of the man, Bob Welland tells the end of the story: "You know in the anti-submarine business you get a change in water temperature, a thermal layer, and if the submarine gets below it, your asdic sound wave just bounces up again and you can't get a ping anymore – no echo. You can't hear it. We couldn't find it, but we were all pretty well satisfied that this submarine had gone to the bottom."

So were the Admiralty. Their Lordships gave *St. Laurent* and *Viscount* a "Probable." A good Probable we must assume since both the Asdic Officer and the Captain got a Distinguished Service Cross.

Not content with this proven expertise, Welland asked for a specialist anti-submarine course and got it. Upon completion he was appointed to Halifax where there was a newly formed anti-submarine school. He was training new corvettes in their work-up period. "My very able assistant was Warrant Torpedo Gunner Pat Budge." It was difficult for a corvette Captain in his primitive ship with no automatic plot to keep track of where the submarine was, so Welland invented one. "I was supposed to be the expert and if *I* didn't know where the target was how could *they*? I devised it so that I wouldn't be embarrassed myself." The Welland Plot. I used it later; so did scores of Asdic Officers. Then Welland was sent to the west coast to set up an a/s school there. He found some vacant land in the barracks and he and a constructor officer named Jack Roper built the school, put in all the equipment, and took in four hundred students. This was accomplished in three months.

In 1942 Welland was back at sea as First Lieutenant of *Assiniboine*, taking over from Ralph Hennessy. The Captain became ill in 1943 and Welland took command. "The sinkings weren't too bad," he said, "We were beginning to get a handle on the submarines by 1943." In June 1944, *Assiniboine* sailed in support of the Normandy Invasion up and down the French coast. One interesting patrol was off *Ile d'Ouessant* – Ushant. This was one of the Germans' only remaining bases; they had from fifty to sixty U-boats there. Our flotilla blockaded the harbour of Brest. There was a battery of four 11-inch guns there – the Lochrist Battery; they had a range of 53,000 yards and (unlike our coastal battery at Singapore) could train 360 degrees and were giving hell to the American troops who were advancing down the peninsula towards Brest. The German battery on the island was 88mm, about 4-inch. Our destroyers had 4.7-inch, and there were six of them.

"We would go within a mile or less of the island. With binoculars we could make out the faces of the German soldiers. They never shot at us. They were afraid to because we would reply with about eighteen 4.7-inch. On the other hand we were not interested in them because they were not keeping us from our main job – keeping the U-boats penned in. We didn't care if they rotted there. It is an interesting impasse when you are face to face with the enemy and you both know that there is absolutely nothing to be gained by shooting at one another. They had a lookout in the lighthouse there and one morning I signalled to him on the lamp, 'Guten Morgen' and he replied 'Good morning.'"

They could do nothing against the Lochrist Battery; when it started to fire at them they made smoke and fled. But, "some great mind decided it would be a super operation to wipe out these guns. *Assiniboine* and five other destroyers sailed from Plymouth as screen to the battleship *Barham* who was to anchor between the island and the mainland and bombard the battery. This was good heroic stuff." But *Barham* would then be a sitting duck for the U-boats, which were to be kept at bay by the destroyers. The bombardment was preceded by about a hundred Flying Fortress bombers that went over to do carpet bombing. Our ships were still some miles off but it shook them – tons and tons of bombs. Then about twelve Lancaster bombers went over with their Spitfire cover. The Lancs used 12,000-pound armour-penetrating bombs. The Spitfires (the destroyers were tuned in on the frequency) kept saying "Hit, hit. Congratulations." Then the battleship opened fire with her 15-inch guns, each of which fired a one-ton shell. Now the spotter aircraft got on the air, "Short. Over. Hit, hit. Congratulations. Hit." There must have been about twenty direct hits. But all this took time, a great deal of time, maybe six hours, time for half a dozen U-boats to come out. The bombardment ended. The battleship weighed anchor quickly – she was only at short stay – and our forces set off back to Plymouth. Operation eminently successful.

Yes, perhaps, but at what seems to small-ship men as considerable risk to a battleship anchored close to many U-boats which were known to be there. Remembering the proven bravery of the U-boat Commanders and the skill and spirit of their crews, it would have been amazing if one of them had not tried for such an attractive target as a battleship at slow speed. One did. Just as our little fleet was approaching the coast.

"We weren't more than ten miles outside the harbour," said Welland, "when my eagle-eyed Yeoman of Signals, Petty Officer Mackie, said, 'There's a periscope astern.' Now Yeoman don't make mistakes like that, and when I looked aft there *was* a periscope astern, about 300 yards, crossing towards the battleship. So I did a full-speed-ahead, hard-a-port, got the asdic dome up because you can't do more than twenty-five knots without damaging it, and got up to thirty knots."

From looking at the feather of spray from the periscope and judging the course of the U-boat a seaman such as Welland could judge how much to aim off to pass over the target and fire his charges in a pounce attack. When the moment came he gave the order over the telephone to the young seaman aft for a fourteen-charge pattern.

"The kid on the telephone had completely seized up. He had *seen* the periscope and apparently it *upset* him. All he had to do was say 'fire' but he didn't and we didn't get the depth charges away until we were a hundred yards past. I did a quick turn and fired another pattern. The U-boat had to be on a certain course if he was going to get the battleship. Should have been easy. As it was, it turned out a real disappointment because that one was in the bag. I *knew* we would have had her."

Nevertheless, *Assiniboine* had done what she was there for – protected the battleship – so her mission was carried out with success. And, as I said, the mission against the Lochrist Battery was eminently successful. Or was it?

Not quite. With, we may imagine, a sigh of relief, Welland looked back at the receding French coast after the bombardment had ended and, "I saw four dirty round puffs of smoke come from the Lochrist Battery and pretty soon the battleship was covered with spray. They straddled her in the first salvo and killed the Chief Engineer who was standing on the quarterdeck."

How did the Lochrist Battery end her days? The British Commandos put six men ashore in a rubber boat, they poured about twenty gallons of gasoline down the gun barrels, and blew up the Battery. Six men in a rubber boat!

After several hundred years of use by the ships of the world, probably starting with the Phoenician explorations in 100 BC, the bottom of the English Channel and the Straits of Dover were liberally strewn with wrecks. I saw a wreck chart of these waters for the first time in 1940 and it was full enough then; the second time, when, in *Sioux*, we preceded the invasion fleet to the beaches of Normandy in 1944, it looked much like a junk car lot.

These wreck charts were essential to any ship engaged in U-boat hunting, for wrecks gave a good echo on the asdic and could be mistaken for submarines. Also, the U-boats had been forced to rely on the tactic of lying silent on the bottom until a likely target passed. With perhaps a hundred anti-submarine warships in this area, anything else was suicide. Off Plymouth and Portsmouth were favoured spots. The trick for our destroyers was, after you got a likely submarine echo and did a pounce attack with no apparent result, no movement of target or Doppler showing on your asdic set, you ran over her with your depth recorder going and reeling out its yards of paper. If you ran over the suspect echo end-on, fore and aft, you got, first of all, the known depth; then a slight rise in depth, then a sudden rise, then the echo trace went back down and tapered off to the known depth of water again. A silhouette of a submarine, in fact.

Bob Welland in *Assiniboine* and David Groos in *Restigouche* were patrolling off Plymouth one day in the summer of 1944 and *Assiniboine* got a classic submarine echo. David Groos said, "After you," and *Restigouche* swung off to the approved position, at right angles to the attacking ship, about a mile off, and pointed so she could hold the echo and do her run after the attacking ship had dropped her depth charges. By that year the British had perfected a radio-beam navigation aid called QH and the predecessor of the DECCA system used later, which enabled a ship's navigator to plot his position within fifty yards. Welland got a navigation fix and consulted his wreck chart. No wreck showed there. But the depth recorder showed the silhouette of a submarine. He fired a twenty-charge pattern of depth charges set to slightly below the depth so they would "cook off" on the bottom – 2,300 pounds of explosive. The trick, in these shallow waters and at comparatively slow speed, would be to get clear of the explosion.

"After the first three or four had gone off there was a most monumental explosion. The sea just came up all around us; the bridge was full of about five feet of water; the ship stopped dead; smoke belched from the funnel; both steering wheels had gone; fire at the bottom of the tiller flat; a lot of steam lines were broken; the ship rolling in the

145

slight sea, helpless. I just knew it wasn't our depth charges, they couldn't do *that*.

"What had transpired, according to an Admiralty analysis was that the target was a dead U-boat sunk by somebody else about a week earlier with all its torpedoes intact. The depth charges had countermined these torpedoes and they had caused all the fuss. It only remained to limp back into harbour, rudder jammed at twenty degrees, steering mostly by engines. It took about three weeks to put *Assiniboine* together again.

Most were sunk, some got away, and some were destroyed twice.

I first met Bob Welland in 1940 when I was a Sub-Lieutenant in the corvette *Moose Jaw* and he went to sea with us when he was in charge of the work-ups of the newly commissioned ships. I met him here and there in the various parts of the North Atlantic during the war, again after the war as he climbed up the promotion ladder – one time I remember was when he was a four-ring Captain driving one of our cruisers and that time I was Staff Officer (Gunnery) to the Flag Officer, Pacific Coast, Rear-Admiral "Herr von" Pullen during the Admiral's sea inspection during his work-ups. Things didn't go particularly well that day. Who could expect aught else in a warship manned with new hands? But I remember Welland saying to the Admiral with equanimity after the day finished in some disorder, "Well, there we are, sir. That's the best we can do, *today*." I have served under some of the best Admirals in the navies of the world. In common with these Welland had that imperturbable mien and a quiet confidence in his own ability that allowed him to tell stories against himself, with wry self-deprecation.

A life as intense as our wartime lives were, with so much at stake – the safety of the ship, our crews, ourselves – must always be subject to SNAFUs (Situation Normal: All Fucked Up). What follows, then, needs no further comment.

Huron with Harold Groos driving and *Assiniboine* with Bob Welland driving, were travelling along independently at about twenty-five knots after escorting a convoy to Russia. When they got about a hundred miles from Scapa Flow they were told to join up with a Home Fleet exercise. Welland says, "This really annoyed us. We were not in the exercise business. We had had a really hairy trip to Murmansk with a lot of trouble with submarines and aircraft out there." When looking forward to a few days in harbour after an arduous voyage, to

146

be told to go and exercise *is* annoying. There were a battleship, about six cruisers, and a lot of destroyers in the screen. The Fleet was steaming south and *Assiniboine* was put on the western side of the screen. Although they didn't know it, there was an anti-aircraft exercise on at the time.

"It was typical Scottish weather – rain, fog – and, if you can believe it, a lookout standing four or five feet away suddenly fell over. We looked at him. There was blood everywhere. It turned out that a spent oerlikon shell from this anti-aircraft exercise had hit this lad in the neck, gone under his shoulder blade, come out through his life-jacket, and rattled around the bridge. It upset the kid and he passed out. The doctor whipped him away and, do you know, he survived perfectly well. That oerlikon shell, which is as big as your finger, didn't break a bone. He was walking around in two or three days."

Then somebody tried to pass *Assiniboine* a message telling them what the exercise was all about. There were without doubt U-boats in the area and again the eagle-eyed Chief Yeoman of Signals saw a periscope off the starboard quarter; the "feather" the periscope made as it passed through the water showed that it was approaching the fleet. Hard-a-port, full ahead, whip around, and fire a fourteen-charge pattern set at 100 feet. Around again for the next attack. Then, up pops a British submarine. Instantly recognisable from her asdic dome on top. A British T-class – HMS *Trusty*. The guns all train on her begging for permission to open fire. NO. Welland is pushing the cease fire buzzers with all his might. NO. ("I still have sore thumbs from pushing those buzzers.") The cruisers opened fire at the surfacing submarine, 6-inch, 4-inch shells, everything just plastering the area. The submarine with her bow out of the water at a twenty-degree angle, stopped. Kaput. Welland got on radio and called "*Cease Fire!*"

"Nothing doing. Everyone is talking. Nobody is listening. I thought, 'Now Welland, this time you have really screwed it up.' So I felt I had better be a hero and steamed my ship across the line of fire between the fleet and the submarine, and luckily they stopped firing. A great silence fell. Then I got on voice radio and said, 'It's one of *our* submarines. Everybody cut it out.' Well the entertaining part of it is that I went alongside and by this time she had managed to pump her stern up and most of the conning tower is out of the water. I closed her to about ten or twelve feet, looked, and there on the bridge is Dinsey Moore. We had spent six months together as midshipmen in *Glasgow*. He looked faint. I said, 'Is that you, Dinsey?' He said, 'Yes, Welland, what the hell are you doing?' His boat was in pretty bad shape, so I put a line on him and towed him back to Scapa. We also got off a few of his men who had been injured; they had their heads banged. Both his main engines had been dismounted, his boat was full of gas from the battery. It was a gone submarine. If it had been German I would have just scored one."

The RN Commodore had a good sense of humour and berthed them alongside each other, HMCS *Assiniboine* and HMS *Trusty*. "I was about to rush off and see the Commodore but he sent for me. I told him that I didn't know there was one of our submarines in the damn exercise. He said he thought we should have a board of enquiry and I said, 'Hear, hear.' The Fleet Communication Officer lost his job. Our troops and the submariners had a good time boozing it up. Dinsey Moore said, 'I knew you were making a pass at me. If I had thought you were going to attack me I'd have torpedoed you, you son of a bitch, and you'd never have made it.' The Commodore said he supposed I had to send a report of proceedings to Canada every month and I said yes. He said he, too, had to send one to Admiralty every month but he didn't have any strong feelings about reporting this and I said that I hadn't any strong feelings about mentioning it, either. All it would have done is caused a lot of trouble. It didn't cost Canada anything except fourteen depth charges."

Welland paused, smiling at the memory, then added, "But it was *embarrassing*, Hal, it really *was*."

Talking about Bob Welland taking *Moose Jaw* to sea for her one-day work-up in the summer of 1941 brings back memories of the ramming and sinking of U-501. We had done a few exercises on our own but we were a long way from being as efficient as a warship should be when we were sent to join the mid-ocean escort force based at St. John's, Newfoundland. Two years after the start of the war the corvettes were manned pretty well solely from RCNVR sailors just a few months off the beach. The RCN, the pre-war permanent force, were nearly all in the destroyers which were more complicated weapons of war and really required professionals to run them. We started the war with about eighteen hundred of these professionals and the navy had increased by this time to more then ten times its pre-war strength. So when we lost a destroyer we lost, mostly, these well-trained officers and men. Our Captain was pre-war RCN, Lieutenant Freddie Grubb, and the rest of us, apart from one Leading Seaman, were reserves. The First Lieutenant had never been to sea before he sailed with us; neither had the other Sub-Lieutenant. The Navigator, Ruddle-Brown, had his Mate's ticket, had come back from twenty years retirement to do his bit. I had been lucky and had nearly two years' sea time. We were put under the command of *Chambly* and sailed from St. John's for three days of exercises. *Chambly*'s Captain, Commander Chummy Prentice, was permanent force. (A monocle was a fixed part of his rig; nobody ever saw him without it, not ever.) He too had "swallowed the anchor" many years before but had returned for wartime service. Ninety-nine per cent of his crew were reserve.

We were told to join up with SC42, a heavily attacked convoy, and we set out at best speed. It transpired that this convoy was attacked by a wolf pack of about nine U-boats. On this particular night, as we were cutting quietly along expecting to make a rendezvous the following day, the Captain came up to the bridge about eleven for a final look around. I had been astern of station on *Chambly* by about five degrees and the Captain had vehement views on being off-station; he was wont to express these loudly and at great length. But I had sensed his presence – it was quite dark – and softly ordered the helmsman to steer five degrees to starboard, which put the senior ship on our beam where she was supposed to be. Now this is alright if the Captain doesn't stay too long; if he does then you gradually drift out of sight of the ship you are supposed to be keeping station on and harsh words come your way. He stayed only a few minutes. All serene. All as it should be. The wind keened gently in the rigging; the bow dug gently into the swells with a soft rush of water up the hawse pipes. *Chambly*'s bow wave shimmered two cables off.

"I'll be in my bunk if you want me, Sub," said Freddie.

"Aye aye, sir."

I altered course to port a bit and cranked up the speed a few revs to get in station and breathed a sigh of relief. Another blast from the Captain avoided. I suppose about an hour passed. Then *Chambly* came up on voice radio, "Have good contact and am attacking." She altered away. I followed. Better tell the Captain. Better still, ring action stations. Before I could, the night exploded. First, *Chambly*'s depth charges exploded, then a tanker went up in a mountain of flame some miles ahead. The convoy! Then another sheet of flame. Then the *whump, whump, whump* of torpedoes hitting their target. Further

depth-charge rumbles from ahead. The escorting destroyer and corvettes must have fired starshell, the convoy ships fired their flares.
Red tracer arched ahead, to port, to starboard.

The Captain arrived breathless, and looked incredulously at the carnage I had apparently wrought. And he had left everything so nice and
quiet. Now, just look at it!

"Lawrence, what *are* you *doing*?"

On the port quarter the geysers of water erupted by *Chambly*'s
depth charges subsided and in the middle was a U-boat. Freddie
altered to ram. U-501 made off in the general direction of Germany.
We followed, trying to overtake and get out on her beam so we could
ram. He kept altering to point his arse at us – he had stern tubes there
he could fire at us.

The Captain's order, "Stand by to ram," was repeated fore and aft,
from truck to keelson, throughout the ship. For the first time I heard
the joyful battle cry of the Canadian sailor going in to ram the enemy
with the certainty of time in harbour for repairs, "Refit! Refit!"

The carnage ahead continued. We weaved and spun at full speed in
pursuit of the twisting, turning U-boat. Our forward gun fired. Then
followed a freakish accident. Our whirling-dervish dance brought the
U-boat and *Moose Jaw* beam to beam about twenty feet apart – so close
our guns could not depress to fire. The Germans boiled out on deck. A
figure balanced on the rolling top of the conning tower and made the
most amazing standing jump I had ever seen. He hurtled through the
air and landed on our deck.

"See what he wants," said the Captain and altered course to open
the range.

We opened, turned in, altered to close, and rammed. Not dead on at
right angles, but refit-worthy. I slid down the ladder to my interview.

"Away boarding party," sang out the Captain. That was me too. I
seemed to be doing everything.

The 4-inch which had been silent spoke again, and hit the forward
gun of the U-boat. Quite ruined it. Now that's a chance in a million,
maybe two. But Bill Spinney, the Gunnery Officer, got really quite
impossible about this. Telling the story later he used to say, "I saw the
Krauts going for their forward gun; so I shot it away."

I dropped with my crew into the skiff and set off for U-501 but Ted
Simmons from *Chambly* was ahead of me and signified that I should
fuck off so I picked up survivors and returned. Go away again and get
more, said the Captain; but this time he buggered off and left me. I

think he had seen another U-boat. Anyway, I got picked up as dawn was breaking, having dropped my second load of survivors on *Kenogami*, "Cowboy" Jackson driving. "Most were dead," he told me later, "although I know they were alive enough when you picked them up." They died of exposure to the wind, which, while not really cold, was enough to kill a wet man. We in the skiff's crew had covered them with our duffle coats but it did no good. This was my first sight of the danger of exposure. God knows we were cold enough and we were dry.

U-501 sank. We lost SS *Muneric, Empire Springbuck, Empire Hudson, Sally Maersk, Baron Pentland, Tachee, Winterswijk,* and *Stagaard* that night. And many more in the days ahead on our way to Scotland – fifteen out of the sixty-four we started with. Other U-boats joined the wolf pack. Some went home with their supply of torpedoes expended. There were up to ten U-boats left that had a go at us.

There is a sad sequel to this story. When Commandor Hugo Förster, the Captain of U-501, landed in a heap on the deck of *Moose Jaw* and struggled to his feet, the words he spoke to me were, "Do not fire. Do not fire on my men anymore. We have stopped firing. We surrender." It is my firm conviction that he made this jump not to save his own life but to save the lives of his crew. But I noticed in the days that followed that relations seemed strained between himself and his First Lieutenant – they were sharing our Captain's harbour cabin. I stood with them when they got their daily airing, ruefully watching the convoy sail calmly on. When it came time to land them at Greenoch, Scotland, Commander Förster asked me if he could say goodbye to his men for they would undoubtedly be going to separate prisoner-of-war camps. I said of course, and we fell in by the brow just as his U-boat crew filed up from aft to get into the waiting trucks. Förster extended his hand to the first man and wished him good luck. The man ignored Förster's outstretched hand, averted his head, and strode ashore without a word. So did all the others.

About ten years ago I heard that in the camp Förster was sent to in the United Kingdom, his court martial was arranged by other U-boat officers in the camp. It was, of course, an *in camera* trial and certainly without the knowledge of the Commanding Officer of the camp or any of the guards. He was to be tried for cowardice, abandoning his ship. For any Captain to be the first to leave his sinking vessel is simply not done in any navy in the world. His motives may be of the highest but this is just not on. Had he been found guilty the penalty would probably have been death – and that could have been arranged. But the camp authorities found out about the intended court martial and Föster was moved to Canada. About two years ago I found out that there had been exchanges of prisoners of war before the fighting had stopped, before Germany surrendered. Sometime towards the end of 1944 Förster was repatriated (if this is the word) to Germany, through Sweden. In Germany there was a board of inquiry and then Förster was tried by court martial for cowardice. The court-martial officers – mark you this, it is important – were not SS officers or Nazi thugs; they were *Kriegsmarine* officers of the U-boat arm. Förster was found guilty and was shot I heard.

Then there was U-94 in August 1942. I was in another corvette then, HMCS *Oakville*, under the command of Lieutenant-Commander Clarence King, DSC. (Rugby and *Conway* was Uncle Clarence, his DSC from World War One when he commanded a Q-ship and sank a U-boat. Back from running his fruit farm in the Okanagan Valley in British Columbia, he wanted to do his bit, sink more submarines, and, presumably, get another DSC; as it turned out he got a DSO.) A real fire-eater, was Clarence, but then, looking back, weren't we all?

We departed Port of Spain, Trinidad, with a fast convoy of tankers, picked up a few more at Curaçao, Aruba, and Maracaibo and on the night of August 28, were on a northerly course just south of Haiti and heading for New York. I was asleep on the upper deck in only my tropical shorts when the action alarm bells jangled; I heaved myself up and bolted for the bridge to join the other semi-nudes. A rumble of depth charges exploding shuddered up through the hull. I was asdic officer and found Leading Seaman Hartman, our senior anti-submarine rating, already on the set and sweeping the a/s beam ahead. He pointed to a plume of water subsiding ahead. A USN patrol aircraft, a Catalina, circled; then she flashed SSSS – submarine! The Captain headed for the spot – dressed as if he were about to call on the Admiral, he always was. I donned the headphones and heard a submarine blowing tanks. I had never heard it before except on a record at the a/s school but that's what it was. In the turbulence caused by the Catalina's depth bombs, I couldn't get a good echo to tell me when to fire our depth charges and the Captain was somewhat annoyed with me. We only got enough to know the target was moving left. That didn't faze Clarence. He aimed *Oakville*'s bow off and ordered me to drop a pattern as we crossed the white foam left by the aircraft bombs.

Ours were set to 50 and 100 feet, our stern reared and the ship shuddered as they went off, the mountain of water they raised mast-head high. A pounce attack. We turned to do a deliberate attack. The black snout of a submarine reared up in the subsiding mist of our depth-charge explosions.

"Ho, ho," said the Captain with immense satisfaction. Not a quote which would go down in naval yarns of joining action with the enemy. Nothing to compare with "England expects. . . ," "I have not yet begun to fight," "Damn the torpedoes. . .," but a bit better than, "What *are* you *doing*?" His next order was better: "Stand by to ram." Again I heard the Canadian sailors reply from stem to stern, "Refit! Refit!" Cheyne, one of our bright eighteen-year-old signalmen, unbidden, fired two rockets which flared heavenward and burst into bright stars. Very pretty, and the "submarine sighted" signal. Cheyne also manned the starboard .5 machine gun, a versatile lad, lots of initiative. We charged in to the U-boat, now fully surfaced, white water cascading off her hull. We had been too close to get a good collision course. Missed! But not by much. The sub grated down our starboard side and fell astern. We ran out to open the range and try again. Now it was the gunner's turn. Our 4-inch flashed out, and again. Then the gratifying red glow of a hit. (Maybe it wasn't as hard as I had thought it was. First in the *Moose Jaw* we hit U-501 with our 4-inch gun and now again in *Oakville*. Lieutenant-Commander (G) Hugh Pullen and others from Whale Island always made such a *fuss* about how *technical* gunnery was; it didn't seem that hard, just point the gun and fire.)

The Captain was now on the starboard wing of the bridge and the sub on the starboard bow. Cheyne, behind his machine gun, let off a stream of slugs that just missed the Captain's ear. You've heard of a standing broad jump but have you ever heard of a standing side jump? No? Well that night Captain King made one of thirteen feet to the port side of the bridge – nearly into the fire of another enterprising signalman, Bradley. Two streams of traces arched ahead, the 4-inch boomed from time to time. The pompom aft was silent; we called it a "pom" because it always jammed after the first round; now, a detached part of my mind told me, it had jammed *before* the first round. It never had gone "pom pom pom pom pom" as the makers and as Whale Island intended; now it couldn't even seem to produce its customary "pom."

The Captain got on a ramming course again. But Otto Ites in U-94 had other views and weaved violently. His guns' crews were blown into the water by our hail of lead but our gunfire, with such a flat trajectory, was not reaching his vitals. Just before we hit, Ites swung to port, and we missed again. Again U-94 passed down our side so close that our guns could not depress enough to bear on the target. Ah, but we had another weapon hitherto untried in the Battle of the Atlantic, indeed, hitherto unheard of, even by us. Stokers not needed in the boiler rooms were on the fiddley abaft the funnel to reload the depth-charge throwers. On the fiddley abaft the funnel was also where the canteen manager stored his empty Coke bottles. Since I had forgotten to fire the throwers, and since an enemy should obviously be fired upon, a constant stream of Coke bottles now sailed over from the stokers with much partisan baseball invective. Also I remember that from port and starboard, from forward to aft, the spitting of the strip Lewis gun was heard; this was Drinkwater, an OD only about five foot four, just a little higher than his gun, galloping gallantly around, gun under one arm and spare ammo drums under the other. *Oakville* ran out yet again, wheeled yet again, and bore in at full speed yet again. The Captain had got the hang of it.

At nearly right angles our stem hit U-94 just abaft the conning tower, our bow rose high, higher. U-94 rolled and was forced under. The grinding and shrieking of tearing metal was bad enough on the bridge; it must have been frightful in the magazines, boiler rooms, and engine room. We slowed as some of our bottom was torn out. U-94 broached just under our stern. Leading Torpedoman Charlie Skeggs, the senior hand of our depth-charge crew aft, had the same fine qualities as one of his professional predecessors, Leading Torpedoman Pat Budge. He saw his duty plain before him and he did it. No orders from the bridge necessary. He set a depth charge to fifty feet and plopped it over the stern alongside U-94. Lights went out, black smoke erupted from the funnel, the stern bucked, telephones shrieked as various parts of the ship phoned in various mishaps: "Gowdyk is dogged down in the a/s compartment which is flooding; may we open up?"

"Yes."

"The tiller flat is flooding; may we evacuate?"

"No, stay and fix it."

Oakville chugged on at reduced speed, wheeled, and headed in again.

"Away boarding party," the Captain roared. "Come on, Lawrence, get cracking. Never mind the skiff. I'll put you alongside."

"Aye, aye, sir." But I thought skeptically of his three misses. Oh well, even my old mum never promised me immortality.

The boarding party mustered on the forecastle. The 4-inch gun had had a misfire and was silent. The .5s on the bridge chattered. Drinkwater leaped about with his .303 Lewis gun squirting a few rounds when he could. The little bugger was everywhere and disconcerted us quite as much as the Germans. It's annoying to have a *brrrrrrrt*, *brrrrrrrt* go off behind your ear when you don't expect it. There had been an Admiralty Fleet Order out on the equipment needed for a boarding party. It was quite firm on the subject and listed what would have seemed a plethora of gear even for the great American tourist except that a camera wasn't mentioned. But I had a length of chain to pass through the conning-tower hatch so the perfidious Hun could not submerge and leave us swimming. All the usual stuff one would expect. We looked like an impudent implausibility of infantry: steel helmets, web belts, .45 revolvers, grenades, torches, a signal light for Cheyne, a bag of tools for the stoker, but no entrenching tools. Dress, tropical informal: since we had been sleeping in an August night in the Caribbean, tropical shorts or underwear shorts, no shirts, no socks, only those who had been on watch had gym shoes.

The chanted litany of the 4-inch gun's crew had been filtering through my subconscious mind unheeded. Now an internal alarm bell rang. I had heard, "Open the breech."

"Breech opening. Stand by."

"Get the whoreson out." (Not in the drill book, that.)

Splash. (As the smouldering round was daintily dropped over the side.)

"Load."

U-94 was now close under port bow; 4-inch was training around towards her – and us.

"Get down, get clear," I yelled.

Clang. The breech block shut.

"Layer on. Trainer on."

I threw myself sideways.

"Fire."

BOOM

I regained consciousness in the break of the forecastle, a drop of about eight feet. Ears and nose bleeding, the rest of the boarding party scattered in an unseamanlike jumble, all out cold.

"Come on, sir. The sub's alongside," said a Petty Officer.

I remembered a phrase of my father's and sang out, "Come on then. You can't live forever."

I vaulted lightly and gracefully over the gunwale and sailed serenely down ten feet to the U-boat's deck wishing I had a cutlass between my teeth. Was I not leading a boarding party onto an enemy ship on the Spanish Main?

U-94's deck surged up to meet me. Instead of the Nureyev-Baryshnikov entrechat and feather-down landing, I had a spine-jarring, heels-first thud.

My exaltation-of-larks' mood snapped. So did the elastic in my tropical shorts. They slipped down around my ankles and I tripped over the other side of U-94.

Swimming aboard on the next swell, the only other conscious member of my boarding party and I lurched up the deck to U-94's bridge. Two Germans appeared from some mysterious hatch I didn't know about. (Since we had captured U-570 off Iceland the year before, we all knew the layout of this 800-ton submarine well; at least, those of us detailed as Boarding Officers did. U-570 was now HMS *Graph*.) Others came from aft. One I knocked over the side with the .45 barrel and the others jumped over.

Oakville was a half mile away, stopped, guns silent. Sinking, I supposed.

Well, I had this boat if she didn't sink too. That's why we were here – to prevent her sinking. A prize of war, codes, prisoners, cyphers, intelligence information beyond imagination, all pukka gen. Up the ladder to the bridge to find the Germans boiling out.

We're two against perhaps thirty. Stop them. They won't stop. They want out. Shoot two. The remainder stay below. What now?

There's a half-open hatch aft. Leave the Petty Officer on the bridge. Skitter back and see if we're going to be flanked from there. As the hull rises, rush; as the hull sinks and the rollers sweep over, fall prone and grab the wooden gratings. It's all dark in the compartment below the hatch. Chuck a hand grenade in and scuttle away. *Whump.*

Oakville's pompom opens up. Finally! But now! Some silly SOBs never get the word. The rounds chip away at the wooden gratings and *whing-whing-whing* off the steel hull. Safer in the water; a sharp pain in left arm. A wooden splinter, some blood. Hurrah. Now I am a wounded war veteran. Swim back on next wave. Climb again to the bridge. Now to get the German crew out so we can get below. This is not easy when you have shot the first two that tried to come out. Turning on what Celtic charm I inherited from the Irish side of the family, I crooned in dulcet tones down the hatch to the dark control room below. None of the U-boat crew seemed beguiled, and in retrospect I can see that this was probably due to my flashlight reflecting back on bleeding ears and nose and the resultant gore on my chest. But they came, hesitant at first, then in a rush.

Goddamn! Now there were a dozen of them and two of us on a bridge which would normally hold five or six. Getting them aft to the gun platform helped; one by one they heaved themselves up and fell in under the .45 of the Petty Officer. The bridge was partially crushed from the ramming, pock-marked from Cheyne's and Bradford's machine guns (our 4-inch brick had hit forward), and spent slugs and broken Coke bottles abounded. The hatch was jammed partially closed, and two or three corpses lolled as we swung broadside on to the twelve-foot seas. A half moon cast a wan light, green phosphorescence boiled as we made leeway, and I dropped below.

It's dark down here but for the orange glow of my flashlight, weak now from constant dunking in the sea. Nothing much here; the controls are one deck below. Down again. Flooded down here, water surging back and forth as we roll. Now ankle high, now chest high. Let's see, where are the controls to the main ballast tanks. The port side. I slipped and went underwater on a long roll. As the water receded I arose. But now which side was port? Ah, this side. And there are the pressure gauges.

Yes, how well the Confidential Admiralty Fleet Order (CAFO) now came back to me. And how painstaking had I been to memorize the details of the insides of a 800-ton U-boat. How well those shore-side administrators prepared us to fight the war at sea. Since I had lost the chance to salvage U-501, I had always hoped for a second chance. Here it was. And it was not too difficult. The CAFO said so:

Unless men boarding a U-boat realize they have an
extremely easy job to perform – *viz.* to prevent
the U-boat sinking – they are unlikely to succeed.

I grasped an unknown valve to steady myself against a violent roll that had a bit of fore-and-aft pitch in it and spat out a bellyful of water and oil from my last dunking. My unknown friend in Admiralty had adjured me to look for the nameplates for the ballast tanks, *Tauchz*, and the vent valve, *Entle*. He hadn't told me where the light switch was. I could have used that. Or where the Germans might stow some flashlights. Mine was now glowing a dull orange like a setting sun on a cloudy evening. I peered myopically for *Tauchz I* and *Entle I* which were forward, *Tauchz III* and *Entle III* which were midships, and aft for *Tauchz* and *Entle V*. Also required were the *Anblasev Tauchz* and to open the master blow, the *Hauptanblasten,* controlled from the *Anschel Anblasevert,* provided there was pressure on the *Druckluff.* There was, as far as I could see, which wasn't very far.

The lively motion of a boat stopped in a seaway had slowed; more sodden now. A thud which shook the hull told me that a bulkhead had given way. The oscillating wave inside the hull was developing greater strength. Twice I was treading water; then it receded to my thighs.

The Petty Officer I had left on deck shouted down, "Better get out, sir. I think they have a scuttling charge set." I would have been surprised if they hadn't, but had been trying to keep this thought at the back of my mind. But if I could blow the main ballast tanks and keep her on the surface the Captain might get the rest of my boarding party over to me and Skeggs would know how to deal with demolition explosives.

So there was *some* pressure. Now open the vents, my Admiralty office sailor exhorted me; indeed, he had truly copied all the letters in a big round hand and copied all the letters so *carefully*:

> It is easy to open the vents, one wheel on the forrard
> bulkhead, port side – one wheel on the after bulkhead,
> port side, and push up two obvious handles abaft the
> periscope. That's all. You must admit that there is no
> difficulty in this operation.

I would *not* admit there was no difficulty in this operation. I couldn't find the "obvious" handles.

The water which had been splashing down from the open hatch through which I had descended was now becoming more of a cascade. She rolled to port and hung there, then a few more degrees to port, and hung there again. The deck canted as the bow rose. These were death spasms. Singing "Hail Queen of Heaven, the Ocean Star/Guide of the wanderer here below," to keep my spirits up, I squirmed up to the deck.

Ah, pale moonlight, a blessed trade wind, white cumulus, to the north the white glow of starshell and snowflake rockets, the red flames and smoke of a burning ship. About a mile away was *Oakville,* stopped and low in the water. Was she sinking too? Running over a submarine and dropping depth charges at fifty feet at slow speed was not the best way to maintain water-tight integrity. My prisoners hung on the rails around the after 20-mm gun. Pulling out my .45 from its holster, I motioned them over the side. With alacrity they jumped in – a drop of only a few feet now – and swam vigorously away. I gestured to my Petty Officer, "You too." He jumped and followed U-94's sailors. I was alone on my prize of war.

So much for dreams. This boat would never sail as a prize into Guantanamo, Cuba, with the Canadian white ensign flying superior to the German swastika. I flicked my torch at *Oakville* sure in the knowledge that the Yeoman of Signals, George Ballinger, or Cheyne, or Bradley, would be keeping an eye on me. Good lads those. I hoped I had not been too hard on them in the past. I flashed PSB PSB PSB PSB (please send boat). I got a T T T T (message received) and then silence. Then *Oakville*'s light flashed again, MRU (much regret unable).

My clothing was now down to one Mae West lifebelt and one revolver belt. I unbuckled the revolver belt and tossed it in the water. Then, feeling rather naked. I picked up a pair of binoculars hung around the voice pipe. (I can use those, I thought. Besides, Macintyre took Kretschmer's.) Then I stepped into the water, rolled on my back, and swam away. Sharks and barracuda were active; I kept one hand on my private parts and propelled myself with the other, gently. I had heard sharks were attracted by splashing. And blood. I swam away from wounded men, too. Not heroic, you say? No. I was just so damn mad at losing U-94 that I just thought "Bugger them all!" The U-boat's bow rose, rose higher, and she slid quietly down into the thousand fathoms to join the Spanish, French, and British ships that had met their end in the Napoleonic wars and before. The senior officer of the escort in the destroyer USS *Lea* came up in a smother of foam and swirling water as his engines went full astern. We all splashed towards his jumping ladder in a most unseemly and noisy race. The U-boat crew started a clamorous chorus around the *Lea*'s ladder. A real scramble of frightened men. Fifteen-odd Germans, and me. This welter of splashing arms and yelling mouths reminded me of the Tuscan army before the Tiber bridge: "Those behind cry 'Forward.' Those in front cry 'Back.' " I had always thought Germans had more sense of decorum, of seniority. Apparently not. It was time to assert my leadership again. "Gangway for a sub-lieutenant," I shouted, "we can't *all* be saved."

All that happened forty-three years ago. But I don't think I'll ever quite forgive myself for not salvaging U-94. If I had only. . . .

If you find strange my lugubrious treatment of these two U-boat kills, you must remember that many of the men I had done my training with seemed to be turning in a much more polished and professional performance than I was. According to them, true, but also according to others.

I didn't meet Roger Hill, DSO, DSC, until the Normandy Invasion in 1944 when he was driving HMS *Jervis*. She and *Sioux* were ordered to cover minesweepers while they swept a channel into the port of Le Havre. Four shore guns opened up on us at about our maximum range, ten miles, so we couldn't do much to silence them and protect the minesweepers. We therefore got to windward and made smoke which comfortably obscured them. The German gunners saw that we were hiding their main target and shifted fire to us for three hours. Then we withdrew. In talking this over with Roger later we got onto the subject of U-boats and I told him of my balls-up. He, more inventive than I, said that when he had commanded *Ledbury* he had worked out a drill that a constant hail of fire would be thrown at a surfaced U-boat while the boarding party went over, to keep German heads down. After boarding, a grenade would be tossed down the conning tower, and the party would go below armed with coshes, knives, and knuckle-dusters and demand that the crew surrender. Like me, they spoke no German but had had cards made up which read, in phonetic spelling, "*Hauptventile zumachen lassen oder ich tote sie*," which meant "Shut the main vents or I kill you," and "*Haupttauch zellen ausblasen lassen sonst tote ich sie*," which meant, "Blow the main ballast tanks or I kill you."

I was envious that I hadn't thought of it but was reassured of the frailty of human nature when he said that, again like me, salvaging and getting cypher and code books were his first priority. Failing that, next were binoculars and booze.

A bit later in the war, *Regina* sank the Italian submarine *Avorio* the first time she was in action. She got a contact, dropped depth charges, the submarine surfaced, opened fire on *Regina* and fled. *Regina* returned the fire warmly and gave chase. A gun duel! For nearly an hour the chase continued. Then the submarine crew began jumping over the side and their vessel sank. It all seemed so tidy, so simple, so professional. Of course Italians did not fight with the same tenacity and courage as the Germans. But still. . . .

Then there was our frigate *Waskesiu* and her first U-boat in the Atlantic. She picked her adversary up on radar, got contact, dropped depth charges, and the U-boat surfaced, helpless. For fifteen minutes *Waskesiu*'s 20mm sprayed the Germans. Eventually most of the conning tower was shot away and U-237 tilted almost to the perpendicular and sank. So *tidy*.

Just a month or so before our *Oakville* kill, our destroyer *St. Croix* had spotted a surfaced U-boat at about four miles. Cranking up to full speed she set out in chase but the U-boat dived when she had closed to three miles. Asdic range was one mile at the best, perhaps a few hundred yards more in good conditions. Thus the U-boat Commander had a vast array of courses and speeds and depths to choose from to elude *St. Croix*; or he could be silent. At the ten miles he had led our destroyer from the convoy, it was certain that no other ship could now hunt him. But the Captain of *St. Croix* had a sea sense and an uncanny skill of getting into the mind of his enemy. And this time he read him correctly. Aiming off by instinct he reduced to a good searching speed:

Ping. . . . .
Ping. . . . .
Ping. . . . . Beep
Ping. . . . . Beep
Ping. . . . . BEEP

There she was! A fine fat metallic echo, correct extent of target for that Doppler, reasonable rate of change of bearing, moving left. A pounce attack first; then the slower deliberate attack. Three times a ten-charge pattern was dropped, over seven tons of TNT.

Oil and wreckage appeared on the surface. Was this a *ruse de guerre*? It could be. U-boats would often discharge wreckage and oil, even sundry clothing and books. But this time there was oil, wood, food, cigarettes, and bits of human bodies upon which shrieking herring gulls plummeted. (This all had to be gathered and landed later for analysis; in the past some of these "human" remains had been pronounced to be pig or sheep guts. Very deceitful, the Hun. War brings out the worst in all of us.) So, was this really a kill? The Captain thought so. Amongst the flotsam and jetsam was a lacy, filmy brassiere. All sailors collect their trophies. This one was labelled, "Triumph! Paris." We were sure that the phlegmatic German Naval

Intelligence (Department of Dirty Tricks) could not rise to so subtle a deceit. Surely even the Chief of German Intelligence, Admiral Canaris, would not, with his Teutonic mind, think of such a Gallic *ruse de guerre*.

Toward the end of July 1942, *Skeena* and *Wetaskiwin* did a pas de deux with biblical overtones to a dirge of death for another U-boat. *Skeena* was investigating a contact and signalled *Wetaskiwin* for assistance, "Acts 16, Verse 9." The Captain in the "Wet Ass Queen" thumbed through the Bible always kept on the bridge for signalling purposes and read:

> And a vision appeared to Paul in the night; there stood a man of Macedonia and prayed him saying, come over into Macedonia and help me.

Wetaskiwin increased speed and swung over while she replied, "Revelations 13, Verse 1," which told *Skeena*:

> And I stood upon the sand of the sea and saw a beast rise up out of the sea having seven heads and ten horns, and upon his horns ten crowns, and upon his head the name of blasphemy.

But these two ships with their large black hunting pennants at the yardarm would make sure that this horned beast would never rise from the sea again. The two-ship hunting manoeuvre which had evolved was for one ship to lie off (let us say to the west) and hold the contact (bearing to the east). The other ship would steam in (say from south to north) and carry out a deliberate attack. The attacking ship would fire when her asdic trace told her she was over the sub; the directing ship would signal when *she* saw the attacking ship pass over the bearing on which she was holding contact. A double check. Then the attacking ship would run out, turn bows on to the echo, and when *she* had contact again take over the role of directing ship while her consort attacked.

Twist and turn as she might, the U-boat was held by the relentless probing sound beam of her two hunters. For five hours the hunt went on; the team worked as they had been trained by Torpedo Gunner Pat Budge; Lieutenant Bob Welland; the Training Commander, Jimmy Hibbard and his staff in Halifax and St. Margaret's Bay and Pictou; and the trainers in St. John's, Liverpool, Londonderry, and a dozen others. They used the skills taught to them by these hundreds of trainers and learned for themselves in the last three bitter years at sea.

The Asdic Petty Officers and the Asdic Officers listen to the ping of their sound waves going out, the reverberations returning as a hundred fish or pieces of seaweed sent back their small echoes: a school of porpoises send back larger echoes which can be identified as does a whale, which is about the right size for a sub, but a whale's echo is soft, not metallic, and a whale turns quicker than a sub can. The ASO's eye follows the sound trace of the U-boat as the eye of God followed Cain across the desert. Signalmen hoist and dip the flag signals and flash visual messages on their lamps; the Yeoman passes messages to the consort over the voice circuit; the depth-charge crews wait; the guns' crews wait, all silently urging the U-boat to surface. And the Captains guide all, in, after three years of battles, almost a relaxed way. As *Wetaskiwin* closes *Skeena,* who has the contact, extracts from the signal logs go on with the story:

WETASKIWIN You direct the hunt. Give me my station and course.

SKEENA Take station on my port beam; 1 mile, course 228 degrees.
(Later) Turn 180 degrees to port together.
(Later) Course 070 degrees.
(Later) I am now over my last contact. Start square search from here.

WETASKIWIN Contact bearing 260 degrees, 1900 yards.
(Later) Contact is firm.
(Later) Contact bearing 200 degrees, 1300 yards.
Attacking. (She drops a ten-charge pattern)
Lost contact at 600 yards.
By my plot you are over sub.
Contact bearing 210 degrees, 1900 yards.

SKEENA Contact bearing 345 degrees, 1600 yards.
Am attacking. Please keep to port. (She drops a ten-charge pattern)

WETASKIWIN Confirmed right spot.
Contact bearing 300 degrees, 1000 yards.
Attacking. (She drops a ten-charge pattern)
Lost contact.

SKEENA Echo bearing 120 degrees, 700 yards.

WETASKIWIN Think this attack mine also.

SKEENA	I agree.
WETASKIWIN	Attacking now. (She drops another pattern)
SKEENA	Unable to gain contact.
WETASKIWIN	I will direct you.
SKEENA	Attacking. (She drops a pattern)
WETASKIWIN	Excellent.
SKEENA	Did you hear an underwater explosion?
WETASKIWIN	Yes. Definitely.
SKEENA	Your turn.
WETASKIWIN	Attacking. (She drops a pattern) Plenty of wreckage over this way.
SKEENA	I am lowering a whaler to pick up guts.

But that was only one less in the wolf pack that was attacking that convoy. Plenty left to provide the excitement that is a welcome change from the more usual monotony. The corvette *Sackville* had her share of fun.

At dusk the next evening she sighted a U-boat and raced out after it. As she did, however, starshell from the other escorts and snowflake rockets from the merchantmen flared in the gloom astern of her. The convoy was being attacked. She spun to help counter the closer threat. And there ahead of her, silhouetted against the glare, was another U-boat. Go after this one. Since this U-boat could not escape *out* from the convoy she headed *into* the convoy.

This isn't as wild a tactic as you might think. Lieutenant-Commander Otto Kretschmer, as I have said, once went down the centre column of a convoy from the van to the rear, shooting torpedoes to port and starboard as he went. Lieutenant-Commander Jimmy Hibbard in *Skeena* in Convoy SC42 in 1941 chased a U-boat down the columns from ahead to astern, firing as he went, the U-boat firing as she went through, the merchant ships firing at the passing U-boat and pointing and yelling encouragement to Jimmy as he passed, "She went thataway."

Oh, yes, we did have our moments. But to get back to *Sackville*. She lost that U-boat, as I say, into the convoy. Another *whump* of a torpedo striking home and a merchantman near her blew up. In the glare *Sackville* saw another U-boat making off into the fog and the gloom. Again she gave chase. The submarine crash-dived. *Sackville* ran over the swirling turbulence and dropped her charges. With the first explosions of the pattern the U-boat's bow reared out of the water, the hull followed to perhaps half her length; then the rest of the depth-charge pattern boiled the sea into a maelstrom. The U-boat hull slipped back. *Sackville* returned for yet another attack. The contact was still there but fuzzy from the aerated water. Another pattern. Then, an underwater explosion that was certainly not a depth charge. An uprush of oil to the surface.

An hour later she sighted another, just a couple of ship's lengths to port. Hard-a-port. But in the fog she lost contact. Thirty minutes later she heard the rapid, smooth thrumming of a U-boat's propellers (quite different from the turbine and the reciprocating beat of a destroyer or a corvette.) Almost dead ahead. There she is. Increase speed. Stand by to ram. ("Refit! Refit!") The U-boat Captain altered *towards*. In under the bow he went, so close that the guns could not depress enough to fire at him. As with *Moose Jaw* and U-501, they went into their *danse macabre, Sackville* attempting to ram and the U-boat twisting and turning to avoid and to remain within the corvette's turning circle so the gun would be mute. But the machine guns rattled away. A miscalculation on the part of the submarine Captain: the 4-inch came on. *Blam.* A hit at the base of the conning tower. The U-boat Captain prudently left his bridge. As the hatch clanged behind him the sub crash-dived. Sweep the area. No echoes. Where is she? No echoes. Whatever course the submarine Captain chose it was the right one for him. He was not seen again. A busy night for *Sackville* and only one of many in a busy life.

If you would like to see her now, Her Majesty's Canadian Ship *Sackville*, the only corvette left of the 123 that Canadians manned, she rests in Halifax, the base from which she sailed to so many convoys and so many battles. If, while you walk through her, you see portly grey-haired men also rummaging around with an air of melancholy illuminated by an occasional smile, the odds are that you have met them in their youth somewhere in these pages.

Five days later, August 6, 1942, it was *Assiniboine* who got into a difference of opinion with our German friends. She was about four hundred miles off Newfie. A wolf pack of about five U-boats had been marauding around the convoy all day. It was sunny with some cloud, but there were large foggy areas, lifting and falling, receding and sweeping in again. Submarines had been sighted all day but as the screening ships dashed over to close the range and attack, they would retreat into the mist. In the last dog watch things quietened down and one watch of the hands was piped to supper. The action alarm bells clanged again. In one clear patch a lookout sighted a U-boat just off the port bow. Full speed ahead. A stern chase – always lengthy. Petty Officer George Vander Hagen was caught with his pants down. I do not speak metaphorically; he was in the shower (in defiance of the First Lieutenant's Standing Orders). He told me, "I stuck my feet in a pair of seaboots, no socks, no underpants, no shorts, nothing, and up to the gunnery director I scoot." For an hour *Assiniboine* gradually closed the enemy and the Captain, Lieutenant-Commander Johnny Stubbs, found this most exasperating as he couldn't fire his guns – and he had two 4.7-inch that could have sunk the enemy if only they could see her.

It was in the gunnery director – at the after end of the bridge – that the aiming and firing of the guns was controlled. Here, high above spray and smoke sat four men: the Gunnery Control Officer (GCO) who directed the fall of shot onto the target from visual observation of the previous splashes; the Range-taker who took "cuts" with his optical instrument and thus fed range to the computer below decks; the Director Trainer who slewed the director in azmuth and fed the bearing of the enemy to the computer; and the Director Layer who, by keeping the cross hairs of his binoculars on the target both corrected for the roll of the ship and fed angle of elevation to the computer. He also fired all the guns and thus was one of the most important specialists in the ship. This man in *Assiniboine* was George Vander Hagen. Like the Captain, he found this elusive target most exasperating. He told me, "It nearly drove the gunnery team nuts to sight this enemy, get the director layer and trainer on, feed their bearings and elevations and ranges to the computer [which then moved pointers at the guns, they followed the director's pointers and were thus on the target]. The GCO gives the order "Broadsides", and the U-boat disappears into a fog patch – in and out, for an hour!"

As the range began to shorten it became clear that the U-boat intended to fight it out on the surface. This is one of the difficult choices of a U-boat Captain. If he can safely do so he will submerge and swim quietly away. Admiral Dönitz – himself a submariner from World War One – had made it clear that the job of a U-boat was sinking merchantmen and warships when they came within their periscope. But when the Captain submerged in the path of an approaching convoy escort, he was very vulnerable for the two or three minutes when he could fire neither his guns nor his torpedoes. It takes about a minute to clear the bridge of a submarine before the Captain drops below – always the last. It takes longer – up to four minutes – to get to depth and trim the boat if he has had a crew manning his forward and after guns. In this time a destroyer will close him by over two miles.

The hot pursuit continued; the range shortened; the U-boat altered toward and opened fire, steering for the magic circle where she would be within the turning circle of *Assiniboine* and Vander Hagen's 4.7-inch guns could not depress enough to hit her. Stubbs altered to ram. The submarine altered away. Stubbs manoeuvred to bring his guns to bear. U-210 countered. Dodging and twisting and weaving, the mêlée continued. Germans had piled on deck to man their guns. The small-calibre weapons of *Assiniboine* had killed some; they were replaced; more were knocked over. The 20mm of the destroyer was replied to by the 40mm of the U-boat. Our heavy guns would not bear but hers had a big, high, long target. The hail of shell hit both adversaries again and again. Vander Hagen had the best view of the action, in his gunnery director high above all others in the ship, "I saw our forward 4.7-inch hit three or four times; one hit the loading number, Ken Watson, he was carrying a 4.7 projectile – just blew him apart." The whole bridge structure was being riddled – obviously U-210's most favoured target and the Captain and Hennessy and all and sundry there swayed back and forth and up and down.

Vander Hagen said, "The guy who got my admiration was the Captain. He never flinched. There was bloody stuff flying all over the place, but he was going to hit that sub and he bloody well did, too. He was a cool one under fire, believe me; just sat in his chair and ran the action from there most of the time." A cannon round hit an upper-deck gasoline-stowage on the starboard. Hennessy said, "Johnny was busy trying to get squared away so he could really have a bash at the sub. Then there was this fire on the starboard upper." Stubbs said, "Ralph, go and take care of that." Amid the hail of lead passing his way, Hennessy went to cope with the fire.

Taking a young signalman with him to act as messenger, Hennessy dropped down to the deck below to be met by a wall of flame and smoke. No good. Over to the port side. No good either. The fire had gone through the sick-bay flat and was coming up that way. Off the after end of the bridge then, onto the mast and shinny down (resolving that there would be an addition to the First Lieutenant's Standing Orders, "Thou shalt not store gasoline on the upper deck"). When he got there everything that should be done had been done by Chief Torpedoman Burgess, in charge of the midships damage control party. Vander Hagen said, "He was the one who saved the day. Thank God Burgess was on the job. He kicked asses and got the fire hoses right into the smoke and flame." Hennessy said, "I got to the fire in time to see that I really could have stayed on the bridge for all the good I could do. The fire party was already advancing on the fire with their spray nozzles going."

After that, the First Lieutenant checked on the damage to the forward 4.7-inch guns. B gun was all right but A gun had only three of the crew left – one killed, Watson, and the rest wounded. *Assiniboine* was hit again and again. The director was hit. The GCO got shrapnel in his back; the Range-taker was hit also. Vander Hagen said, "There were splinters flying all over inside the director. A piece clipped my cap. I was wearing the fore-and-aft rig cap and a piece of shell fragment just clipped the peak of my hat in two. I never even knew it until after." (George must have donned the hat in addition to the sea boots; sartorial elegance being a mark of the gunnery branch.)

For half an hour the battle waxed and waned, swung and turned. Stubbs tried to open to either bring his guns to bear or to get on a collision course. The U-boat followed. Hard-a-starboard; she went hard-a-port. Hard-a-port, stop starboard. Midships. Full ahead starboard, stop port. Every machine gun and rifle and pistol hammered at U-210. The rapid engine and helm changes were rapped out by the Captain and relayed to the Coxswain in the wheelhouse.

This was Chief Petty Officer Max Bernays. He was at the helm himself and he watched the two telegraphmen relay the Captain's engine movements. As the flames licked the scuttle and door to starboard he ordered these hands out to help fight the fire and shut the door behind them to keep out the flames and perhaps some of the flak. Shell splinters hit him in the face but every one of the Captain's orders was carried out – one-hundred-and-forty-one of them. Stubbs was now behind the voice pipe to Bernays, bending down to give his orders; on the bridge of the U-210 he could see the German Captain bending down to his voice pipe and giving *his* orders. Burgess continued to fight his fire; others broke out, were fought and quelled. The battle continued. Who would make the first mistake? Tenaciously Stubbs held on and hammered away.

The U-boat Captain made his play. He estimated he had time to dive. At twelve knots he just had to dip his horizontal fins and, in effect, he would disappear. He held a steady course for a few seconds. His bow tilted down. Stubbs wheeled and bore in. His bow hit just abaft the conning tower and slid away – a glancing blow but it threw the sub off her trim. Hard-a-starboard and come in again. Stubbs caught her squarely this time, rolled over her, and let go depth charges. As he opened again the after 4.7-inch gun fired. A hit.

U-210's bow rose in the air. Her Captain was dead. She sank.

The stories of our destroyers sunk are told in this book: *St. Croix, Fraser, Margaree, Ottawa, Skeena,* and *Athabaskan.* Six. Twenty-eight RCN destroyers fought in the Atlantic in World War Two. For every one sunk there were two or three who were damaged in action. In 1939 the RCN destroyers had only numbered six.

In the RN, which ranged further around the world, 132 destroyers were sunk. This, too, was about their pre-war strength.

The RCN lost twenty-four ships of all classes, armed yachts, minesweepers, corvettes and frigates; 1,234 Canadian sailors were killed.

Over a thousand U-boats were built during the Battle of the Atlantic and over eight hundred of them were sunk. Of about thirty thousand U-boat sailors, about twenty-six thousand were killed.

Looking back on these battles, one's admiration and respect for the German submariner is heightened. By 1943 they knew they would lose the war. By 1944, they knew that if they survived two patrols they were lucky. By 1945, for them, death had risen from a possibility through a probability to a certainty. Yet, when hope was gone they went forth in obedience to their orders to unmarked graves. They went because their Admiral, Dönitz, had so ordered. They did have one forlorn hope, it is true. If their modern MK XXIII boats had been able to come into production. . . . That this U-boat would have prolonged the war is certain, that it would not win it is equally certain, now. But the Battle of the Atlantic was a near-run thing.

When I was about nine or ten there was much made of Regulus in the Latin class of the school I then attended. He, when besieged, was asked to surrender. It was against his orders, he said, but, if the Carthaginians would allow him to go to Rome, he would make a request to the Senate. The Senate said no. Regulus returned with his unaltered orders and was slain with his men.

It is impossible not to have admiration for those who die without hope of reward, and, in the case of the pagan, without hope of eternal life. I have to thank the Jesuits of Regiopolis College at Kingston, Ontario, for bringing to my attention in the 1930s the story of The Three Hundred at Thermopylae in their war against Persia. As Simonides tells it, they wrote their own tombstone before they died. "Stranger, if you go to Sparta, tell them how you found us lying here in obedience to their orders."

The analogy is apt, I think.

The early days of the German submariners were, like ours, an apostolate of laughter, the love of friends, of adventure, of the sea. The luminosity of a happy life devoted to duty. Some of us now go to reunions in Germany of the wartime U-boat sailors. They are muted affairs and the war is not much discussed. We in the RCN honour our dead on the first Sunday in May, Battle of Atlantic Sunday. In recent years we have taken to honouring their dead, too.

On the evening of the fourth of May in this year of our Lord 1985 a large group of the Band of Brothers gathered at *Royal Roads*. The tables were set for two hundred and fifty-one. It was the eve of Battle of Atlantic Sunday but it was, this time, more than that. It was the seventy-fifth anniversary of the founding of the Royal Canadian Navy. Rear-Admiral Bob Yanow, the Commander of our Maritime Forces, Pacific, was at the head of this venerable gathering. Around him were fourteen retired Admirals, some fifty other retired officers, the Honourable George Rogers, Lieutenant-Governor of British Columbia and a soldier who had landed on Juno Beach in Normandy forty-one years before, and the Mayor of Esquimalt. The remainder were serving officers in our navy today. Each retired officer was seated between two serving officers. I was between two young Lieutenant-Commanders who had just been appointed to their first commands. It was with considerable nostalgia that I thought of myself at that age with my first command. It was the same for all of us grey-beards. These two were pleased when Rear-Admiral Pat Budge came over to talk to us during one of the breaks that Admiral Yanow allowed out of deference to the amount of wine consumed and our ageing bladders.

Five who had lived in Admiral's House before Yanow were there, Rear-Admirals Jimmy Hibbard and John Charles among them.

Charles Dillon, while well enough, didn't think he was quite up to it and prudently stayed home. We had drinks in the castle from seven on, went up Neptune's Walk to the dining hall at eight-fifteen and took our places. The naval band played the good old songs throughout dinner, the queen was toasted about eleven, and we rose at two-thirty to go back to the castle where the junior officers played silly buggers as they have since time immemorial. We ancient mariners watched with amusement and wonder that we too had performed similar japes, just yesterday it seemed to us. We judged the show to be stridently suitable but not, of course, quite up to *our* standards. About four I found myself talking quietly to John Charles about previous ships. The sun was coming up when I got home. The youngsters, and Bob Yanow, were still at it when I left.

I'll not forget that dinner. Today's officers in their mess dress; we in dinner jackets and miniature medals. A brave sight. "Heart of Oak" was sung with gusto. At eleven in the morning we mustered again for the Battle of Atlantic Sunday church service. We gathered around the naval ensign at Duntze Head, sang "Eternal Father Strong to Save," and said the naval prayer.

Oh Eternal Lord God who alone spreadest out the heavens and rulest the raging of the sea. . .

As I stood there, head bowed, I thought of the generations of British and Canadian sailors who had said this same prayer in this same harbour. In my mind's eye I saw *Rainbow* sail past Duntze Head in 1910; her sailors too, said this prayer. And life goes on. . .

Survivors

Had we lived, I should have had a tale to tell of the hardihood, endurance, and courage of my companions which would have stirred the heart. . .our dead bodies must tell the tale.

At the South Pole, Robert Falcon Scott (1868-1912)

I saw it first in HMS *Alaunia* in 1940: it is heart-rending to have to steam through survivors in the water. They shout, even cheer, as you approach; the red lights of their lifejackets flicker when they are on the crest of a wave and are dowsed as they slip into the trough; their cries turn to incredulous despair as you glide by, unheeding, keeping a stoical face as best you can. But the cold logic of war is that these men in the water belong to a ship that has bought it and that a couple of dozen more ships survive and must be protected, for if they don't get their cargos through we will lose the war. "The safe and timely arrival of the convoy" is the overwhelming, the prime, the cardinal, the only rule.

I saw it again in HMS *Seymore*, in HMCS *Moose Jaw*, *Oakville*, and *Sioux*. I never got used to it. A lot of my friends and I were at sea from the autumn of 1939 to the summer of 1945 apart from short technical courses. I from Trinidad to Russia and from Halifax to Scotland; they, besides the Battle of the Atlantic, in other battles the world over. Although we kept stoic faces, each time was as bad as the first. We *never* got used to it. Perhaps the most pitiable cases were those where men had to leave their friends in the water – friends from another ship in their flotilla, friends they could see struggling for their life a few feet away. "Hang on, Jack, hang on; swim this way. . . ." But they had to leave.

Many men of the Royal and the allied navies died – blown up, drowned, or, more slowly, succumbing to thirst, hunger, or cold. This was their job. They knew this when they joined. But the men of the Merchant Navy were really civilians. They could leave at the end of any voyage. Yet in the main they didn't. They sailed yet again – for five-and-a-half years. Between 180,000 and 190,000 men served in the British Merchant Navy; in the allied merchant navies perhaps as many again. British merchant ships lost 32,952 men in the Second World War. That is 17 per cent, about three times the number lost by the army, about double that lost by the navy and air force. But then came the rescue ships. The shortage of escort vessels in the first year of the war did not permit the protection of convoys all the way from Canada to the United Kingdom, but with the startling growth of the Royal Canadian Navy this became possible in 1941. Also, on January 11 of that year, there sailed in convoy the first of the rescue ships, SS *Hontestroom*, of the Hollandsche Stroomboote Maatschappij Line. She was twenty years old, 1,875 gross registered tonnage, speed about eleven knots, and she was followed that month by SS *Toward* and SS *Copeland*, both sixteen years old, 1,526 tons, eleven knots. *Zaafaran* and *Zamalak* of the Pharaonic Mail Line were at sea later that year.

In the battle between the Austrian and the Italian fleets on July 20, 1866, nine hundred men lost their lives when their ships foundered. This aroused the public conscience. How to help distressed mariners? Rules were drawn up for the employment of hospital ships and these were embodied in both the Geneva Convention of 1868 and the Hague Convention of 1907 which remained in force during the two world wars. These were the progenitors of the rescue ships, a comfort to see butting sturdily along in the aftermost positions in the convoy columns, their green flag with white diagonal bar streaming in the wind.

History was made when *Copeland* became the first rescue ship to cross the Atlantic and steamed into Halifax in February 1942. There her Master forged the war-long link with the Canadian Red Cross. By March, 834,164 tons of shipping had been sunk: that is about five hundred ships of the size of the rescue vessels. On October 27, SC107 departed Halifax for the U.K. and was sighted by off Cape Race, Newfoundland, three days later by the U-boat patrol. They drew in for the kill but two were sunk by the RCAF. There were enough left – seven. As the convoy passed out of the range of air cover on November 1 the attacks started.

To the Master of the rescue ship *Stockport* it seemed a never-ending stream of survivors. The first ship to be hit was *Empire Sunrise*; her entire crew of fifty were saved. Three hours later the British *Dalcroy* was hit; her entire crew of forty-nine were picked up. Then the Greek steamer *Rinos*; twenty-six out of forty-one. *Stockport* almost collided with the wreck which was floating bottom up. *Stockport*'s Chief Officer went over the side to help but when it came time to return he fell back into the sea in exhaustion. Willing hands hauled him out. *Empire Antelope* and *Empire Leopard* were hit simultaneously; the whole crew of the former were saved but *Leopard* blew up and only four were saved. The weather deteriorated; by five in the afternoon of November 4 it was blowing hard.

Stockport was backing and filling ahead and astern to get alongside the torpedoed American *Parthenon* when her propeller cut into an abandoned steel lifeboat. Part of the boat remained jammed between screw, rudder, and pintles and for the next eight hours every revolution of the screw gave a metronomic thump, thump, thump. Speed was reduced to eight and a half knots. Twenty-three out of the twenty-nine men on the *Parthenon* were rescued, however. While *Stockport* was flogging along to catch up with the convoy, *Hahoie* was torpedoed; fifty-six out of fifty-nine were rescued. Captain Fea of *Stockport* now had 256 survivors on board. They made Iceland. For this effort Captain Fea was awarded the Order of the British Empire, but before it was gazetted – on February 24, 1943 – he and his gallant ship had been sunk with all hands on another rescue operation. Besides the ship's crew there were ninety-one survivors on board at the time.

I was nineteen, a midshipman, very salty from about six months sea time, but I had yet to hear the guns speak in anger. Another snottie, Bob Gauvreau, and I, were quaffing our port with the best of them in Admiralty House when we met Captain Patrick Dove, who had dropped in for a noggin. Oh, with what starry-eyed questions did we ply him! For he had been the Master of the merchantman *Africa Shell*, sunk by Captain Hans Langsdorff in the German pocket battleship *Admiral Graf Spee*. The *Graf Spee* had had a merchantman in company to receive the prisoners Langsdorff allowed to leave their ships before he sank them. After *Graf Spee* had been scuttled off Montevideo, this prison ship, *Altmark*, made for Germany north about the Denmark Strait, Iceland, the Shetlands, the Faeroes and south down the Norwegian coast. In Jossing Fjord, Norway, *Altmark* was stopped by Captain Vian in HMS *Cossack*. With cutlasses flashing, our sailors boarded *Altmark* with cries of, "The Navy's here!" (As part of our training, we snotties had been taught how to use a cutlass and one of my daydreams of glory was to board an enemy ship on the Spanish Main, "Have at ye, ye lubbers.") This was what we had joined for! Captain Dove had dined with Captain Langsdorff at sea in *Graf Spee*. What was he like? A most courteous and humane gentleman, pleasure to know him, liked him better than Vian, he had shown "many acts of kindness."

In the years that followed I sometimes wondered how Captain Dove was getting on, was he still alive? Well, in November 1942 he was. He was picked up by the rescue ship *Perth*.

Perth had made fifteen voyages with only four rescues – it wasn't all *Sturm und Drang* – but on the night of November 17, her convoy was set upon by a U-boat wolf pack and two ships were torpedoed simultaneously. *Mount Taurus* sank quickly but thirty-eight of her crew were plucked from the water, from boats, from rafts. Survivors from the other ship were not found. At three in the morning the American *Parismina* bought it. *Perth*'s crew went over the side on nets and ladders to get them out, stiff and numb with cold, fifty-four of them. Then the French *President Sergeant* was hit. *Perth* searched for those survivors in lifeboats, found them, got them inboard, went back to the wreck, took off the remaining ten, and one of them was Captain Dove. One of the crew had jumped from the bridge and landed head-first in a boat. The doctor operated for a compound and depressed fracture of the skull, a broken wrist, and paralysis down his left side. Since the two sick-bay tiffies were busy with the other survivors the radio officer acted as anaesthetist. The Master put the ship on an easy course but when a U-boat was spotted on the starboard quarter overhauling them, he ordered, "Full ahead. Hard-a-port. Open fire." These tactics were effective but the U-boat was lost. Now more U-boats were sighted on the port bow approaching the convoy. The corvette *Rose* harried them. *Perth* took up her station in the convoy. He of the depressed cranium was now conscious and resting comfortably. *Perth* steamed into Halifax. And Captain Dove was again on the beach, without a ship, but he soon got another.

"Had we lived, I should have had a tale to tell. . ." said Scott. Well, a lot of us did live and so we tell these tales.

The ramming and sinking of HMCS *Fraser* in June 1940 is a good example of the dangers of the sea under wartime conditions. To go to sea with no radar on dark nights in snow squalls and rain showers, zig-zagging in front of the convoy or changing station at high speed, was not exactly a way of earning money that made life insurance salesmen rush to us with fountain pens outstretched.

Fraser and *Restigouche* had been assisting in the evacuation of some sixteen thousand of our troops pushed back to the sea by the *Wehrmacht*. They left St. Jean de Luz under the orders of HMS *Calcutta* and shaped course to return to England. No one had had much sleep for the previous ten days but now they were going home at a fair rate of knots on this dark night with a fresh breeze, moderate swell, and a visibility one to two miles. *Calcutta* ordered the destroyers to take station astern of her. Fraser, on her starboard bow, turned inward to comply. *Calcutta* thought *Fraser* was crossing her ahead and altered to starboard. *Fraser* wasn't. She was committed to her inward turn to port to pass down *Calcutta*'s port side. She was hit just abaft the bridge and sliced in two. The two halves drifted apart. *Calcutta* lowered one small boat and swept on, signalling to Lieutenant-Commander Lay in *Restigouche* to pick up survivors. He was not told that *Fraser* had been rammed and was amazed to find that the after part of her was floating perfectly well – but that there was no bow, no bridge, just the funnels and the stern. It was now just after ten at night. The easiest way to get the survivors off the after end was to go alongside – never mind the risk of holing his side or damaging the inboard propellor. The ships bumped together for about ten minutes and about fifty-five hands were taken off.

Tom Kellington was a Stoker on watch in the engine room of *Fraser* at the time of the ramming. The engines were still going astern. The lights went out. Not much of a shock, no bumps, no grinding noise. Silence. Chief Engine Room Artificer Kent sent him up the hatch to see what had happened. He saw what he thought was a rammed submarine tilted upwards. But it was *Fraser*'s forward end. *Calcutta* had sliced *Fraser* with her bow which had torn aft to the daymen's mess, then the stokers' mess, then the mess of the engine room artificers and then broken Fraser's keel. The forward boiler room was flooded and "the tank suctions came whack-a-mess and everything died." Kellington went to pick up some of his jerseys hung up to dry on a line around the air pump. Whe he got back the engine room was empty, so he got out, fast. He jumped over the side and was hauled into *Fraser*'s whaler. "Give me an oar," he said, and set to work with a will. Those who were left onboard *Fraser* started passing medical supplies to their doctor, Blair McLean, who was now in *Restigouche* – bottles of medical supplies and bottles taken from the officers' liquor store. "The Doc did a great job on the boys, getting fuel oil off wounds and eyes. Many injured, some badly."

After all had been taken off, Lay heard a lot of noise ahead, went to investigate, and in the ten-inch searchlight saw the *Fraser*'s bow floating high in the water, keel up. Both of the forward 4.7-inch guns fell out as he watched (it is only their weight which keeps them seated in the mounting-rings), and she righted again. Those who had been trapped below tumbled out and rushed to the side nearest their consort. *Fraser* turned turtle again and they were flung into the water. Boats, carley floats, and lifebuoys were lowered and they were picked up. *Restigouche* was already carrying the evacuees from St. Jean de Luz, including the two Polish Generals Kukiel and Kleeberg. On board also were the Embarkation Officer, Captain Allan, RN, several women, and a Basque priest, for a total of fifty-nine survivors. Now these fifty-nine survivors had been joined by eleven officers and ninety-six men from the fore part of *Fraser*. There were more guests than crew.

These survivors were covered with oil. Kellington rushed back and forth to the engine room to heat water under the air pump (no hot water taps then) and take it to the doctor who would wash off the oil and give the wretch a tot. Kellington would have a tot and then repeat the process. There was little space for the injured; they lay on the deck where they could. After a few hours things came under control and Kellington had a chance to get his head down. He was lucky to find a free place on the deck. "I went to sleep very fast and about five in the morning I woke stiff as a board. Stiff, and I couldn't move. I let out a scream that you could hear over half the Atlantic Ocean. All I could do was move my lips. I screamed. Then it passed."

While Tom Kellington was sleeping, the Captain had sent *Fraser*'s Engineer Officer and some of his engine-room staff back on board the after end to scuttle it. "They were gone a long time and I suspect some of them were salvaging their personal gear," Lay told me. One of Lay's officers was David Groos, whose brother, Harold, was First Lieutenant of *Fraser*. All her officers were now accounted for except three: the Captain, Wallace Creery; the First Lieutenant, Harold Groos; and The Gunnery Officer, Bill Landymore.

In the morning light *Restigouche* approached Plymouth. There was *Calcutta* ahead.

"Look. Her bow is all bent back from ramming *Fraser*."

They peered through their binoculars as they drew even closer.

"That's not *Calcutta*'s bow. That's *Fraser*'s bridge!"

And it was. *Calcutta*'s stem had sliced through the hull of *Fraser* but *Calcutta*'s forecastle deck had slid under the bridge superstructure, lifted it up, and carried it back to harbour. Wallace Creery, Harold Groos, and Bill Landymore, together with three hands of the bridge staff, had stepped off the *Fraser*'s bridge on to *Calcutta*'s deck.

Lay had now been on the bridge of *Restigouche* continuously for sixty hours and in the five days before that he had had only a nap here and there. By the time the court of inquiry assembled, he was not, therefore, feeling charitable to Admiral Burgess-Watson in *Calcutta* who had rammed a Canadian destroyer, dropped one small boat, and not stopped to pick up survivors, instead speeding on into harbour. Lay met Burgess-Watson.

"When you sank the after part of *Fraser*, Lay, I suppose she *would* have sunk anyway, shortly afterwards," said the Admiral.

"No," snapped Lay, "I'm sure the after part of *Fraser* would have floated for at least a week."

War is as unfailingly funny as it is unfailingly sad and the dichotomy is commonplace to those who have fought. There is, for example, the sinking of our destroyer *Margaree* in October 1940. A random confluence of events has, perhaps, more effect on sailors than landsmen, given that sailors look for an underlying significance to the apparent whimsicality of the dangers of the sea. No sailor I know has heard of the inscrutability of God's motives and the apparent contradiction of God's foreknowledge and man's free will; not in those words. They are the words of a theologian or a philosopher. But sailors are painfully aware of the problem – too true!

Thus it was that the sinking of HMS *Duchess* seemed a presage to the sinking of HMS *Diane*. *Duchess*, *Diane*, and three others of the class were escorting the battleship HMS *Dragon*. They had sailed from Gibraltar for the River Plate to help *Ajax*, *Achilles*, and *Exeter* in their brouhaha with *Graf Spee*. On reaching the equator and finding that their help was not now required they were diverted to screen the first Canadian troop convoy. On entering the River Clyde, Scotland, the night was black as a tinker's pot, and *Dragon* ordered a turn to port.

Five destroyers and the battleship altered to port, but *Duchess* altered to starboard. *Dragon* was fitted with a ram bow of 1914 design; she hit *Duchess*, who heeled over, keel up, and swung alongside, propellors slowly turning. Her bow reared up, scuttles started popping open and heads came thrusting out. But shoulders couldn't get through – the scuttles were too small. There were no escape hatches. She drifted astern. Her depth charges blew up. One man was saved.

Sub-Lieutenant Bob Timbrell in *Dragon* had seen this and remembered *Duchess* when he commissioned *Diane* – now renamed HMCS *Margaree* – in October 1940. She was the replacement for *Fraser*. An omen? No, *Margaree* would be a lucky ship the hands assured each other. Goering's blitz was reaching a peak; there were twelve ships tied up close to *Margaree*. All were hit but not her. A lucky ship! Another night a stick of bombs straddled her and one sank under her but did not explode. The next morning the dockyard mateys manned her lines and pulled her a few hundred yards down the jetty. And when she was clear – *Boom.* "Great. She's a lucky ship."

She sailed to Londonderry, a shake-down and work-up cruise. One Sub-Lieutenant had to sleep in a cabin forward, under the bridge, not at all comfortable. The two Subs flipped a coin. Timbrell won and so slept aft, near the wardroom. After Londonderry she sailed as escort to a convoy. Two nights out and the weather was rough, rain squalls, lessening visibility, no radar; after midnight *Margaree* dropped back to maintain visual contact. As a squall passed, SS *Port Fairy*, a freighter, discerned *Margaree* near and fine on her starboard bow. *Port Fairy* went full astern, but did not lose headway immediately. *Margaree* altered to port across her bow, and was cut in two just abaft the bridge. The forward end drifted clear, turned over, and sank.

Timbrell had come off watch an hour earlier and was thrown out of his bunk aft. A fuel tank had ruptured and the deck was covered with oil. So was he.

It's cold outside, October, slip on a greatcoat and rush to the ladder. There is the torpedoman whose watch is at the electrical switchboard and the doctor, Blair MacLean, a survivor of the ramming of *Fraser*. "She's sinking," says the doctor – he's reliving the sinking of *Fraser*. The hatch is jammed. Their combined pushing and banging won't budge it. They need something to batter it with but there is no lumber. Timbrell is the lightest and the longest so the doctor and the electrician up-end him, he holds his legs rigid, they use him as a battering ram. The hatch bursts open, they drop him, and he falls back down the ladder breaking three or four ribs. The ramming party scuttle out, the "ram" picks himself up and follows, they squirt out on deck, and *Port Fairy* is right alongside. The forward end of their ship is just not there. A weird feeling – no bridge, no forecastle, just the funnels and the after end. Twenty-nine hands on the after end – the engine-room, the boiler-room, and the depth-charge crews, and those sleeping aft. Both ships are stopped, a nasty sea has got up and the hulls grind and screech, steel on steel. Twenty-three of the crew get over to *Port Fairy*, two are crushed between the hulls as they scramble up the ladders. The ships drift apart and four are left on board *Margaree*.

These are the First Lieutenant, Pat Russell; the Gunnery Officer, Bill Landymore; the Sub, Timbrell; and the torpedoman who had been in the battering-ram team. There are ten depth charges set to fifty feet and these have to be set to safe. The memory of *Duchess* is all too clear. Some depth charges are careening around, loose. "Got them all set to safe, Sub? Good. Now go and get the money from the safe. There's all the payment for the crew in it." Down into the dark again. What's the combination? Ah, yes, left to seven, right to. . . .Bloody thing won't open. Try again. No luck. What *can* be the matter? Oh my God, I remember. The Captain changed the combination yesterday and didn't give me the new one yet. Frig it! Let's get back on deck. Now, how to get off? There is a small carley float on top of the torpedo tubes. Timbrell and the torpedoman climb on the tubes, crank them athwartships over the side, and grab either side of the float.

It was by now about two-thirty in the morning, cold and dark. *Port Fairy* is not in sight, the convoy has gone on. There is a fresh breeze, they are five hundred miles west of Ireland – a long way to swim, even to paddle in a raft. Timbrell passes the raft's painter to Landymore, neither the tallest nor the heaviest man in the RCN. He takes a turn of it around his wrist and grasps the end. Timbrell and the torpedoman heft the raft, adrenalin pumping, hearts pounding. One, and two, and *over* the side she sails – nearly to Ireland. The painter snaps taught. Landymore sails over the side, comes up spluttering, oil streaking his face. He looks up at the three on deck, they look down at him, the First Lieutenant speaks. "Landymore, did I give you permission to leave the ship?"

But they all joined him in the raft. The after end of *Margaree* sank, *Port Fairy* turned and picked them up. So ends a yarn which illumines the dark narrative of the loss of one of HMC destroyers and 141 of her men that October night of 1940.

Captain Tommy Pullen is a brother gunnery officer of mine; he from HMS *Excellent* in 1941, I from 1945.

He was appointed First Lieutenant of *Ottawa* in late 1941. In the summer of 1942 he got a new captain, Lieutenant-Commander Larry Rutherford. "Age twenty-five, capable, efficient, everything a destroyer captain should be," he said, "Work hard, play hard, which seems to be the usual naval procedure. But I realized I was going to have to work really hard to meet *his* standard. I don't know how many convoys we did back and forth from Newfie to 'Derry. Many. We never were attacked and I remember commenting on how dull life was. I was to regret that statement. We went out westbound with convoy ON127 and were attacked by thirteen U-boats. The action went on for two or three days and eventually we were torpedoed on the night of September the thirteenth at eleven-thirty.

"I was turned in aft and at about 11:20 I heard the propellers increase speed rapidly; a sure sign that *something* has happened. I got to the upper deck – calm, dark, no moon. Over the sound-powered telephone I heard a voice say, "Port fifteen." After a few seconds there was a shattering explosion; the sky momentarily lit up. Then absolute silence. Then a rain of bits and pieces falling into the sea around us. 'Good God! We've been hit!' I was alone on the quarterdeck, the lifebuoy sentry had disappeared somewhere, and I stood for a moment in a state of shock, before rushing to my cabin to get my lifebelt, my luger, morphine syrettes, and a flashlight. I went to the bridge to report to the Captain that I would be below inspecting the damage. Below there was nothing left. The bow had gone, right back to B gun. It was a shambles in the passageway: broken glass, wreckage, dark. I went down to what was left of the stoker's mess – abaft the seamen's fore lower mess where the asdic is. It was a scene of carnage and chaos. The force of the explosion had driven the men in their hammocks up to the deckhead – not a pretty sight – and the wreckage of the mess deck had piled against the door of the asdic hut. It's a door that opens outward and so the asdic ratings inside were trapped. The ship was open to the sea. There were voices. There were people seriously injured. It was hard to know what to do. Then the second fish hit; just about the bulkhead between number one and number two boiler rooms.

"The ship began to break up. My damage control party and I scrambled up the ladder and I went to the bridge to report to the Captain. It was obvious we were sinking. He was the only one still there. She started to roll on her side and the two of us climbed over and walked down the side of the ship. As I climbed out of the bridge my cap hit the fore-stay of the mainmast and fell back in. I went back to retrieve my cap, put it on, and climbed out again. I abandoned ship properly dressed.

"Then the Captain and I walked down the ship's side to the bilge keel and jumped into the sea. I had my seaboots on and went straight down. I kicked them off and popped up again. We drifted off and I never saw Larry Rutherford again.

"I swam away from the ship through about five inches of fuel oil. (Don't speak to me about pollution, I say to environmentalists who get excited about anything.) *Ottawa*'s stern stood straight up on end, I noticed the after canopy and X gundeck slide off and plunge into the sea. And, to my horror, about 125 depth charges broke loose from their stowage. I wondered if they had been set to "safe." It would only take one to countermine the rest. I waited for the explosion. I found later that the Torpedo Gunner, Lloyd Irwine Jones, had set them to safe before he jumped over the side.

"Then it was a question of hanging on. The carley float was a mass of unrecognizable, oil-soaked figures. I hung on to the float with one hand and to a dan-buoy that happened my way with the other. I guess we floated around about four hours, five hours. The convoy went through us. We had gone ahead of the convoy to rendezvous with *Witch* who was coming from St. John's to take over from us. We were four hundred miles east of Newfie. What we had done was blunder into the U-boats' marshalling area where they got ready for the night's fun.

"I have to say that the cries of those hands trapped in the asdic hut could be heard coming up the voice pipe. A sad business. Nothing could be done for them. A tanker went by us with a bloody big hole in her side; she was in ballast. I didn't know why she didn't stop to pick us up and I was explaining to her in words of one syllable that I didn't think it was too much to expect, under the circumstances. Then we were alone.

"It was very lonely. As you know, under these circumstances one's thoughts dwell on the fundamentals of life. It was a beautiful night, actually, clear, no moon, but stars. Face to face, with what. . . ? If you have the *will* to survive as long as it is physically possible. . . . The thing that struck me most forcibly during this business was how many men gave up. They were not mentally prepared for the shock of what had happened, so suddenly, so completely. They couldn't cope with it. I think they were physically able to hang on but they just let go and drifted away. It was more than they could handle. I think that's an accurate description. Some were injured, of course. I'm sure some gave up because of the pain. There was one stoker, I remember, his name was Skilhen, he was down in one of the boiler rooms when the second torpedo hit. You can imagine the chaos – super-heated steam escaping, the flooding. He had the wit to get down into the bilges while the live steam was spouting and he floated up. As the water rose in the boiler room he went up with it. If he had not done that he would have been scalded to death. He was badly injured but he survived.

"Eventually, a *presence* was sensed and we looked around the gloom and saw the corvette *Celandine*. They knew we had been sunk from the messages we had sent. I gave my luger to the Chief ERA as I came over the side. He took it away and cleaned it for me. My morphine syrettes were extremly useful to ease the pain of the wounded. They took us into St. John's. So that was the last of the *Ottawa*. Rescued were sixty-five officers and men. I was the senior surviving officer. In Newfie was the usual court of inquiry. Then I went on survivor's leave. I was going on leave to Oakville anyway after that trip to marry Betty. Ralph Hennessy lent me his cap. Some tailor whipped me up a uniform in a three or four days, and I got married.

"She was a good ship, *Ottawa*. I remember that that's the last thing Larry Rutherford said to me as we stood on the bilge keel, just as we jumped in, 'She was a *good* ship.' I was told later that he had given his lifebelt to one of the hands."

By 1943 the tide was turning in our favour in the Atlantic but it wasn't yet evident when Winston Churchill said in February, "The U-boat warfare takes first place in our thoughts." The army's success in Africa was by now certain but from the time of their landing on African soil in Operation Torch, millions of tons of supplies had to be taken across the Atlantic to the United Kingdom and then via

Gibraltar to the Mediterranean and Malta. The landings in Sicily and Italy would need millions of tons more. The Russian armies were hammering Germany from the east but millions of tons of supplies had to be taken to Iceland and the United Kingdom and thence to Murmansk. In 1943 Admiral Dönitz replaced Admiral Raeder as Commander-in-Chief of the German navy. The Mediterranean had become a grave for the U-boats from whence they had only a five per cent chance of returning. The key to German success lay in cutting the Atlantic lifeline. Dönitz pursued this policy with his customary vigour.

That winter was judged particularly bad even by old Atlantic hands; ships foundered in gales or turned turtle from iced-up superstructures. In January alone four merchant ships were driven ashore, eight foundered, one rescue ship sank under the weight of ice. In another convoy the Commodore's ship split her seams and went down with all hands. Mountainous seas driven by eighty- to one hundred-knot gales, snow, sleet, and freezing temperatures took their toll. Of the 196 Canadian and 35 British ships under Canadian command, 30 per cent were in for repairs at any one time. U-boats were coming into production faster than we could sink them. Merchant ships were being sunk faster than they could be built. In March we lost 627,000 tons of shipping. By April and May there were several packs of U-boats, each of ten to twelve boats, forming a barrier around our Halifax–St. John's seaports in an arc of six hundred miles. We were losing the battle.

This was the year that *St. Croix* bought it. She had had her successes, mind you. In March she and *Shediac* had sunk U-87 on the U.K. to Algiers leg. Then in April she sank U-90. In August she and her group were diverted from a Bay of Biscay offensive sweep to help beleaguered convoys to the north. A slow convoy had set out from the U.K. on September 12. Three days behind it was a fast convoy which steadily overtook the slower. U-boat signals abounded. The two convoys were ordered to form one. The British destroyer *Icarus* and corvette *Polyanthus* and the Canadian destroyer *Gatineau* and corvettes *Drumheller* and *Kamloops* escorted the slow convoy. The Canadian destroyers *St. Croix* and *St. Francis* and corvettes *Chambly, Sackville, Morden,* and the British frigate *Itchen* were ordered to join the combined escort.

The evening gloom of the twentieth merged with a menacing fog as the sixty-three merchant ships joined up. A difficult evolution. As one Escort Commander put it, "The two convoys gyrated majestically around the ocean, never appearing to get any closer, and watched appreciatively by a growing swarm of U-boats.'' The U-boats had taken to heckling the escort with rude remarks. We replied in kind and some of our Captains were hard to beat in vulgar invective. So much for the days of chivalry. Darkness fell and the attacks started.

The British *Lagen* swept back to make contact with the supporting group, sighted a submarine, pursued it, and had her stern blown off by another U-boat. A short time later *St. Croix* started out on the bearing of another sighting. She was hit by two torpedoes and began to lose way. To *Itchen* she sent the signal, "Am leaving the office." These were her last words. She was hit by another torpedo and in three minutes she was gone.

Itchen had to leave *St. Croix*'s survivors in the water to pursue the attacking submarines; she told *Polyanthus* to pick them up. On the way to do so *Polyanthus* took a torpedo up the stern. Thirteen hours later *Itchen* got back and plucked out of the water eighty-one hands from *St. Croix* and one from *Polyanthus*.

On the twenty-first the combined convoys steamed on. That night the U-boats were fought off. On the night of the twenty-second the attacks began again at 9:30. *Itchen* swung over to a contact, opened the shutters of her searchlight, and saw a submarine a few hundred yards ahead. Other ships heard bursts of fire from her 20mm guns. "Then there was a tremendous orange-coloured flame from the position where *Itchen* had last been seen, and an ear-shocking explosion."

Only three men were saved. One from the crew of *Itchen*, one lone survivor from *Polyanthus*. And, of the eighty-one survivors pulled out of the water by *Itchen* after *St. Croix* sank, one. Out of *St. Croix*'s whole ship's company, just one lived. We heard that he turned a little strange. He kept asking, "Why me? Why only me?"

In October 1944, *Skeena* was making up to Iceland in a howling gale. Every so often she would hit what sailors call a "milestone" – she'd rear up on one unusually high wave, and, instead of soaring over the crest and into the trough, she'd crash on the crest of the next. Spray covered all. A heavy *Slam*, a thud which makes the whole ship quiver from stem to gudgeon, from truck to keel. It seems to bring her up all standing, her next refit leave therefore closer and is greeted with joyous crys of "Refit. Refit."

Skeena's navigator, Peter Chance, was discussing the weather with his Captain, Pat Russell; they were glad that they could stay out and

185

not have to enter Reykjavik; the old girl could ride out anything if hove to. Then the shore authorities ordered them in. They didn't want to go but the senior officer signalled "Follow me" so in they went.

By nine-thirty that night they were anchored off Videy Island, near the harbour. Chance knew the bottom was mostly volcanic ash and not good holding ground for their anchors, but what could they do? The gale rose in strength. Snow flurries driven by eighty-knot winds made it hard to see anything as the ship strained this way and that against her bar-taught anchor cable. There was not, of course, anything visible on which to take bearings to check their position; but around midnight the Officer of the Watch, between snow squalls, sighted Videy Island. It was closer than it should be. The wind was now blowing about 100 knots. The second anchor was dropped. The engines were put at full speed ahead. All to no avail. *Skeena* yawed and then, lifted on a great swell, her stern struck the off-shore rocks. Another sea caught her and swung her broadside to the seas, hard aground. Now that she was not bow-on to the swell, waves broke over her. Ninety tumultuous yards away was Videy Island. It first seemed the ship would capsize and sink. Waves swept her deck from stem to stern. The starboard seaboat was smashed. When the port seaboat was lowered, it foundered. Only the carley floats on the lee side offered any chance of abandoning ship. They were released and swung to their painters.

Fifteen men who manned three of the carley floats were carried past the island and drowned. Chance said, "Although every effort was made to hold the lines, it was so cold that oil and snow on the upper deck had formed a kind of slithery slush, and, even though a couple of turns had been taken around a stanchion, the lines couldn't be held."

A few others were swept onto the slippery rocks, battered, and only half conscious. Some found refuge in caves or abandoned crofters' huts.

At three in the morning two British landing craft from Reykjavik hove into sight but it was neither possible to take men off nor to land them in the surf. An Icelandic pilot, Einar Sigurdsson, headed a rescue party from the leeward side of Videy Island, and, at seven-forty in the morning, arrived on the windward side. *Skeena* shot a line ashore; a heavy hawser followed and was made fast. The rest of the crew were landed with the help of Sigurdsson and British sailors shoulder deep in the water.

The fifteen dead were buried in Fossaburg cemetery with full naval honours. Today can still be seen the fifteen white crosses, each with

186

the man's name and official number. The cemetery slopes down to a bay and the white mountains around Reykjavik can be seen a few miles away.

Peter Chance took passage in one of our destroyers back to Londonderry. He says, "There is always something funny, thank God. The Chief Yeoman of Signals and I were always good pals, he on the bridge a lot and me the Navigator. We were also jointly responsible for the ship's canteen stocks: soap, cigarettes, candy bars, soft drinks, tooth brushes, and all that the navy doesn't supply. We got all our stock on credit, of course, from the Navy Army Airforce Institute, good old NAAFI. As obliging a grocer as Gieves was a tailor, and with much the same benign views on money owed to them. Even though there was a lot of water around, we salvaged all the money in the canteen before we abandoned ship. English coins are notoriously heavy and we had pounds and pounds of these pennies and shillings, as well as wads and wads of pound notes. I went into NAAFI in Londonderry with these sacks because I knew we owed a lot of money to them. The NAAFI man said, 'Oh, *Skeena*, It's alright. You don't owe us anything.' I said, 'You cannot be serious.' The NAAFI man said, 'Well, your bill is paid.' I said, 'That's marvellous!'

"So Pat Russell and I divided it up into fifteen parts, it was well over a hundred pounds, I guess, and we sent it to the families of the dead. It was a large pot of money in those days. Also there was quite a lot of the wardroom liquor saved and we shared that with the survivors. I had a couple of bottles of whiskey which I shared with my wife, Peggy (she was a Wren in Londonderry) and some friends. New Years' Day in 'Derry! But the money to the families of the hands who were lost was kind of a nice finale. It was a gesture, which was all it could have been, after all, for their loss."

The skeleton of the once-proud *Skeena* rusted for a year or so upon the rocks of Iceland, reminding us all that the price of safety is eternal vigilance and good luck. I know that a little part of Jimmy Hibbard's heart died with her. In 1945 she was sold and broken up for scrap. A second *Skeena* was launched in Vancouver in 1957; she is still sailing out of Halifax.

The naval saga of Craig Campbell started in 1937 when he joined the RCNVR as a Midshipman; then, as a Sub-Lieutenant in 1942 he went to *King Alfred* and, after that, got command of the crash boat *Creol II* plucking survivors out of the English Channel. Next the destroyer

Bulldog intercepting German convoys off Calais, then *Mackay* running our convoys from Harwich to Hull where German E-boats and aircraft had many a go at them. From there Campbell got another command in 1942, a fairmile, a motor launch, ML090. The U-boats were just starting to move over to the Canadian side of the Atlantic; his patrols were off Cape Breton Island and, after that, Bermuda until 1944. Now the U-boats were really strong off the Atlantic seaboard – up to twenty at any one time. It was when the Battle of the Atlantic had moved to within two hundred miles of Quebec City that Campbell got HMCS *Clayoquot*, a Bangor minesweeper used for convoy escort. Campbell was an acting Lieutenant-Commander by now. It was in her that his naval saga nearly ended when she was torpedoed off Halifax on Christmas Eve, 1944.

On the twentieth of December Kapitänleutnant Klaus Hornbostel in U-806 was on patrol nine miles off the approaches to Halifax coping as best he could after 5,000 miles of cold, fog, and the strong currents that swirled around Chebucto Head and Sambro lightship. Convoys in and out of Halifax had for the past two years been a fertile killing ground. Between there and the approaches to St. John's were the wrecks of HMCS *Ottawa*, *Windflower*, *Valleyfield*, *Esquimalt*, *Otter*, and, in the approaches to Quebec City, *Shawinigan*, *Bras d'Or*, *Racoon*, *Charlottetown*, and *Chedabucto*.

Besides conventional straight-running torpedoes Hornbostel had "gnat" torpedoes which homed on the propellor noise of targets. To counteract this our ships streamed astern "cat" gear – two light iron bars which set up a terrific din and attracted the gnats before they got to the propellors. Hornbostel heard these and the British "foxer" (same thing but weighing three tons), the *thump thump thump* of reciprocating engines and the constant, whine of turbine engines, the eternal *ping ping ping* of our asdic sets and the ever-present acoustic anomalies of disturbed water, thermal layers, the songs of whales and porpoise, and the flutter of schools of fish. A confused aural picture. Oh for a visual picture.

On the twenty-first of December he raised his snorkel (which allowed fresh air into a submerged boat) and swept the sea with his periscope. Fog patches, but clear at times. Then he saw a small convoy departing Halifax. He manoeuvred to attack and fired a spread of torpedoes. Missed. Then he fired a gnat at one of the rear ships. Hit. The SS *Samtucky* stopped; he made another hit and slipped silently off. A massive Canadian search would surely follow from the naval base only an hour's steaming away.

Also on the twenty-first Campbell was in Chester on Christmas leave and was having a noggin of rum when the phone rang. He was to return to his ship said Captain (D), Halifax, "Come back *immediately*, there's a flap on." He got to his ship by midnight.

On the twenty-second Hornbostel fired another spread at a merchant ship escorted by a corvette. Missed. U-1231 and U-1232 were now in the area.

On the twenty-fourth the 8,100-ton troop ship *Lady Rodney* was en route to St. John's. *Clayoquot, Kirkland Lake,* and *Transcona* were sailed to sweep ahead of a convoy bound for Boston, then to screen it when it formed up off Chebucto Head. At about eleven in the morning Hornbostel sighted them at two miles. Half an hour later the convoy was in view, forming up. The three escorts probed with their asdic ahead of it. When the convoy was formed into columns they would station themselves, one ahead and one on either bow.

The signal flags for "Take up previously assigned stations" streamed from the senior officer's yardarm. In the two consorts the answering pennant flew, "signal understood." When the senior officer hauled down his hoist, the answering pennants would be hauled down also and all would peel off, increase speed, and take up their stations. Hornbostel watched this with interest.

"Execute," said the senior officer and his hoist ripped down. So did the answering pennants.

Campbell had gone to his cabin to read while the sweep ahead of the convoy was going on. ("I was at a rather exciting part of the book.") The "Take up station. . ." signal was then flying, his answering pennant was close up. Better take the chance to get his feet up; it might be another long night. He gave the officer of the watch the course to steer when the signal was executed. "Increase to full speed, alter to that course, and call me."

Hornbostel watched.

The signals were hauled down, "Captain, sir, execute. I'm altering and increasing speed."

"Very good. Full ahead both. I'm coming up."

Hornbostel saw *Clayoquot* alter towards him with a bone in her teeth while he was taking bearings on the convoy to fire his straight-runners. She must have detected him on asdic. She was attacking. He fired a gnat to home on the attacker's screws.

Campbell arrived on the bridge.

The gnat hit.

"I was knocked flat on my ass. Things flying in all directions. A large chunk of the minesweeping winch from aft landed on the fore-castle," said Campbell, "and a piece of a depth charge landed on the galley stove. The cook was putting the roast in. There was an awful racket from escaping steam; you couldn't hear much. The signal lockers disintegrated. One of the artificers came out of the engine room through the fan trunking; but he had forgotton his Dunhill pipe so he went back to get the damn thing. Both his ankles were broken and he didn't know it."

Hornbostel had dived deep to avoid the explosion of his torpedo, now he surfaced for a look. His gnat had countermined the after magazine. The two explosions had blown the whole of the stern to the vertical. This jammed the hatch of the after cabins. Fortunately, most of the hands were forward for the grog issue. Only eight were killed. Two officers, the Navigator and the Sub-Lieutenant, were trapped below, their heads out of scuttles as they shouted for help. Boats and floats were lowered in a seamanlike manner. No panic.

"Abandon ship."

She listed further. Nothing could be done to help those trapped below. When all the hands were off Campbell slid down the ship's side to the bilge keel and stood there a while. "All the hands were yelling at me, 'Get off, sir, get off ' thinking I was going to play the bloody hero and go down with her."

He slid into the freezing water and swam to a float. *Clayoquot* sank. From torpedo hit to sinking – nine minutes.

"I turned and swam on my back. I had heard that exploding depth charges would play hell with your guts if you were on your stomach. Then there was a *carrumph*! and I was lifted nearly clear of the water. A dreadful blow! We were only three miles or so from Sambro Light so I knew we would soon be picked up but to give the hands something to do I led them in singing Christmas carols. In under an hour *Fennel* picked us up. I was put in the Captain's bunk with a rum and coffee and about four blankets. Then I got the shakes, violent tremors; cold or shock, I don't know. I kicked the blankets off and went forward to see how the troops were. They were having a jolly time, so I went to the bridge with the Captain who was looking for the boat that fished us. I remember smoking a cigar. We couldn't find the U-boat so we were landed in Halifax."

"I got two weeks' leave and went home to Victoria. On the way back I stopped in Ottawa to see the Captain who looked after officers' appointments."

"Oh, hello Campbell," he said, "I suppose you want a cushy shore job."

"No, sir, I want a frigate."

"Oh, you do? We have no frigates that need a Captain, but how would you like a brand new corvette? The *North Bay*?"

So the *North Bay* is what Campbell got. He joined her a few weeks later and took her on the Newfie to 'Derry run.

Yarns Spun in the Dogwatches

*The web of our life is of a mingled yarn, good and
ill together: our virtues would be proud if our faults
whipped them not; and our crimes would despair if they
were not cherished by our own virtues.*

All's Well that Ends Well, Shakespeare

The dogwatches – the first from 4:00 P.M. to 6:00 P.M. and the last
from 6:00 P.M. to 8:00 P.M. – are the recreation time of the navy. The
working day, as landsmen understand it, is over at about five. Not so
with us. After the last dog comes the first watch – from 8:00 P.M. to
midnight; the middle watch – until 4:00 A.M.; the morning watch – to
8:00 A.M.; the forenoon watch until midday and the afternoon watch
from midday until 4:00 P.M.; then the dogwatches again. You might
think that the first watch of a twenty-four-hour day would start at midnight; but no, that is the middle watch. Don't try to understand it; it
has always been thus.

On board ship, a sailor will always have one of the night watches and
the ship's business and equipment maintenance is carried out during
the day. That leaves one of the dogwatches, the first or the last, for
supper and socializing. The hands gather in groups on the upper deck
in good weather or around the mess tables in bad; the officers on the
quarterdeck in good weather or in the wardroom in bad. We spin our
yarns of past ships, foreign stations, battles, shipwrecks, collisions,
girls met in our odyssey thus far, Lothario-like encounters of the past,
and predictions of certain successes in the port we are headed for. We
talk of the heroes of our youth, and of ourselves and our shipmates.

Cadet H. G. DeWolf was at the Naval College of Canada from 1918 to 1921. Eleven cadets graduated that year but a reduced naval budget allowed only four to be taken into the navy: he and Nelson Lay were two. They joined the battleship HMS *Resolution* for their Midshipman's time. She was a Plymouth ship, a west-country ship, the Home Fleet. Each spring the Home and the Mediterranean fleets would meet at Gibraltar for exercises. The second year *Reso* was sent post-haste to Smyrna where the Turks had driven the Greeks into the sea; there had been a massacre and Mustaphah Hanel was taking over. We were supporting the Greeks. The Turks had forbidden the British ships to enter but they ignored this. DeWolf remembers the various trips he made in his picket boat taking senior officers to other foreign warships and ashore. "Not much happened, our Admiral decided to leave, having established a British presence and made known the views of H.M. government. The Turks said we couldn't leave because they had mined the entrance to the harbour. But we sailed anyway." They went up to the Dardanelles, off Constantinople, and kept a presence there all summer. Other nations were represented, "I remember there were eleven because at eight o'clock in the morning when the colours were hoisted, we had to stand at the salute while eleven national anthems were played."

Canadians serving in RN ships on September 3, 1939, were ready to help sink German ships, but Canada had not yet declared war. It was the same in 1923 for cadets DeWolf and Lay. Our Prime Minister, Mackenzie King, had said that Canada did not support the British position. Yet his nephew, Midshipman Nelson Lay, stood ready to help in the bombardment of Turkey. Also there was the usual trouble in the gunroom. "The Sub-Lieutenant in charge had the power to award six strokes of the cane – Midshipmen and Boy Seamen were the only ones subject to caneing – but in our case we were older than the RN mids, usually by a year or two. There were the usual good-natured rough-and-tumbles in the gunroom. We had twenty-four Midshipmen and Sub-Lieutenants. Of these, four were Australian, one New Zealand, and four Canadian, so we were up to strength when the Brits cried, 'Out the colonials.' There was a royal battle and these can get strenuous, but we were *not* removed."

Resolution returned to England after nine months away. "I remember that at church service on the first Sunday on the way home, ninety-nine banns of marriage were read. I suppose the same banns were being read in the parish churches in England." After Sub-

Lieutenant's courses DeWolf returned to Canada in 1925 and went to HMCS *Patriot* as Navigating Officer and general dogsbody: correspondence (done by hand), confidential books, mess secretary, wine and tobacco caterer. Winters were spent in Bermuda exercising with the British North America and West Indies Squadron – at least, that was the intent, but money was running out. *Patriot* and *Patrician* were told not to join the squadron at sea but to stay in Bermuda. Canada had no money for fuel. The next year was even worse; there was not even enough money to steam our destroyers to Bermuda; the crews went in the Canadian National Steamship *Chignecto*. "I had hoped to spend another winter ashore," said DeWolf. "The previous year I had met the girl who was to become my wife and I was looking forward to spending more time with her. I had made out a list of what ships everyone was to go to. I had put myself down for *Cairo* which I knew was in refit. No luck. We arrived a day late and the RN had different lists and I had to go with twenty-five men to the *Cape Town*. So I had to get word to my girl that I wouldn't be seeing her for some time. We went south to the Falklands, through the Patagonian Channel, north up the west coast of South America to the Panama Canal, and back to Bermuda."

Because he had picked up a year's seniority for high marks in his Sub's courses, he was promoted to Lieutenant early and went to *Argos*, a merchant-ship hull with a flight deck. "She was very old. The bridge was a little hut that went up and down – down when we were landing aircraft. Then I was alone on the flight deck with a voice pipe to the helmsman to keep the ship heading exactly into the wind so that aircraft could fly off. We had Blackburns and Fairey aircraft, pre-Swordfish if you can imagine anything that old. One of the Squadron Leaders was RAF; he was very skillful and when we were uncertain if there was enough wind to fly, or if it was too rough, we'd send him up first. One day one of the Blackburns was landing and the Pilot decided he was going too fast and would go around again. The Navigator in the rear seat decided that the Pilot had left it too late and jumped out – at about twenty knots, about ten feet up. The plane dipped almost to sea level then slowly, painfully gained height and landed. The Pilot was furious when he found that his Navigator had deserted. 'I'm the Captain of the ship and you'd no right to leave,' said he. To this the Navigator replied, 'If I hadn't left you wouldn't have made it.'"

A specialist navigation course followed, appointments ashore, a staff course, and a stint at naval headquarters. Then he got command of one of our coal-burning minesweepers, *Festubert*. "I got a dollar a day command money. I was drawing hard-lying allowance, and my sixty cents a day as a Specialist Navigator. I was rich."

Skeena and *Saguenay* had replaced the ancient *Patriot* and *Patrician* and DeWolf next went to *Skeena* as First Lieutenant for two years before going again to naval headquarters. For a warrior of his renown and a man who as Chief of the Naval Staff as a Vice-Admiral made many important decisions, I found it intriguing that, while he is diffident about relating his time in battle or his time as Chief of Naval Staff, he is, for him, nearly loquacious about his time from 1935 to 1937 as a Lieutenant-Commander on staff. "We wrote a five-year plan, this civilian officer and myself. Edsell was his name. We had to get modern destroyers. It was clear that war was getting closer. We worked out the costs that would be required over five years. The RN had four that we could have. The *Cygnet*, *Crusader*, *Comet*, and another of that class. These became our *St. Laurent*, *Ottawa*, *Restigouche*, and *Fraser*. When war came we had six modern destroyers: *Saguenay*, *Skeena*, and these four. Good thing too. After war started, Nelson Lay got *Restigouche* and I got *St. Laurent*."

On September 15, 1939, *St. Laurent* and *Saguenay* escorted the first outward-bound slow convoy from Halifax to the United Kingdom. On the seventeenth, *Fraser* escorted the first fast convoy. More followed in October and November. Five days at sea; two days in harbour. Fuel, store, and out again. Then came troop convoy number one on December 10, 1939 – TC1 – carrying the soldiers of the First Canadian Division. *St. Laurent*, *Restigouche*, *Fraser*, and *Ottawa* led *Aquitania*, *Monarch of Bermuda*, *Empress of Britain*, *Duchess of Bedford*, and *Empress of Australia* out of Halifax. Big ships were based in Halifax by then: *Resolution*, *Revenge*, *Barham*, *Malaya*. One of these would be the ocean escort.

These troop convoys had their hairy moments, mostly due to an enemy more persistent and wide-ranging than the Germans – the weather, which was often foul. DeWolf said of TC1, "I'll tell you exactly what happened. I came on the bridge before dawn. You know, it is usual to have action stations at dawn in case you sight something. This was before radar. Well, it was foggy and I found that we had lost touch with the convoy. We'd been keeping in touch by asdic and we'd got off into the wake. We had to speed up. I did this and closed in ten degrees to the convoy. It wasn't long before we heard foghorns. That's when I should have got wise. It was one of the big liners. Fine, we're on the right track. I was at the back of the bridge and I looked over my shoulder and there was the buff upper-works of the *Aquitania*. Hard-a-port, full ahead. I am looking straight *up* at the sheer of her bow. Our stern swung over and almost slapped her. The Engineer came to the bridge, white-faced, 'I could have touched her with a poker.' I realized we were now shooting ahead so I slowed speed but before I knew it I was on the quarter of *Resolution*. I made a signal, '*Aquitania* on your starboard quarter.' She acknowledged it but didn't tell me to get back on my station which was way out on the beam. So I stayed there. I thought this is nice and safe – right with a battleship.

"For the rest of the day we were between *Aquitania* and *Resolution*. *Aquitania* would edge in a bit and I'd increase and edge over. I was afraid of getting pinched between a 60,000-ton liner and a 40,000-ton battleship. The distance between the two was not more than a hundred yards. A narrow slot to keep station in. Then the Captain of *Resolution* sent me over to see where the *Monarch of Bermuda* was. I slid back past *Aquitania*, dropped astern of her, then went up the other side and used her as my point of departure to set off a course to find the *Monarch*. She was supposed to be out on the starboard wing. I found her and steamed back the same way, tucked in under *Aquitania*'s stern, steered slowly up her side, and sighted *Reso*. 'Yes, she's there,' I signalled.

"We could only stay with the convoy two days – just to the tip of the Banks, the Newfoundland Banks. Then I was detached, went ahead sounding my fog signals, eased over to get clear of the big ships, and set off at my best speed to Halifax. I came down the coast on a line of soundings, the forty-fathom-line is a good one. I had done that often going from Cape Breton to Halifax. You could pick up Egg Island fog signal fifteen miles east of Halifax; then you would hear Chebucto Head. It's not difficult. We could pick our way in qute easily. But *Aquitania* was *big*. There was no question of the modern navigational aids we have today. I looked up and saw her because I heard or felt something. There is something different in the sound, with that great ship so close, a difference in the waves. *Something* caused me to look up."

Commander Chilli Manfield told me that "HMS *Curlew* came to Vancouver in 1927, shipped a detachment up to Chilliwack for a parade, and I was *smitten*! I joined up and my father took me over to Esquimalt to the barracks. He asked to see Commander Nelles, who was the Commanding Officer, and I was taken off to do my in-routine. At noon I came back, my father was still speaking to Nelles, I said, 'I'm in,' he said, 'It's about time.' His parting words were only, 'Be careful of the girls.' Then he left. I was in for seven years. I was seventeen.

"Rate of pay was fifty cents a day and they kept ten dollars a month until you went on leave. We had Saturday and Sunday afternoons off until nine P.M. We had to ask for money to go ashore from our divisional Petty Officer; he'd dole out five cents for an ice cream, ten cents for streetcar fare; we always walked: two extra ice creams. Make-and-mend on Wednesdays was spent running around the football field chased by Nelles who was trying to teach us rugger. I wrote the first part of the educational tests and passed. I was a rarity because most of the lower deck could barely read or write. Now I was eligible for the higher educational test. The schoolmaster taught me general knowledge, an Electrical Artificer taught me electrics and magnetism but navigation proved a problem. Schooly came in one day and said he'd found a young Lieutenant who would take me on. This was one Lieutenant (N) H. G. DeWolf. He was very patient and kind and spent many, many hours with me until I had it as well as I could get it. I got a second-class in navigation and pilotage, first-class in general knowledge, and second-class for magnetism and electricity.

"Harry DeWolf and I have crossed paths many times since those days. He was always good. I remember he always suffered from sea-sickness, but he would carry his bucket with him up to the bridge, hang it on a voice pipe, use it if necessary, and afterward carry it down and wash it out himself. I thought that was a damn good show.

"In 1929 I was promoted Ordinary Seaman and joined *Vancouver*. Then I became a real salt. I was put in the rattle for throwing some broken bottles over the side. I knew they were useless, being broken, but didn't know I should have saved the remnants to turn in to the storesman. Four days' extra work, polishing the brass guard rails on the quarterdeck. Now I had a crime sheet.

"I got rated to Able Seaman. As an AB I was cabin hand, looking after the officers' cabins. They used the term "officer's servants" as they did in the RN. We found the term odious and called ourselves "cabin hands."

"By now I had my nickname, "Chilli," from Chilliwack. From Ordinary Seaman to Commander I was Chilli Manfield. I went to Whaley to qualify Seaman Gunner and after a spell in *Warspite* was sent to *Skeena*. Scotty Brodeur was Captain. He was called "Scotty" because when he first went to the RN the troops had never heard a French-Canadian accent before, didn't know what it was, so called him Scotty for lack of more accurate information. In a shoot one day – I was on X gun [A and B guns were forward, X and Y guns were aft] – I got things ass-about-face and followed the wrong pointers on my gun. The rest of the guns fired to starboard on the up roll. I fired to port on the down roll. Scotty yelled aft, 'Who dat man on hex gun? He won't be Seaman Gunner long.'

"Morale was good in the messdecks. The leading hands of the mess were very good; so were the Petty Officers. But there was a great lack of understanding between the men and the officers. Sailor was sailor and officer was officer. It was a caste system. In the West Indies sailors were not allowed on the "white man's beaches." We had to swim with the natives. In many places there was a sign, "Sailors and Dogs Not Allowed." But the officers who were good were very, very good. We had the other type, of course, but they wouldn't have fitted in anywhere. I served with Tommy Pullen, Ralph Hennessy, Mickey Stirling, Johnny Stubbs, Bob Welland, Jimmy Hibbard, Larry Rutherford, and a dozen more. There were none better."

"Why did I join the navy?" asked Frank Caldwell. "Well, I can't think of a time in my life that was not military, but the navy was where I ended up. As a child I lived in Amherst, Nova Scotia, and the prisoners from the *Scharnhorst* and *Gneisenau* were interned there after the Battle of the Falklands. The family talked about that battle when I was a lad. In 1917 the Gallipoli affair had ended and troops were being brought across Canada by train to go to Zebrugge; they were stranded at Amherst by the Halifax explosion and my parents were host to several of them, mostly Chief and Petty officers. My father had been invalided out of the Canadian Mounted Rifles; he was sour about this and therefore inclined to the navy. We as a family signed up in the Navy League. Because of this connection we were invited to visit the Special Services Squadron when it visited Halifax in 1926. *Hood, Repulse,* and *Renown* were doing a world tour to thank the participating countries for their help in the war. *Hood* was just *beautiful*. And what *style*. I saw the Admiral's Rolls-Royce being manhandled ashore by a party of bluejackets; no cranes – all hand-raulic; they picked it up bodily and moved it. I was about nine and it started me thinking that the navy might be a good way to spend my life. About 1930, my brother, Jack, went to the Royal Military College, so I went the next year.

"My first two summers' training – between RMC academic years – were in the minesweepers *Festubert* and *Ypres* and the destroyer *Champlain*. In 1934 I graduated from RMC and was full time, a Midshipman. We went to the training cruiser *Frobisher*. Besides the Brits we had mids from the Royal Indian Navy and the Chinese navy. We went to the Med but because King Alexander of Yugoslavia had been assassinated in Marseilles entertainment was low-key; we went up the Adriatic to Dubrovnik. The next cruise was to the West Indies, uneventful except that the tanker *Val Verda* was on fire, we helped them put it out and then towed her to Bermuda. It took twelve days. The Captain applied for salvage money and each cadet got twelve pounds, fifteen shillings. He got two thousand pounds. After the summer cruise to Copenhagen, Oslo, Trondheim, we were part of the fleet review for King George V's Diamond Jubilee. Two hundred and forty ships were present, mostly Royal Navy but all other countries represented.

"I must tell you of the first military invasion by Canada in the West Indies. In 1936, this was. An armed party of Canadians stormed and captured Swan Island.

"Three Canadian mids, two RN, and one New Zealander, were sent to HMS *Dragon* in the West Indies Squadron – the "Patagonian Navy," it was called in those days. We were sent down south to keep an eye on all German and Italian ships. We had gone up the Amazon to Manaus – about fifty miles from the mouth – then all the way down the coast. The German and Italian ships we reported were quite hostile in their demeanour to us. On the way north again, after Christmas in Bahia, we were in the Gulf of Yucatan. The Swan Islands are a dependancy of the Caymans, which in turn are a dependancy of Jamaica. These islands had long been claimed by Great Britain, for what purpose, I don't know. They were only little things. But during World War One the Americans had established a meteorological station there. This was continued after the war for the benefit of the American United Fruit Company cargo ships. But somebody on the islands was in the pay of the Foreign Office in Whitehall and had reported this. My Captain was told to investigate. I think with tongue-in-cheek he said, 'Well, I'm not going to get my fingers burned on this one. Let the Canadians go and find out what's going on.'

"We armed ourselves with .45 revolvers, gave the troops rifles, and told them to hide them under the thwarts. Eric Boak was in charge of the landing party and I was in charge of the boats. We also took along a bit of trade goods for bribery – flour, beans, anything that would impress the natives if they were not *too* unfriendly. If they were, we had guns. Sure enough, there was an American flag flying. Boak landed and the hands marched up the hill, arms at the high port, carrying the Union Jack. Pure Hollywood! The local commander was a Cayman Islander and he was most cordial. He had raised the Stars and Stripes only because someone had asked him to. Boak said, 'Would you mind taking it down?'

" 'Oh no. Not at all.'

" 'And put this one up?'

" 'Oh, okay, Fine.'

"So down came the Stars and Stripes and up went the Union Jack. Then we gave them some pickles and flour and beans and everyone was smiling. And that's how two Canadian midshipmen brought the Swan Islands back into the Empire.

"In the Spanish Civil War I was in the *Royal Oak* on non-intervention patrol in the Bay of Biscay. I've quite forgotten whose side we were on but we were escorting any bedraggled little steamer that wanted to get goods *into* Spain, up to the three-mile limit. After that they were on their own in dealing with the Spanish authorities who were trying to keep them out. It was monotonous, but every now and then we went to St. Jean de Luz for leave, mostly having a little walk ashore; it was very pleasant. One of our clients was "Potato" Jones who had a little ship from Barry, Wales. He was always in trouble with the Spanish. I think he used to taunt them. But we escorted him; it was the policy of HM government, that was good enough for us, and that was our contribution to the Spanish Civil War. I somehow doubt that world conditions are much affected today because of it. But imagine a 42,000-ton battleship escorting "Potato" Jones's little 1000-ton tramp steamer.

"We were sent to learn the mysteries of naval air in the carrier *Courageous*. We had the first of the Blackburn Sharks and the Fairey 3F torpedo bomber. We had a flying-off deck and a landing-on deck. To take off on the lower of the two, you gunned the engine inside the hangar, taxied out of the forward door at as good a speed as you could get, out into the daylight, then you had maybe one hundred feet of deck to get airborne. When we landed it was on the upper deck, of course; landing through a hanger door on the lower deck would have been too much to ask, even of our intrepid Pilots. Some of the Pilots were air force and some were navy; the Navigators were all navy. We Midshipmen had to spend so many hours in the air. There were no closed cockpits and above 11,000 feet it was (A) very cold, and (B) you were gasping for air – no oxygen masks. We had what we called the "Rat Club." If a pilot saw he was going to make a boo-boo of a landing, he'd pull the nose up, climb out, jump, and let the plane go in by itself; he'd land in the water. I think we had four in the "Rat Club." Then there was the "Rat Trap Club." This was for the Navigator in the rear seat. If he thought the Pilot was going to make a boo-boo, he'd jump out.

"I went as First Lieutenant to Harry DeWolf in *St. Laurent* just before we were sent to Dunkirk with *Restigouche* and *Skeena*. As we came into Plymouth in a slight fog a plane went over; we opened fire, too late, and missed. The Captain was *not* pleased and, believe me, he was quite definite in telling everyone what he thought. The plane, it was an Anson, came back and signalled, 'Poor shooting but at least you are awake.' This didn't soothe the Captain one little bit. Our first job was at St. Valery where the 51st Division was pulling back from the original line. General Fortune decided that he could hold on one more day and let more troops escape. But he was wrong. While we were there General Rommel's troops made the coast and the first thing we knew we were being potted at from the cliffs. We fired back. I don't think we hit the German guns but it made us feel better. All we took off was about fifty French. We had to land them at Brest but they were not that happy.

"The next event was the arrival of the Second Canadian Division in July. Britain was alone and glad of help. Sir John Tovey was C-in-C Home Fleet and came down to greet the Canadians. *Fraser* had arrived by herself from Bermuda and so we had four Canadian destroyers screening *Hood* and a couple of cruisers. We joined Tovey the night before we met the Canadian troop convoy. It was cold, wet, miserable, no radar, all eyeball. Tovey wanted the destroyers to sweep ahead of him for mines. He told us this at ten at night. The hands turned to and in the dark on the slippery decks we had this damn minesweeping gear ready to slip at two in the morning. Came nine o'clock he decided he didn't want it any more and we had to recover it. If there is one back-breaking operation it is getting inboard the wires and floats and boards and everything else connected with destroyer minesweeping. We met up with the troop convoy, circled around them, and escorted them up to Greenock. It was a nice gesture to the soldiers. All we got out of it was a signal from Sir John saying that our station-keeping was abominable.

"Harry DeWolf hated to stop his ship at sea; so would any Captain; so did we. But we were sent out to get survivors from the *Arandora Star* which had been torpedoed. She was outbound to Canada. Even at best speed we were seven hours getting there and by then there were over eight hundred in the water. We knew there were U-boats in the area because we had sunk one. But we stopped and started hauling them inboard. Some were exhausted and we had to go over the side to get them up on deck. We went in amongst them slowly, getting them from the boats, the rafts, flotsam.

As First Lieutenant I had to wash, feed, and billet them. We had them on board from about three in the afternoon until noon of the following day. We washed them off as best we could and gave them dry clothing. We had to shut down one boiler room and put some survivors in there. We had on board – crew and survivors – one thousand people in a ship that usually carried about two hundred. They weren't hungry the first night but in the morning. . . . We used all the bully beef we had, gave them each bully beef, porridge, and a hard-boiled egg. We didn't have enough mess utensils so when they got to the head of the queue they'd take a porridge bowl, get a ladle of porridge, then a ladle of sugar, then a piece of meat and an egg. They'd eat it standing up, wash off the bowl, and return it for others. They didn't complain. We were lucky to have picked up two Austrian doctors with this lot. They bent over backwards to help those who were suffering from the fuel oil they had absorbed. We had to leave all *Arandora*'s lifeboats there. Lovely things; big, well-built, teak lifeboats. We liberated one boat's compass and gave that to the Captain as a memento.

"All the survivors, except the ship's crew and the guards, were German or Italian prisoners of war, either that or foreign nationals who had to be interned. There we were picking up the enemy and risking being torpedoed by a U-boat. While we were picking them up we had an RAF coastal command Sunderland overhead. Harry sent him a signal, 'Most of these people are Italians and Germans.'

"He sent back, 'How bloody funny.' "

These next few stories were told to me over the years by Ralph Hennessy, a man I first met in 1940 when he was a Sub-Lieutenant, I a

Midshipman. At one point in our naval careers, when he was a Commander and I a Lieutenant, he discussed with my class for a couple of hours a week – for a year – the qualities that are the mark of a good leader of men. Like true leaders of men we all arrived at our separate answers according to our personalities. He never really gave *ex-cathedra* pronouncements about what he thought – just encouraged the discussion. But now I notice that a quiet confidence in one's own academic and professional ability and a certain insoucience were not on his list of desirable qualities, although forty-five years later, I see these qualities in him as I put his yarns to paper – the start of his rise from scrub nurse to Vice-Admiral.

"When I was First Lieutenant of *Assiniboine* and after our brush with U-210 – she banged us up a lot, you know, holes everywhere and a good fire burning aft – we refitted and went back to convoy screening. I thought I had had fairly extensive training in naval subjects but, of all the schools I had been to and all the ships I had served in, I realized one day that there was a gap. I had had no training in medicine.

"We had gone off on a convoy in January and February and you know what the weather was like, and in the midst of this storm, the doctor, Arne Johnson, comes along to the Captain and says, 'I'm going to have to operate to save a man's life.' This was in a full Atlantic gale. The Captain said we should heave-to as best we could astern of the convoy. The doctor enlisted me as the scrub nurse, 'because Hennessy has got about the strongest stomach in the wardroom.' I wasn't sure if that was a compliment or an insult.

"We used the Captain's cabin. We double-lashed his dining table in position to use as an operating table. Then came the time when we were all set to go. The doctor had previously asked the other destroyer if he could borrow their doctor to act as anaesthetist. In the midst of the gale a whaler came over from this other destroyer, just absolutely beautifully done! The Coxswain laid his whaler alongside, she came up on the wave and the doctor with his little black bag just stepped over the guard rail and staggered down to the operating room. I knew this doctor, a fellow called McKenzie. "I said, 'Mac, that was a beautiful piece of boat work', and he replied, 'Most of the crew are Newfies.'

"We got on with the operation and Arne was having problems getting himself set to cut the guy open, because the ship was bouncing around. He jammed himself up against something, we offered to tie him but he said no, he needed more room. He was just using sheer muscle power to hold himself against the table. I was sterilizing the instruments. McKenzie was sitting there keeping a running commentary going, which he thought would ease the tension.

" 'If you don't mind, doctor,' he said to Arne , I'm going to give the patient a wee drop of mother's ruin.'

"He pulled a bottle of ether out of his pocket, and just sprinkled a little of that onto a pad to help keep the patient subdued. Then he said 'Do you know, doctor, I remember when I was taking surgery instruction at the university. And the old professor said to me "McKenzie, if you have got to do an appendectomy, make a full cut, man." I remembered that when I did my first appendectomy, I made a bold cut and got right through to his liver.' With which Arne, without batting an eye, just went *psssht* with his scalpel – and the operation was on.

"It took an hour and a quarter; you know, normally, doctors do those things in about ten or fifteen minutes, but of course labouring under those conditions. . . I was making a private bet with myself as to when the sick-bay tiffy was going to upchuck into the wound. Fortunately he managed to survive. He was turning greener and greener. Then the scrub nurse distinguished himself. The doctor asked for a drainage tube. I'd been having trouble all the way because he would say 'scalpel' or something, and I wouldn't know the scalpel from a hole in the ground, but the drainage tube I knew. I picked the drainage tube up in the pincer tongs and dropped the bloody thing on the deck, and said, "Oh fudge," or some appropriate naval oath, picked it up and handed it to him. Well, he nearly blew a fuse; there was a small delay while I resterilized it. The guy lived. He was fine.

"I remember when I was a snotty in my first battleship, *Resolution*, during the Spanish Civil War. We were sent directly to the 1937 Spithead Review from the Bay of Biscay for the coronation of King George VI – another sailor King.

"All the other ships had been painting and titivating themselves up for weeks. We looked quite dreadful, rust-stained and so forth. We were told so by the Commander-in-Chief, Admiral Sir Oliver Backhouse. I remember Sir Oliver because I was one of the snotties driving the steam pinnace and I had to take my Captain to pay a formal call on C-in-C who was wearing his flag in *Nelson*. This was when I started my career in what you might call ship-bashing. There was a good chop on and I approached the starboard after-ladder perhaps with too much verve, too much of a charge might be more accurate. I walloped into the flagship's ladder with a hell of a crash. Sir Oliver was up top watching this great manoeuvre, leaning over the rail. I practically dumped him on the seat of his pants on his own quarterdeck. My Captain, Lionel Arthur Doveton Sturdy, who I thought would take this opportunity to blister me for shaming him, said, very quietly, "Hennessy, that was *not* well done." Harry DeWolf once told me that I was an *aggressive* ship-handler.

"But I loved the independence of boat work. Your first command, really. Two ABs as bowman and sternsheetsman, a Petty Officer on the helm, a Stoker killick in the engine room, and me in charge – eighteen years old. And that lovely brass funnel and she would *chuf chuf chuf* across the fleet anchorage. . . .

"I went from *Resolution* to *Neptune* and we set off for the South Africa Station, for Simonstown, via a lot of West African ports. In all these we were at anchor and that meant a lot of boat work. I had a pinnace.

"We had a lot of liberty men to land at all these ports and the Captain sent for all the mids who ran the pinnace. He said, 'What I am going to tell you is probably against the Naval Discipline Act, but so be it. You will find if you are running a late liberty boat most of the sailors coming off will be under the weather, markedly so, if not screaming, fighting drunk. They'll get into the native shabines and drink the locally distilled coconut juice. Literally, some of them will go berserk in the boat. What you are to do at all times is to carry with you some piece of wood or metal and in the event that anyone goes berserk you are to hit him over the head.'

"So I found a ten-inch spanner and my Coxswain had a spare oak tiller about three feet long. My Coxswain let it be known throughout the ship that any time he and the Yank were running late libertymen – that's what I was called in that ship, "the Yank" – anyone causing trouble, regardless of rank, would get bonked. The Captain had made it clear, 'I will not have anyone drunk and fighting mad on my quarterdeck.' I never had to use my spanner but the Coxswain had to lay about him a few times. I remember one Stoker Petty Officer screaming that when he got on board he was going to murder one of the engineer officers, ' 'oo 'ad done 'im 'ard.' The Coxswain, a Leading Seaman, belted him and laid him out in the boat. We had to get a couple of hands to carry him on board but he had not 'performed an act to the prejudice of good order and naval discipline in that he did attempt to murder his lawfully appointed superior officer. . . .' No charges need be laid. Pragmatism. We learned a lot through the pores. It's not in a manual. So, from Captain Sir John Anthony Veremorse, Bart., DSO and Bar and other gongs, and from Leading Seaman Jack Saxon, I learned a bit about taking charge.

"I had another interesting collision after pranging the ladder of *Nelson*. I was driving a destroyer; it was after the Normandy landings and I was running convoys back and forth between Portsmouth and Le Havre. I was having a kip in my cabin and the Officer of the Watch picked up on radar the port-wing ship of an approaching convoy at twenty thousand yards staying on a steady bearing. A steady bearing! The thought suddenly percolates through his mind that there is something about a steady bearing he should remember. Oh, yes. A steady bearing means you will collide. My God! Hard-a-port! Then he freezes and leaves the helm on. The second Officer of the Watch senses that something is going on that perhaps the Captain would like to know about and presses the panic button to my cabin. I come charging to the bridge still trying to pull my sea boots on and everywhere there are red, green, white navigation lights. And by this time we've hit something and the whole ship is shaking. What he had done is turn the ship through four hundred and ten degrees and ram a merchant ship up the ass. Four hundred and ten degrees! He had passed his original course and was going round for the second time! It didn't hurt the merchant ship because she was going away. But our bow was jammed in more than somewhat.

"When we got back to Portsmouth, I knew I was scheduled to go back to Canada to pick up *Micmac*, so I asked the Chief of Staff if I could have my court martial as quickly as possible. I didn't see any sense in hanging around.

" 'My dear Hennessy,' he said, 'You are about fourteenth on the list. Do you know anyone in London?'

" 'Yes, sir. I have some friends there.'

" 'Well why don't you *go* to London, dear boy? Enjoy yourself. Leave your telephone number with my secretary. We'll call you when we want you.'

"So I did and I had great fun for a while but eventually the secretary telephoned and I went back for my board of inquiry. I had "Incurred the severe displeasure of Their Lordships. . . ." And my Officer of the Watch? Nothing. Captains are always responsible. But I would have liked to have *shared* it with him.

"In early 1941 when Johnny Stubbs was still driving *Assiniboine*, we were running troop convoys from Portsmouth to Gibraltar with *Ot-tawa, Restigouche, Piorun, Blyskawika*, and a couple of Free French ships. One day we came across a lifeboat carrying nine survivors – one woman and eight men – from a British freighter. They had been floating around for days and it was cold, February or March. The woman was in the best shape of all of them; the men had made sure she was properly warm and fed her the most of the daily ration. The men themselves were in pretty poor shape. We got them on board. Johnny Stubbs gave up his cabin to the woman. We all gave our cabins to the men. They were really in bad shape. In fact, one of them developed gangrene. Either he had it or he developed it, and he left his leg in my bunk. It just fell off. The smell was *unbelievable*.

"You absorb a lot from your Captain. Johnny Stubbs was always calm. When jousting with U-210 he hardly raised his voice, only enough to be heard over the gunfire. Later in 1941 I went up from Navigator to First Lieutenant and we were to take Winston Churchill back from his meeting with Roosevelt in Argentina. We took station on *Prince of Wales* and went like bats out of hell. We overtook an eastbound convoy and then Winnie decided that his battleship and his escort would drive through this convoy, from stern to bow. *Prince of Wales* took the centre aisle and we took the others. A following sea, and you know what that does to a destroyer. We were yawing like mad. Signal flags flying everywhere. Some cheering. I guess Winnie was making his V for Victory sign somewhere but we were too busy staying alive. Yawing like mad. All we needed was one merchant ship out of line and it would have been a disaster. I thought Johnny was looking a little white-knuckled.

"By 1942 the naval reserves were flooding in and only our Chief and Petty officers were pre-war, properly trained. After refit we came off the marine slip in Dartmouth on December 24. We were towed across Halifax harbour; it was iced over, too; it was *cold*! We ammunitioned ship until 2:00 A.M. Christmas morning. Then a quiet Christmas Day. On Boxing Day we stored ship, fueled, ammunitioned, and left harbour at 4:00 A.M. Eighty-five per cent of our ship's company had never been to sea before in their lives. Our strength was in the CPOs' mess, largely untouched in over a year.

"But it was interesting. We set foot on shore again twenty-eight days later. We took this convoy up to Iceland, howling bloody gales all the way, and this teaches a young seaman quite a lot in a short period of time. We anchored off Reykjavik, up Hvalfiord. It was absolutely wild. On one occasion I remember sitting in the wardroom and we got a message, an urgent message, 'Gale coming in.' We got twenty minutes' warning. We had no steam to move the engines; we were doing a boiler clean. A pretty dicey situation. We were berthed on the depot ship, which was anchored in the middle of the fiord. A group of destroyers nesting; we were fourth or fifth ship out. Dicky White and I raced for the forecastle. The duty watch was still mustering. We let both anchors go. Twenty minutes later the gale hit. *Whammo*.

"The Captain said, 'Hang on at all costs.' Under the stress of the wind the wires were popping like pieces of spaghetti. The anemometer showing the wind force, the one on the mast of the depot ship, blew off at 120 knots. I cleared lower deck except for the hands putting the boilers together and lined them up, physically hanging on, while the chief boatswain's mate and I rushed up our last storm hawser. We hauled it out of the tiller flat then we hung on like grim death. All the hands straining to hold on – physically holding our ship to the next. Then we just blew away. I raced to the bridge to report this sad news to the Captain, that we were adrift. I got there just as Johnny answered the telephone from the engine room. It was the Chief Engineer. He had steam for slow speed. On one boiler. From torn down to ready to go, *in one hour*. It was just *magnificent*. It really was.

"For the next thirty hours Johnny was on the bridge. With both anchors down, sometimes he had revolutions on for fifteen knots just trying to stay in the same place. The seamen on the forecastle had to be lashed to the guard rails, backs to the wind. *Thirty hours* Johnny Stubbs was on that bridge! And through the daylight period we saw a wonderful piece of seamanship. Another destroyer depot ship – USN. Like us she had both anchors down and she was caught in irons, as it were. She was a big, slab-sided thing and her Captain couldn't turn her into the wind. He went sideways. Jiggling back and forth. He went through the whole of the combined fleets. About fourteen or fifteen miles down the fiord – sideways. Avoiding this ship by going ahead, that by going astern. A *beautiful* piece of work. Finally her anchors caught a bit of good holding ground and she swung into the wind again. Between the fiord and round the corner at Reykjavik there were eighteen ships aground that day.

"We took another convoy back to Newfoundland after that. The crew got ashore again in St. John's twenty-eight days after we left Halifax. And man! They were *sailors*. You better believe it, Jack!

"Johnny Stubbs left that year to a shore job as Operations Officer in

St. John's. Lieutenant-Commander Pat Tisdall took over but in the U.K. he had to go to hospital and so I got command. I drove *Assiniboine* for one convoy as a Lieutenant. The first night out I was in my sea cabin and we got in a bit of a gale, not much, the usual. The Officer of the Watch called down, 'Captain, sir, I've got a bit of a problem. Could you come up, please?'

"So I went up and said, 'What's the problem?'

" 'I don't think I'm in my proper station, sir.'

" 'And where do you think you are?'

" 'I think I'm in the middle of the convoy, sir.'

"This is about two o'clock in the morning and black, pitch black. So I got on the radar and he was right. Dead right. He was in the middle of the convoy. You know, it takes a certain genius to get there by accident; it's hard enough to do by design. Now there was what you might call a dull pregnant pause, and I was waiting for somebody to do something. Then I sensed that everybody on the bridge had either their eyes or their ears trained on *me*. And that is when the phrase "the loneliness of command" first struck home. There was nobody else. I was *it*. It took me an hour and a half to get us back to where we should be. When we got into harbour I thought that I would have a sherry in the wardroom before I took my bath. When I went in everyone stopped talking and stood up.

"I then realized that this was not my home any more. My home was on the other side of the wardroom flat. I was one of the young Captains – twenty-four. We all learned fast.

"I joined the RCN as an Ordinary Seaman in April 1938," said George Vander Hagen. "My father was Flemish, my mother Dutch. They had lived on the sea before coming to Canada and used to tell me stories of the sea. My grandfather was a fisherman, and I used to read stories of the sea. We had a farm in Dunleath but I didn't want to farm so my father said why don't you join the navy? I said I'd love to. I was seventeen. I'd never been more than a hundred and fifty miles from home. The biggest boat I'd ever seen was a seven-foot punt on old Soda Lake. My Dad wrote our MP but he said the navy had taken in its quota for the year – fifteen. After a year my father went to see Judge McPhee – his son, Big Art, had joined the navy. Four weeks later I got a letter. I was in.

"About eleven prairie boys took the train for Vancouver. It was a great adventure. I'd never seen anything so huge as Vancouver in my life. I was just awed by the hustle and bustle of it all. The closest town to our farm was Yorkton with a population of 3,000. We went on board one of the *Princess* ferries. We arrived at the old CPR dock in Victoria and were met by a couple of brawny ABs and the Master at Arms, Chief Petty Officer Wilf Pember. We took the street car to Admiral's Road – six cents, we didn't pay, Pember did – got off and walked to the barracks. They opened the gates and we all walked higgledy-piggledy carrying our suitcases, an AB on either side. One was a two-badger – eight years' good conduct – but we didn't know what that was. The first thing they showed us, the very first thing, was how to sling a hammock, because we had to sleep in it that night. The "Stripey" called me over;

" 'Vander Hagen. You and two others, you and you. Over here.'

"The clews and the lanyards and the lashings didn't mean anything to us but we had lots of help from the older hands in the messdeck. At four-thirty they said they'd have a mug-up. They brought out a bunch of cracked cups, and so help me Hannah, I thought they were kidding. Great big white mugs, cracks in them, handles off, cracked plates, a great big aluminum urn with a cylinder down the middle where you put the tea and then poured boiling water in – a tea fanny, it was called. And the tea! Black death! *Phleau.* An Indian name the RN troops picked up when in Bombay or Trincomalee or somewhere out there. Tea is *phleau.*

"The man who signed me up was Chief Petty Officer Danny Rigg who I was shipmates with in *Sioux* in 1944 when he was a Torpedo Gunner and I was a CPO. Wilf Pember was there, of course. Me standing prim and proper trying to look my best. '. . .and do you swear to bear true allegiance to His Majesty King George and his heirs and successors according to law so help you God?' I said, 'I so swear.' Pember said, 'Sign here.' And I was in for a seven-year hitch. We got through the first three days. What a shaker! Horrendous! 'March here. Double there. Stand straight. Hands behind an imaginary seam at the side of your trousers.' (In the old bell bottoms there was no seam there.) 'Stand still. Shoulders back. Head up, chest out. Eyes front. Keep silence in the ranks. Don't squirm. Motionless, I said.'

"Six months' ordinary seaman training. Weekends was the only time we got leave and we had to be back aboard at 6:00 P.M. We had an afternoon off on Wednesday, a "make-and-mend"; sailors had stopped making their clothes long before but we could mend our clothes and get them chamfered up a bit, study, write letters. Leave on Saturday

210

until 10:00 P.M. That sure played havoc with your dating life. You take a girl home at nine on a Saturday night and that's the last time you see her. Church service every Sunday, of course.

"When we passed out as qualified ODs I was drafted to *Ottawa* and we sailed after Christmas for the Caribbean to exercise with the east coast destroyers. That's the first time I saw a fleet, the Royal Navy's America and West Indies Squadron: the cruisers HMS *Apollo, Ajax, Exeter* – with Harwood as Captain, he who sank the *Graf Spee* two years later – and the four Canadian destroyers, *Ottawa, Restigouche, St. Laurent*, and *Fraser*. We had 4-inch, 6-inch, 8-inch guns banging away; much more fun than the farm. And now we had leave each night in harbour until eleven.

"After seeing the guns firing in the practise shoots we had in the West Indies, I wanted to be a gunnery rating so I applied for a Gun Layer 3rd-class course, LR3. I got it in Halifax and went back to sea in *Ottawa* taking convoys out for the first few days of their voyage. Later, we went to Scotland. I got my LR2 course in Plymouth after the air raids had started. One air raid we got the windows blown out of the classroom. Then we froze our butts off at the end of the room while the instructor stood with his backside to the stove at the other. The class was me, a Brit, two South Africans, a Welshman, and a New Zealander. One air raid the roof came off. I passed and now I'm a one-badge AB LR2! Then I went to *Saguenay* and we did fast convoys. I remember we met Winnie when he came back from Newfoundland in *Prince of Wales*. I saw him walking back and forth on the bridge. Johnny Stubbs I remember, very dapper; he was my skipper later in *Assiniboine*. In 1942 I was drafted ashore to do my LR1 course in Halifax. I had been dating Connie for quite a time and Connie was from Halifax and we got married. After the course ended I asked for marriage leave. They said, "You're supposed to go back to *Ottawa*," but I had leave coming. So they said, "Okay if you can get someone to stand in for you." In the course I had just finished was a Petty Officer, a young RCNVR from Saskatoon, McKenzie. He went in my place. A week later he was dead. The ship was torpedoed. The Captain was Larry Rutherford and the First Lieutenant Tommy Pullen. They were both fine officers. Rutherford everything you would want in a Captain and Pullen, too – strict but fair. The Captain was drowned and some other officers and over a hundred of the men.

"Mac was sleeping in the bunk I'd been sleeping in. I missed the torpedoings every time. I either joined a ship after she had been torpedoed or left her before she was torpedoed. But poor Mac bought it.

"It was in *Saguenay* I saw my worst gale. The most horrific storm I ever recall. We left Newfie, picked up a convoy and were just off Iceland when it hit. And it hadn't been *that* good up to then. Phil Haddon was our Captain and he brought us through. The Navigator estimated the height of the waves at one point to be fifty-five feet. The wind was gusting over a hundred knots. We hove to for about four days. The engines were just turning over enough to keep her nose into the seas. We lost fifty-five miles in one day. Fifty-five miles in twenty-four hours. It's hard to believe, isn't it? Fifty-five miles *backwards*. It's in the ship's log book. That was the most horrible storm. It was nerve-shattering. We never thought we'd make it. Some of the guys were even paying off debts, figuring they had no use for the money anyway, so they were going to go out with a clear conscience. Old Haddon brought us through that one. He was on the bridge for most of eight days.

"The seas ribbed the barbette of our forward gun, actually ribbed half-inch steel, high-tensile steel. Every boat was carried away. We didn't have a guard rail left on the upper deck. There was nothing left standing on the upper deck. I was in the wheelhouse and steering was not easy. First primary steering broke down, then secondary. So I was sent aft to the tiller flat to the emergency steering.

"I was steering the ship from the tiller flat and if that steering gear had gone we'd have all been dead. Only one small steering motor left. You had to look over your shoulder to see the compass. Eighteen hours we were down there. Me and a Leading Seaman, Taylor. I was a Petty Officer. The compass broke off so one of us had to hold it while the other steered. We took it turn about. We got helm orders on a sound-powered phone from the bridge. The Captain asked me once, 'Is she handling any better, Vander Hagen?' I said no. He'd order starboard thirty and I'd put thirty of starboard wheel on, hoping she'd come round and she'd just sit there, and hold, and hold. And when she did come, look out! You had to put thirty of port wheel on to meet her. That was the only way we could hold her. The Captain didn't want to use the engines too much.

"After six or seven hours you got hungry and thirsty, jammed down there, getting tossed about, with your feet against the tiller motor box and your back up against the bulkhead, so we told the bridge. The paymaster said there were dry provisions on either side and to help ourselves. That's another time we knew it was bad; paymasters never say help yourself. Taylor jams the compass between my feet with a couple of rope fenders so as I can watch it, he grabs a fire axe, whomps the locks off one of the screens, hauls out a box, and it's full of canned peaches. Oh, that's marvellous! We eat peaches; slimy, juicy peaches. We drink the juice. We drink out of the cans and it slops down our front. We smell of peaches. We smell anyway, I guess; we'd been at sea a week. Then we figured we had enough of peaches and we said, well, we've got permission, so we opened another case and this was tomatoes. That helped a lot after the sweet of the peaches. We ate that too and that made more mess of our clothes. The ship was pitching mostly but rolling, too. Then a few more peaches. I have to think twice about eating peaches even to this day. We must have gone through two gallons. From there on in, when we had peaches for duff, for me, never! Connie still buys them for dessert but I rarely eat them, only in a cake or something. To go to the heads we used the bilges. It was eighteen hours before we got out of the tiller flat. The seas were washing over so that they couldn't get to us. But the old man got us through. The storm damage was so great that we had to go into refit; eight weeks in refit. Then went back to *Assiniboine* and Stubbs who had been navigator was now my skipper. Hennessy was First Lieutenant. Good men, both. So was Haddon for pulling us through that gale.

We did Russian convoys in *Sioux*, mostly, and strikes at shipping off the Norwegian coast, and the Normandy D-Day. We bombarded about a mile off Juno Beach where the Canadian soldiers landed. We had a good lot in *Sioux*. That was the finest ship I ever served in and one of the most efficient I've been in. Doug Bruce was an excellent First Lieutenant, Boak was a good Captain, and I had Stubbs and Haddon and Pullen to judge him by. We had a bunch of characters. The cook wasn't a cook but he was full of fun. Dave Rollins was the messdeck moaner. Every ship had one and we had Rollins. If you said good morning he'd prove it wasn't. And our forger – one day the Gunner's Mate was in a fury because the flotilla Gunnery Officer was coming and the Captain was ashore and had not signed the gunnery log, the magazine logs, and all the rest. We had this kid in the gunner's party, he said, "What's the problem?" Then he signed the Captain's name just as nice as you please. You couldn't tell the difference. We all knew what the Captain's signature looked like. He had it exact. The Gunner's mate said, 'What did you used to do?' and the kid said, 'I was a forger.' We had a real cross-section of humanity in that ship. One was

Lawrence who was always looking for gunnery targets, coastal batteries, when we were off the Normandy coast on D-Day and after. One day we were anchored off Le Havre. We found out later that we were decoys so that the coastal batteries would open up. There were Wellington bombers circling upstairs to bomb them if they fired at us. We were at defence stations and I was in the director. Lieutenant Tom Wall was Officer of the Watch. A nice fine calm day, warm sun, just a brisk breeze.

"I'm sitting on top of the director and Wall and I are chatting back and forth when I saw Lawrence up on the forecastle, past the forward gun, past the capstan, up to the eyes of the ship. We had half the guns closed up. Then I hear this horrible freight train coming from some place up in the sky. I could almost feel the wind of it, it was so close. Lieutenant Wall and I looked at each other and I said, 'shore battery.' Lieutenant Wall said we'd better up anchor and he called the Captain. Lawrence looked around and the shells fell ahead of us; he had his binoculars, never without them. The shells landed ahead and the splashes went up and up. Big-calibre guns, 6- or 8-inch. More fell closer, about two hundred yards, fragments flying everywhere and going *ching ching ching* on the upper deck and funnel. Another salvo went over us with a rushing sound. Everyone was now flat on their face. Lawrence was looking shoreward trying to see the wink of the guns when they fired. No tin hat on. Alarm bells going off. He keeps looking; he's trying to locate them so he can fire back.

"I said, 'Geez, he's going to get hit.'

"Lieutenant Wall says, 'He's a gunnery officer. He'll be all right long as he gets hit in the head.'"

"I remember my time as a Boy Seaman in Esquimalt in *Naden*. My grandfather was a North Sea fisherman and my Uncle Bob was at the Battle of Jutland in a battleship, the *Barham*. I'd always wanted to be a sailor like them, I guess. And in that summer of 1938 I became a sailor or I got my start, anyway. Boy Seaman Richard James. I used to play a lot of sports and was in good physical condition so the running and the doubling didn't bother me. I enjoyed Boy Seaman training. I can honestly say that. Gunner Johnson was quite a character. He used to creep up on the boys in the gun battery and if you weren't doing what he liked, he'd boot you up the stern. He booted me several times. But the whole staff was top line and all you had to do was keep your nose clean and you had no problems. We only got leave on Saturdays until nine at night. I did a little boxing, not too much. Young Dick James was never going to be fleet champion.

"At first everyone was terrified of Gunner Johnson, he was so gruff. But they were all kindly underneath it. I ran into the same thing later at Whale Island. There you had Petty Officers teaching Petty Officers and they gave you a hard time during the day, but after the day's work was through we'd all have a beer in the mess.

"When I reached age eighteen I got promoted to Ordinary Seaman and my pay went up to $37.50 a month. The same day I got promoted to OD I met my wife, June. I'm still married to her, incidently.

"I went to my first frigate in 1944, *Beacon Hill*. All the officers were wartime reserves and in the lower deck only the Coxswain, the Yeoman of Signals, and myself were pre-war navy. But by the time we finished our work-ups we were all ready for the Atlantic, except for a couple. The Gunnery Officer didn't know much; nice fellow though. Another officer, one of the bridge watchkeepers, got the ship pointed right at the convoy. I was PO of the watch. The Captain came to the bridge, chewed him out, and said don't *ever* come on my bridge again. He never did. They were the only two bad officers. We had a good doctor, a good First Lieutenant, and the Captain was great. He had a DSC from sinking a sub early in the war, in *Chambly*. Also he had been mentioned in despatches a few times, I think; and he had a DSO. He was also Escort Group Commander, EG 26. He was so good that once he had to be taken off to hospital – complete exhaustion. You know what the English Channel and the Irish Sea were like. Wrecks everywhere and all gave a good asdic echo. You couldn't get all the crew up to go to action stations every time we got an asdic echo. We were in cruising watches – four hours on and eight off – and, since we got so many echoes, we had the hands attacking with the cruising watch. But the Old Man had to be up for them all. We lost a destroyer on Hallowe'en night, the USS *Whitaker*. A beautiful night. Just at dusk. We were all on the upper deck, shooting the breeze, and up she went. The torpedo got her right in the bow, in the hedgehog magazine. It wrapped the bow right back to the bridge, killed ninety-four.

"We did a funny thing one time. All went in line abreast about two hundred yards apart, a dozen escorts, we went toward Lough Swilley, firing everything we had, depth charges, hedgehog, squid. We chased a U-boat into the lough. We heard it was sunk by a coastal command aircraft later. Another time, we were coming out of Londonderry and went downstream to fuel and get the boys sort of sobered up from their boozing in Ballykelly or 'Derry. Next day we just got out of Lough Foyle up by Inishtrahull and *New Glasgow* ran smack bang into a submarine, right on the surface, she glanced off her conning tower. We stayed on top of the U-boat for two days. You know, the bad currents and the poor asdic conditions. But we forced her up. Two days. She scuttled. We picked up survivors. U-1006, I think. Another time we assisted in a kill off Land's End. We were outward bound with a fast convoy and we got this contact, ran up to it and fired our hedgehog. Hedgehog was better than depth charges; by firing those mortars ahead you didn't lose the sub's echo in the ship's wake or get the turbulence from the depth-charge explosions. We had to go on with the convoy but when we got back someone else had sunk it. The survivors were all on the surface.

"The U-boats were on the run in 1944; Our bad year was 1942; over a thousand ships sunk. The next year was better – less than half that. In 1944 we hadn't had many ships torpedoed and we were sinking more subs. I found out later we sank over eight hundred total. The survivors were all kids, too. A shame. I was nineteen and they were younger than me – fifteen, sixteen. They were all scared to death. I guess they had heard stories about the monstrous things the Allies did to prisoners. They were no different to us. I don't think they wanted to be in this conflict any more than us.

"On VE Day we were with a convoy off the white cliffs of Dover. Peace! So Commander Simmons said, "To hell with it. Let's go," and took the whole flotilla into Portsmouth. I was in London the day after VE Day. Most of the pubs were dry, if you can figure that. I guess they drank it all the day before. Fantastic! Everything all lit up like the day before Grey Cup. Waving flags, shouting, all boozed up, naturally.

"We went back to Londonderry and a lot of the surrendered U-boats were there. They knew *Beacon Hill*, they knew our pennant number, K407, they knew that Commander Simmons was what they termed "dangerous." He was a fine Captain to us."

"Every time we got into Londonderry the Wrens would come down to the ship. They were a fine lot of girls. They manned the port war signal station, handled most of the visual and radio communications, drove the cars and trucks, and for me they were great because the Ordnance Wrens, about three of them, would come down and clean all the rifles, brens, stens, Lancasters, 9mm revolvers. I was the Gunner's Mate of the ship. It gave the gunner's party time for other things and a better chance to get ashore. These three girls did that for all of us – and there were fifty or sixty ships based there. When we left we fired a gun salute to them. We were going downstream past the Wrennery, past Broom Hall, all the Wrens came out to wave to every ship that went by, and we fired our salute. We didn't have saluting charges so we used the regular cordite charge. A great belch of flame and *blam*.

"Our whole group was going back to Canada. We got a few days into the Atlantic and Ted Simmons, being the type he was, said, "Bugger it, let's go," and took off full speed. The rest of the group tore along astern as best they could. A great race to Halifax. Then we got ready for the war in the Pacific. One of our cruisers – the *Quebec* – was out there already."

In 1935 Tom Kellington finished grade eleven at age sixteen. "I had applied for the navy in 1934 but they weren't taking anyone, so I joined the Canadian Scottish. What else was there to do in the Depression? I got as far as Sergeant but I couldn't even get a beer in the mess – under age. After a little over two years in the army I was able to join the navy – as a Stoker, Second Class, the same as Ordinary Seaman. I left Work Point Barracks at 7:30 in the morning and went to the naval barracks, *Naden*, and the first one to greet me was a Chief Gunner's Mate, an old friend from football when the army and the navy used to tussle. I think I had one hand in my pocket so he let out a *bellow*. It shook me rigid. Next thing I knew I was doubling. Wilf Pember (good man, Wilf) was the jaunty and, as the main man in naval police, he was looking after the incoming hands. He took me to see Lieutenant-Commander Wurtele. He was a very conscientious man, quiet, a wry sense of humour, a wry smile. He said, 'And what are you going to be, my boy?' I said, 'I'm going to be an engineer.' He turned to Pember and they laughed. But I don't know anyone who didn't like Wurtele; he never had an enemy.

"We started training on the parade ground, of course. I had to learn to come to attention without stamping like a pongo. Then I went to *Fraser*. Rastus Reid was Captain and Tisdall was First Lieutenant. He gave me the only entry on my crime sheet I ever had in thirty-four years. I was out of the rig of the day. I was sunbathing. I was off watch so I didn't see any harm in it six hundred miles off Mexico. I got ten days' extra work. Harold Groos was a Lieutenant, a good man; if you had a problem he didn't mind discussing it with you. He was First

Lieutenant later on with Gus Miles as Captain when *Fraser* was cut in half in the channel. He looked up all the survivors when he got back to Canada. I was with her the whole time. I was a Stoker First Class by then, doing Leading Stoker's duties looking after auxiliary machinery, evaporators, and that sort of thing.

"In 1937 we did a cruise to Mexico, Peru, those places; next year we went through the Panama Canal to the West Indies and exercised with the east coast destroyers and RN ships of the America and West Indies Squadron. In August of 1939 we were in Vancouver when we got word to sail for Halifax. We set out at twenty-five, twenty-six knots; get out your pencil, it's 7,700 nautical miles. Fourteen days to Halifax. Actually, thirteen days, twenty-three hours, and some minutes. We collapsed our boilers and had to re-brick them when we got there. But we took the first convoy of the war out a few days later.

"In December 1939 the first troop convoy – TC1 – was to sail. The big thing for me was that my kid brother was in it with the advance guard of the Princess Patricias from here in Victoria, Work Point Barracks. I went over to see him. I was standing in the big foyer, three decks high, when I heard a 'Brumph, brumph, brumph.' It was my old colonel, Calhoune. He thought of me as a deserter and he told me so. Even though I left his regiment to join the navy, he thought of me as a deserter. The navy was the senior service so he couldn't stop me. But I had to buy my release. A hundred bucks, a lot of money. I was only getting forty a month.

"By February 1940 we are down south, working out of Kingston, Jamaica, looking for German merchant ships running the blockade back to Germany. There were a number that had run into Aruba, places like that. We'd lie over the horizon and watch their smoke. If they came out we'd head for them and chase them back in.

"I remember our dhoby wallah in Jamaica, old Mary, a little old West Indian. She picked up our laundry when were were in Kingston. She'd come into the mess decks to collect it and we'd be skylarking around. You'd get a character coming in with a towel around him after a basin bath. He'd bounce around. But one old fellow, an old-timer in the mess, flicked the towel off, 'Hey, Mary. Look at this.' And Mary would say, 'Aw, man. Mary no more dhoby ruined pieces.' When we rushed off to England we had to leave all our laundry behind. Mary went to some business men in Kingston and told them. They sent it to us and we got it all when we were in Plymouth. But we hadn't paid for it so I went round and collected all the money and sent it to the same business men. I got a letter from Mary thanking us; that arrived after *Fraser* had gone down.

"I don't think that many of our hands were lost. I think only one or two – except those who were in the daymen's mess when *Calcutta* hit, about eight stokers. One guy that got away with a whole lot was Russ Milray. He was badly crushed. He spent nearly two years in hospital in Devonport. He had more breaks in his body than you could shake a stick at, green gangrene set in. But he had a marvellous young doctor. He said to Russ, 'Do you want to do everything I say? Operations, you're going to have a hundred of them. You're either going to come out of them alive or you're not getting out of here at all.' He was a hopeless case, Russ. They had to shorten his legs and then gangrene would set in so they'd take off some more. I took a Leading Stoker's course, that was three months; and after that I'd go and see him whenever I could. Me and the others were over there for five months after *Fraser* went down.

"After *Restigouche* took off all the *Fraser* survivors and landed us in England, we were put into compartments with sentries over us, so one group couldn't talk to the other. There were two or three merchant ship crews as well. We started counting noses and we thought, 'Gee, *Calcutta* may have some.' Finally those who were okay were kitted up and sent on survivor's leave. The Brits have a great way to get your uniform size. The supply guys at the wicket peer at you through a hole about fifteen inches by fifteen inches. Depending on what part of your body they see, that's your size. If they see your head, you must be short. If they see your stomach, you're tall. From side to side they know if you're fat or thin.

"All us Stokers from *Fraser* wanted to go to *Margaree* but they wouldn't let us. We had to finish our course. So they sent four RN Stokers in our place and they went down in her. It struck me, 'Jesus, there but for the grace of God, go I, or, rather, go the four of us.' After the course was over we were sent to different ships. I went to *Niagara* and was promoted to Engine Room Artificer. Before I left the navy I got up to Engineer Lieutenant-Commander. I showed Alfie Wurtele my engineer's stripes.

In about 1947 my wife and I were standing in the queue at the old Dominion Theatre and I saw Russ Milray and his wife. He was looking as healthy as all blazes.

Peter Chance joined the RCNVR in 1938 when he was a student at Lisgar Collegiate in Ottawa. "I had never seen salt water except when my mother took my brothers and me to England in 1930 to visit relatives. But I lived next door to a reserve officer, Victor Browne, otherwise known as Starchy Browne because of the fact that, on one occasion, when Commodore Miles had seen him coming off from shore leave very late – or early in the morning – he'd said, 'Browne, the only thing that's holding your head up is the starch in your collar.' I joined as Midshipman. The next summer, in my best uniform and sporting my dirk, I reported to Halifax for summer training and lived in Admiralty House. There I met Teddy Orde; he was very kind and helped me a lot. The Staff Officer (Intelligence) was Lieutenant-Commander Gauvreau who set me to work learning naval cyphers and coding and decoding. Gauvreau was very interesting and intensely engaging.

"Ships from the West Indies Squadron visited in August, *Berwick* and *York*, and, because everyone was going to their reception one particular evening, I was to do rounds at the barracks. I had never been Officer of the Day. I hadn't a clue what I was supposed to do. It was as quiet as a tomb at 2100 when we were to start rounds. I was led by a very old, gnarled Chief Petty Officer (so it seemed to me then; he was probably thirty-five) in front of whom was a bugler and a hand carrying a lantern. "Still for Rounds," someone kept shouting but there was nobody in sight until we got to the wet canteen where all the hands were drinking beer. The Chief said, 'Don't worry, sir, it will be all right.' There was much shuffling and a stand-to-attention noise, and I passed through looking straight ahead. I didn't know what else to do. It really is quite frightening for an eighteen-year-old, that first time you are put in charge.

"Teddy Orde sent me to join *St. Laurent*. Lieutenant-Commander Harry DeWolf was Captain. He is a man for whom I have enormous respect although in those days 'trepidation' would have been a better word. He didn't smile a great deal but I feel certain he had a sense of humour. He was a great teacher and he taught by example. I've never forgotten one occasion where he showed his navigational ability. We and *Fraser*, *Restigouche*, and *Ottawa* were sent out with a troop convoy; in December, it was. We would take them out to the limit of our fuel and then return to Halifax. They were escorted across the Atlantic by a battleship and RN destroyers met them at the other end.

"As we departed Chebucto Head the fog set in. There wasn't much of a sea running and there wasn't much breeze. The convoy Commodore had ordered a zig-zag and at seventeen knots we were surging along in this fog. We went along this way for thirty hours or so; pretty nerve-wracking stuff. I was on the bridge and looking aft when suddenly I saw the hands on the quarterdeck move quickly forward. I could see just that far. Then I saw this enormous fountain, 'My God. What's this?' Then I knew it was the bow wave of a very large ship. The Captain was on the bridge and ordered full ahead. We surged forward. This also was dangerous and after a minute or so the Captain slowed again. The next thing we knew we were lapped from the wash of this large ship which had overtaken us; this on the port side. It was *Aquitania*. Then I heard a bugle to starboard. This was *Resolution*, and there was a Midshipman and a marine buglar doing rounds, I guess. Harry DeWolf went full ahead again and got clear. Then he dropped back and we stayed between the two for a while.

"When it was time to leave Harry got out ahead, crossed over – crossed the T, as it were – and altered for the coast. He said, 'I'll just have a look at the chart' and in a while I was apprised of what he was doing. He was looking for a fathom line. We had the depth recorder going. We hadn't seen anything since we left Halifax days before but we surged back in this dense fog at twenty-four knots. We got back to a certain point and Harry said, 'That's about it, I guess.' I *guess*! He altered to starboard and we went smack-on into harbour. Bingo. Chebucto Head. I've never been so astounded in my life. There's Halifax. And that's Hard-Over Harry: damn good officer, terse, man of great capability; in ship-handling, he was a master.

"Just as I was about to be promoted Acting Sub-Lieutenant, the Captain asked me if I was still interested in transferring to the permanent force. I said yes. I then retired to civilian life, swotted up for my entrance examinations, and joined the navy again as a cadet. I seem to be going backwards – from Midshipman to cadet. My class went to the Naval College at Dartmouth but first met the naval tailors Messrs. Gieves, by appointment to the King, the Queen, the Lord Louis, kings of various other countries, way back to before Admiral Nelson's time. They took us in hand, we'd need solar topees, arctic equipment, swords, a dozen of this and a dozen of that. . . . I had an allotment out of my pay going to them for the next twenty-five years; still get my suits there. We were billeted near Hyde Park for a while. The air raids were on; they were going for the London docks. We decided to join the fire brigade; we were so keen and wanted to do something. We got down the river, down below London Bridge, until the fire became so hot we couldn't go any further. A startling and horrifying sight! We were happy to find some sandbags to jump behind when His Majesty's not-so-loyal opposition dropped a stick of bombs. Presently we went to pastoral Devon at the mouth of the river Dart.

"The usual training of cadets at the Naval College, Dartmouth – driven by Chief Petty Officers, navigation, engineering, seamanship, sailing, the lot. At the time after Dunkirk when we were expecting a German invasion, we had to man the trenches at night. We dug them ourselves with trenching helves. We had Lee Enfield rifles but they had no bolts. What we did have was bayonets with which to repel the Hun hordes. Nothing came of it. Hitler called it off. The regular Dartmouth-entry cadets we didn't see much of. They came in at about age thirteen. We were the public-school entry, all around nineteen. We had Pakistanis, Indians, Australians – RAN, South Africans – RSAN, a couple of Corsicans, some Free French, an interesting lot. On graduating, Benny Benoit and I went to a light cruiser as Midshipmen. (I'm on my way back up again.)

"In *Mauritius* the snotties' nurse was Charles Godwin, DSC, known as "Flash Alf." He was a physical training specialist and had got his DSC at the time the Germans were overrunning France. He was in a taxi retreating at a good rate of knots from German tanks firing at him and exhorting his driver to go faster while he threw fulminite of mercury primers at these tanks.

We went to Scapa Flow to work up but before we did much we were sent out to look for the two German battle cruisers. We were no more prepared for that than flying to the moon. Our ship was certainly seaworthy but not worked up. We put to sea and the Captain, 'Black Derrick' Stephens, spoke over the tannoy to the ship's company; 'This is the Captain speaking. As you know by now, I suspect, we are at sea with the entire Home Fleet and we are proceeding at best possible speed. The purpose of this is to intercept, engage, and destroy the *Scharnhorst* and *Gneisenau*. Now I realize that we are not yet prepared to acquit ourselves all that well but I am certain you will all do your best. Good luck.' We were delighted that we didn't meet the enemy.

"At that time in Scapa a young man was hauled in front of his Commander as a defaulter. This was in the battleship *Rodney*. He had made improper sexual advances, apparently, to a sheep. It's hard to know the truth of the matter; there are many versions. 'I was very drunk, sir, I'd had a lot of beer and I thought it was a Wren in a sheepskin coat.' This story delighted the fleet. I was one of the Midshipmen driving the forty-five-foot launches: we carried perhaps forty liberty-men. On one occasion shortly after this, we were passing *Rodney* on our way to shore. The libertymen set up a chorus of *Baaaaaa, Baaaaaa,* as we passed. Sheep jokes became quite the thing. 'What ship are you from?'

" 'Roooooodney.'

" 'And where are you based?'

" 'Scaaaaaapa.'

"The Commander-in-Chief became quite incensed and sent a signal that this was to stop.

"We went to Bathurst in Gambia and there I had the Captain's motorboat. I was told to put two depth charges on the transom of the boat and patrol outside the harbour because there was a U-boat reported in the vicinity. I was told, "If necessary, attack and drop your charges, and, er, good luck, Snotty.' It was one of those beautiful tropical nights, as bright as day, and I could see the ship about five miles away. Here I was, steaming back and forth across the estuary. I was a happy lad when the sun rose and I could return for breakfast. The crew were equally delighted. The water was so shallow that had we fired the charges the chance of getting away was pretty slim. Death or glory days.

"Benny Benoit and I were the only Canadians and, as our pay was higher, we had more money than the rest, two shillings sixpence a day more, so by the time we got to Simonstown we had twenty-five quid each. Benny and I had a Friday-night leave of considerable dimen-sions. July 1941. Delmonico's – an enormous pub set like a hollow square, galleries all round, over the upper gallery the ceiling was painted deep blue with all the stars painted on and lights playing over it.

"We went on to Mauritius and the Seychelles either taking troop convoys or looking for German raiders – they had a lot and were sink-ing quite a few of our ships. We got to Adu Atoll and set up a base there. It was to be the Indian Ocean's Scapa Flow. I remember the day we had to call on the Sultan. Henry Leach was mid of the Captain's boat – just back from a terrible bout of sunburn; he was fair and burned easily. We were all wearing our Gieves solar topees. Hot sun, clear water like crystal, seventeenth-century designed bugaloos sailed by bare-footed natives. A vessel approached from the shore, oar-driven: stroke, pause, stroke, pause, stroke, pause. In majestic rhythm she glided up. The Sultan in a sarong, bare-chested, fez. Behind him the Prime Minister. I knew he was Prime Minister because he was holding the umbrella over the Sultan. They brought an array of fish which they laid on the quarterdeck. Next morning the Captain returned the Sultan's call: guard, band, bugles, salutes, pipe the side. Henry Leach had been working since six on the boat and had all sorts of finery, rope work, all tiddlied up. The Captain doubled down the ladder, stepped lightly into the boat, and put one foot in a pail of soapy water. 'Snotty, three weeks in the boat.' Henry's punishment pleased us; he took our turns as Midshipmen of the boat as well as his own.

"This was good comic relief to our daily routine of patroling, working, patroling, working. . . . Food was poor, lime juice and oatmeal; herrings in tomato sauce. The milk came in blocks two feet square, was shaved into a powder, mixed with water and tasted like chalk. The temperature was 120 degrees below decks – the scuttles and deadlights were closed so we got no fresh air. We all had prickly heat. Besides our regular duties we had classes; trying to learn calculus under those conditions is hard. We had trouble with our firemains; there was more water in the ship than outside it. I had a Coxswain, a square-rig three-badge Petty Officer, who became upset. He locked himself away and we couldn't find him for three days and when we did he was dead.

"Eventually we got up to the Jahore Straits for a refit – the naval dockyard about seventeen miles north of Singapore. It was obvious things were going to get hot. Our troops had bren-gun carriers and bicycles, the Frontier Force Riflemen and the Dogras to withstand the Japanese attack. The Japanese had landed December 6, the day before they bombed Pearl Harbor. Benny and I were on leave but we rattled on back to our ship. They bombed Singapore the same night. Three parties of men were landed, each commanded by a Midshipman; the whole commanded by Flash Alf. Our job was to board some junks which 'appeared to be armed.' We dumped our grenades pretty quickly and there were a few killed – not us, them. It was a pity; they were only carrying cargo; they were not a threat. I remember leading my first landing party. Armed to the teeth: grenades, Lancaster automatic rifle, trenching helve, whistle with lanyard, .45 revolver, in my plimsolls and shorts, frightened to death!

"It wasn't long after that that *Repulse* and *Prince of Wales* were sunk. The Captain of *Prince of Wales*, John Leach, was Henry's father. *Mauritius* had to store, fuel, ammunition, get her electrics back together. Every night Japanese aircraft bombed us at 21,000 feet; our anti-aircraft guns could only reach 19,000; the enemy planes never even broke formation; you could see them in the searchlights. We had a fuel barge on one side and took ammunition on over the other side – everybody but the Captain humping ammo. In seventy-two hours we put to sea. A moonless night. We came out of the Jahore Strait and made a dash up the Malacca Strait over to Trincomalee. We couldn't have fought if we had met an enemy. Then Henry learned his father was dead. He had been a carefree youth, Henry, a good student, a good officer, nothing of particular note. But that day he changed. From that day on, only his best was good enough, only the top was good enough. He ended up Admiral Sir Henry Leach, First Sea Lord.

"After *Mauritius* went back to Portsmouth for refit I went to a Hunt-class destroyer, *Liddesdale*. Twin 4-inch guns fore and aft, splendid vessels, scaled-down fleet destroyers, specifically used for inshore work covering convoys. Our patrol area was from Sheerness at the mouth of the Thames River to Rosyth, once we went through the Pentland Firth down to Cape Wrath. But it was mainly E-boat Alley. I suppose E-boat Alley proper is the Straits of Dover; nonetheless we had our moments of excitement, albeit there were long periods of boredom plodding along at eight knots with the convoy in two columns about seven miles long going up or down the swept channel, minefields on either side – both our own and German. The mines, the E-boats, and low-flying aircraft were the main threat.

"One evening in the spring of 1942 we saw a long line of aircraft leaving our shores – we were off Norfolk – and heading for the continent, heading east. It seemed to us to be a pipeline of aircraft, bombers of every type. I suppose it was the start of the thousand-bomber raids. What was interesting was that we had specific orders that any aircraft at less than one thousand feet heading west – back to Britain – was to be considered hostile. In the early hours of the morning there was a low-lying mist hanging over the sea and visibility was perhaps a half a mile. I was on the bridge and we heard an aircraft approaching from starboard, from the east, it was going west and from the sound, flying low. 'Alarm Aircraft Starboard, Green nine oh,' I cried. All the guns trained around and loaded. The Captain was on the bridge. It was getting closer and obviously near us. 'Open fire.' Everything opened up in a barrage of sound and shell. To our horror a Wellington bomber whistled overhead and splashed into the drink. Clearly, we had success in the gunnery field but that was all, not in international relations. It was a Polish bomber returning from their first strike at the enemy that had invaded their homeland in 1939. To the Polish aviators it was the return from a victory. We hustled over and picked them up. They were furious. But I am pleased to say that when we landed them forty-eight hours later, they were warmed through in many ways and left us with good feelings.

"The E-boat crews were able, and crafty. They used to tie up at any one of the buoys that marked the fairway. This saved fuel and when we picked up a radar echo we expected it to be there – the buoy, not them. Then they would start up and roar out. They were capable mariners, brave, daring, and all the rest of it. Mind you, they had a pretty easy target. A long line of ships parading past in pairs at eight knots. We didn't see them too much but other convoys got clobbered. The Captain, of course, was on the bridge practically the whole time and this was quite a strain on him. He had had a previous destroyer, the *Vimera*, shot out from under him at Dunkirk. He loved the bagpipes. When we were returning to Sheerness on one occasion we heard the wail of the pipes on the forecastle. We thought that pretty funny; we knew the Captain played the pipes but didn't think he should be on the forecastle doing so when we entered harbour. The First Lieutenant said to me, 'Look over the bridge.' I did. There was the Captain playing away without any clothes on; he was naked. So our West-Country, capable First Lieutenant took the Captain gently in hand and led him back to his cabin. He went quietly. After a rest he was perfectly okay and went back to full duty. The strain hit different people different ways. He had had Dunkirk and then night after night and day after day in E-Boat Alley.

"I finished my Midshipman's time in the battleship *Anson*, the pride of the fleet at this point. I was senior mid and we had seventy-five total. We were working with the Home Fleet but we snotties were cramming for our final examinations as well. *Anson* has 15-inch guns and 15-inch armour plate, 55,000 tons – most of it below the waterline. When we went to our studies it was six decks down, large block and tackles lowered the armour-plate hatch above us and sealed us in. We worked from six in the morning until nine or ten at night. The only relieving feature was Chinese checkers. Someone had scrounged a set of Chinese checkers and when we simply had to have a break, had to have a change of pace, we played Chinese checkers. I finished these exams and went off to do my Sub-Lieutenant's courses, to *Excellent* first of all.

"Even getting back to Canada after Sub's courses proved eventful. Benny Benoit and Bill Howe and I went to the *Jamaica Planter*, a 2500-ton merchantman; we picked her up at Avonmouth. Three confirmed Sub-Lieutenants! We had the world by the tail! But *Jamaica Planter* was sunk in the January 1943 gales off Milford Reach. An Esso tanker hit us and we sank, right off the beach there. But war has its amusing side. There was a nurse-cum-stewardess with her bulky cork life-jacket over an expansive bosom calmly handing out cocoa to all hands as the ship was quietly settling. A lighter came alongside and our gear was off-loaded.

"So we were back in Swansea. Great air raids going on and we three thought we should do something to help and joined the local fire-fighting force. We got as far west as Llannelly and met some interesting characters and had great fun with fire hoses during the air raids. This was the time the Germans were using phosphorescent fire bombs. Nothing wildly explosive but they made a hell of a mess, everyone was very busy. Finally we got another merchant ship and set off back to Canada without too much trouble except that the customs inspectors thought our navigation tables were secret cyphers. Fascinating but infuriating.

"We went in convoy, continuing gales – that winter was bad; one day when we were rolling thirty degrees each way, Bill Howe was lying asleep in his bunk and a scuttle burst. He was doused with a six-inch jet of icy water. For three days we made three knots sternway as we went north-west of the Shetlands, over to Iceland, then in the Denmark Strait; off Greenland we ran into ice; it stopped us for two days, pack ice. We got clear of that and made a landfall down Labrador and so on to Halifax. We had on board Monsieur Willoquet, the French Ambassador to the Phillipines, who had been captured by the Japanese and spent a lot of time in a four-foot square cage. He had bluffed his way out of POW camp and was on his way to join DeGaulle's staff in Washington. To us young bucks his story was pretty harrowing and he was obviously a man of enormous courage.

"It took us thirty-two days to make that passage and when I got home I was not feeling that good. This was the result of the last three years at sea, the bad food, and perhaps the incessant sea operations. I also had a six-week bout of a recurring jaundice I got by virtue of my time in Malaya. After leave I was appointed to *Skeena* on the Newfie to 'Derry run.

"Until we went aground in Iceland I had some good times in her. Scattered memories. We got a piano fitted in the wardroom. Some people in 'Derry gave us one but there was a great to-do as to how we were going to get it down to the wardroom. We knew a USN Lieutenant, a 'Mustang,' a man who had been promoted up through the hawse pipe from the lower deck; that's what they called them in the USN. He cut a great hole in our upper deck – the deck head of the wardroom – and lowered it in. The USN were *great*. No paperwork; just ask. Probably a bottle of rum changed hands. It was not a *huge* piano, thank goodness. That evening we had the USN on board and had a rollicking good time. An officer from an American destroyer played for us. It was Eddie Duchin. *Duchin*! He and his band had been playing in New York's Waldorf Astoria Hotel before he joined the navy.

"The weather stayed bad. One night changing watch at midnight, it was wild, the kind of thing one hears about. You know, people getting washed over the side and the next wave washing them back in again. I remember that before we left the bridge we were sometimes with one foot on the deck of the bridge and another on the side as she rolled over, rolled over, and sometime stayed there for a good time before she righted. Everything is worse in the pitch black of night; it is a kind of vertigo. But we always came back. The righting moment is very good in those ships. The bow would rear up, practically all the ship out of water back to the bridge. Then she'd crash down and all the sailors would yell, 'Refit! Refit!' We had a lifeline that ran along the upper deck and we would wait until the ship was more or less on an even keel and then we'd run for it. We were in those heavy leather seaboots. Neil Fraser and I came off watch together and made our run aft but got caught. We both got washed into a carley float by a wave that sloshed in; the float got lifted off its seatings and flopped about. We both managed to get off and Neil made a break for it before I did. He made it. Then when I tried I got caught. Another wave caught me and the only thing that saved me was that handrail around the after canopy. I grabbed that. I don't know how much we rolled but I was hanging on and as the wave surged down the ship's side I was stretched out *horizontal* to the deck, maybe three feet above it.

"It was like that a lot of the time. Summers were better, of course. But mostly it was cold. It was part of our human condition. It was cold. It was very rough. It was dreary and often it was very wet and very cold.

"Besides convoys across the Atlantic we had some in-shore work.

228

Five of us went out on the U-boat blockade outside Brest; they used to try to come out and were heavily escorted by flak ships, trawlers armed with 20mm and 40mm and larger guns. We had good intelligence when they were coming. First we went south and then we went west, right in under the shore batteries. The trick was to get close to the Germans as quickly as possible; then the shore batteries couldn't open up. We used to go in at twenty-three knots. We'd turn to a parallel course at about 4,000 yards and open up and bang away. The flak ships would open up and there would be this cherry-red tracer arcing towards us – but it was of no real consequence. We sank some flak ships but no submarines. We had a stripped-down Lewis gun on the bridge, mounted on a peg sort of thing. The AB manning it got really excited one night and sprayed the *inside* of the bridge. We thought, 'Oh my God. We've all been shot.' Another night in Audierne Bay south of Brest we fired at shore installations and German soldiers trying to get off in barges. It was about the only way they could move up and down the coast. They were trying to get out of Britanny. There was quite an exchange of fire but we suffered no particular damage. But in the mêlée we had got quite close to the beach and had to alter 180 degrees to get off. A great fog of gunsmoke everywhere. We turned but our next astern didn't and *Qu'Appelle* was close; we nicked a corner off her stern and had to get our bow repaired.

"When we were in drydock my Captain said to me, 'Look, if you're interested in that girl you'd better do something about it.' After our first trip we'd been to Londonderry and on to Portrush where a generous Irish family had turned their house and grounds over to the Canadians so we could have a break between our endeavours in the Channel. Tennis courts I remember. That's how I met Peggy. She was one of the twelve Wrens who were running the control station for the western approaches. I found it astounding the amount of responsibility that was placed on these young women. They were very good; they did it extremely well and had an enormous night life as well. I don't know how they managed to stay awake. So I dashed back to Belfast and proposed, she accepted and we duly informed our respective parents in Shropshire and Ottawa. We were married in Plymouth in the old chapel called Stoke Dameral, just outside the dockyard gates. We spent our honeymoon in the rubble of Plymouth. It was badly knocked about, believe me. We had seven days in Plymouth Hoe and then we went back to our respective jobs; she was then working in the cellars of Belfast Castle.

"After *Skeena* went aground I got back to Londonderry in December 1944 in the *Seacliff*. Eric Harrington was Captain, a very gung-ho type, Eric, a terrific guy. A couple of days before we got into 'Derry he and another corvette got a U-boat contact southwest of Ireland and severely damaged it. I was on the bridge and saw it blow to the surface and all the crew bail out. There were fifty-two; we got them in large numbers including the First Lieutenant, an Austrian, only twenty-one and a nice young fellow.

"The Germans didn't want to speak to us and I was the only one who had any German, high-school German from Lisgar Collegiate. But the Austrian First Lieutenant had a little French so between French and German and a German-English equivalence handbook, we managed to get some conversation going. The problem seemed to be that there was an SS officer on board. He was a Technician by rank but he reported directly to the SS, not the Captain. He was there to make sure that everybody toed the party line. Harrington said, 'Look, I'm going to solve this problem of the Germans not talking. Put the SS man in solitary. Put the rest of them down in the stoker's mess.' Then, at very slow speed and with considerable danger to the ship, I might add, he let go a whole raft of depth charges set at shallow. Of course the ship shook considerably and the Germans thought they had been torpedoed. That shook *them* considerably because the stokers' mess is mostly below the waterline. Now the depth charges upset the Germans very much and they remembered our depth charges which sank them, 'Our boat was just like a salad,' they said. 'Everything was so mixed, all mucked up because of your depth charges.' They were unnerved. Then they talked, a lot.

But when they were landed and lined up on the jetty to be marched off to POW camp they gave three cheers for our ship. This was a bit strange.

Jack McClelland had always liked the sea, so, while he was taking engineering physics at the University of Toronto he joined the RCNVR at HMCS *York* as an Acting Probationary Tempory Sub-Lieutenant. "I was determined to get into the navy. I did my interview board at *York* in a room full of Admirals, it seemed to me. I was nervous and one asked me the question, 'Have you been sailing all your life?'

" 'No, sir, just since I was about five years old.'

"I felt such a bloody fool. I thought I had blown my chance but I guess the quality of the other applicants was not that high and I managed to get through. Then I went to *Royal Roads* for four months' training.

"The Captain, John Grant, was an extraordinary human being. A First World War type. The staff were good and they ran us ragged. If you were in bad physical condition when you went to *Royal Roads* you would have been *dead*. They got us into very, very good physical condition, which turned out to be useful and important. We learned sailing, navigation, pilotage, rules of the road, seamanship, traditions of the service, that sort of thing. We learned the responsibilities and the duties of being an officer. We were taught that you do your duty because there is nothing else you can do. That is *it*! The instructors were good.

"I remember the Gunner's Mate. Everybody hated him and loved him at the same time. One day I was in charge of the squad drill and he was in charge of me. He was running late and had to be somewhere else so he cut out the usual routine, which I knew, and said, 'Sub-Lieutenant McClelland, gobblede gabble gabble gabble *now*.'

"I didn't get a word of this strange new language, 'I beg your pardon, Chief?'

" 'Gabbledee gabble gabble gommel, *now*, in three ranks.'

" 'I can't tell them that, Chief. They won't understand me.'

" 'Don't argue with me, sir. We haven't time. Tell them to fall in in three ranks in front of you. Do it *now*.'

"So I raised my voice and addressed the parade square, 'Fall in in three ranks in front of you, now.'

"Well, the class went off in all directions. To my dying day I'll never forget my total embarrassment. It was a completely unmitigated balls-up.

"Another instructor was the Gunnery Officer. I remember one day when he said that he had been in the navy for two and a half years and he hadn't yet been to sea. I said in a stage whisper, 'I hope I can say that when I've been in the navy two and a half years.'

"I was joking, of course, but he picked it up. 'Who said that?'

"Silence.

" 'You said that, McClelland.'

" 'Yes, sir. I did.'

" 'I'm going to get you for that. If I do nothing else I'm going to make sure that you go directly to sea after you finish this course. I'll *guarantee* it.'

"He must have had a lot of influence because I was one of the few who did get to sea and I was at sea ever after that. He eventually did get a ship and I saw him later. I'm sure we discussed it many a beery evening.

"I went to a Bangor minesweeper and we were escorting convoys from Sydney, Nova Scotia, to Quebec City. It didn't take me long to find out that there was a war on. I joined *Chedabucto* in Gaspe one night and the next day a ship was torpedoed. It scared the hell out of me. I never wanted to go below decks again after I saw this happen. I was on watch, the four to eight, the morning watch. I was looking at the convoy and suddenly a great explosion and this merchant ship sinks. Then several other ships were hit, I think. The submarine came up and all the convoy opened fire on it. It was ahead of us and the Captain altered away. I always thought we were supposed to ram them. Maybe it was the gunfire of the merchant ships. I don't know. He was not the greatest Captain of all time. But she was a good ship. We had a good First Lieutenant and Navigator. We had a good bunch in *Chedabucto* and we had great fun. She was rammed and sunk off Rimouski, later, by the cable layer, *Lord Kelvin*. Anyway, after five or six months in her, I applied for small boats and left.

"I went to a Fairmile flotilla working out of St. John's. A great bearded character was flotilla leader, Jim Davis, called 'Fog Horn' Davis because of his voice. A great practical joker. He had a sea-going monkey jacket with gold braid up to his elbows, and over. He said if he was going to be a senior officer he should look like a senior officer. He also had two dozen bits of coloured cloth where we put our medal ribbons. I should say where the First World War sailors put their medal ribbons; we didn't have any yet. Except Jim Davis. He had them coming down from his shoulder and disappearing into his breast pocket. He wore one large gold earring. One night when he was in this rig he got sent for by Captain (D), he was to come *immediately*. He went up in his duffle coat. It was hot in the office and Captain (D) kept asking Davis to take his coat off and Jim kept saying no thanks, I'm quite comfortable. Or he finally did have to show his ribbons and stripes? Captain (D) was angry? Captain (D) was amused? I don't know. There are many versions of the yarn.

"Anyway, my own Captain was Sam Garlick and he was a marvellous guy. Our job was to go up to the Conception Bay area and patrol there; many ships were freighting iron ore from the Wabana mine. We went on patrol there in pairs. One would circle the island and the other would lie up in Portugal Cove, 'Portigal Cove' as the Newfies called it. We are now moving into 1943 and in the year or more I was based in Newfoundland I was in several Fairmiles and then got command on my own. In winter the weather was formidable. We pitched so much and our bow would be out of the water so far that the joke used to be that the asdic would ping off aircraft. We weren't encouraged to fire our guns too much and weren't even sure they'd work if we ever did fire them. Very rudimentary radar; it didn't train around; it was fixed dead ahead and you had to alter the ship around. The U-boats had long been in Canadian waters. We flushed two, I think.

"Our first submarine was detected on asdic one night; the operator said it was on the surface but we couldn't pick it up on radar. The asdic operator was very insistent, however, that it was a sub and so I sounded action stations and closed the bearing. It was either a sub or it was a ship that wasn't supposed to be in the area. I did a quick radio check with St. John's and found out there were not supposed to be any surface ships there. It was about three in the morning and very black. Then we got an echo of sorts on the radar. Some people saw the submarine and some didn't see it. But whatever it was it disappeared rapidly. We could only do fourteen knots. We reported this to St. John's and it was very clear they didn't believe us. But the next morning they found out we weren't joking. A freighter was sunk in a mine field that had been laid outside the harbour.

"The boat we had intercepted had laid her mines and then come up for a look. When we intervened with starshell it had already accomplished its main aim and took off. It was one of the new boats, which explained its speed. That mine field was a serious hindrance to shipping.

"I learned a lot about mines. I had seconded to my boat an incredible character called Rundle, George Rundle, a rendering-mines-safe officer. He had a George Medal and Bar, I think. I retained command but was under his direction. The next three weeks was a very exciting time. One of our crew. . .no, I think it was two of our crew picked up DSCs. I got a Mentioned in Despatches. We would follow the minesweepers and every so often the moorings of a mine would be cut and it would bob to the surface, if it didn't explode. Then Rundle would get into one of our small boats and tow this goddamn mine to an uninhabited cove and land it. His job was to take this thing apart and find out what made it tick – or what made it bang. He had been doing this for years. He was one of the few *living* officers who had taken the original mine-disposal course in London. He would take off the cap of the mine, and if it started ticking he either had five seconds to get the hell out or he had a minute. He never knew which. He'd get it near a boulder he could throw himself behind. He was leading a very dicey life because when he was with me he rendered about seven mines safe. I remember that before he'd tackle a mine he'd lie quiet in the deck for ten minutes and try and relax. Then he'd get up and do the job. Then he'd come back and be violently ill for maybe half an hour. Then he'd start drinking and get blind drunk – for which nobody could blame him.

"The weather was always a problem. Just after I got command we were coming back from Conception Bay after a week on patrol and it was such a sunny warm day we were all stripped down to shorts, sitting on the upper deck. It was beautiful. Suddenly we were in the thickest fog I've ever seen in my life. My Navigator did a fast check and said, 'I know where we are. I saw a point I recognise. I've charted a course.' I decided that the fog was so bad that I better get into harbour and keep out of trouble. I altered in and tried to get the cliffs on the radar but couldn't; the operator said any echo was lost in the ground wave. I slowed the engines. Suddenly, right in front of me, are cliffs, *not* the harbour entrance. A sheer cliff with white breakers at the foot. I went full astern. I almost pulled the handle off the engine room telegraphs. I remember everyone on the bridge *pushing* against the after end of the bridge *willing* the screws to catch and take her astern. Our bow went into the breakers before the full-astern caught hold. I must have backed out ten miles before I even slowed down. The night had turned rough and windy. A convoy had arrived off the harbour entrance and couldn't get in. Nobody could get in. You had maybe thirty ships going back and forth across the entrance and trying not to collide. Everybody wanting to be first into port the next morning. Any U-boat commander there would have had a field day.

"I saw my second submarine coming out of St. John's. I had closed the crew up at action stations as we left harbour as I always did and, my God! There ahead of me was a submarine on the surface. About a mile ahead. I increased speed and flashed the challenge. It didn't answer. Good Lord! I didn't know whether to cry or jump overboard or what. The guns' crews were ready to fire but we were no match for a U-boat's guns. Then the port war signal station started flashing like mad. We had challenged and they had not replied and I was going to open fire. I had no choice. But my Signalman was reading the port war signal lamp and told me the submarine was one of ours. The number of stupid things that happened in the navy. God, I would hate to think of all those.

I'm remembering the time I was disciplined and sent to Halifax in disgrace. This was fairly early on and I had had a grave disagreement with my Captain. I didn't think he was particularly competent and said so. I said he was not fulfilling his position properly. Anyway, Halifax sent me as First Lieutenant to another Fairmile building in Toronto. The whole flotilla was built between Georgian Bay and Toronto. Bill Moore of Orillia was my Captain, a marvellous guy, a good seaman, and as a Lieutenant-Commander he was the flotilla leader. We partied all the way down the St. Lawrence and then worked up in Saint Margaret's Bay. Then, back to Newfie. They were useful ships, Fairmiles. I remember when *Saguenay* was in collision off Cape Race with the Panamanian freighter *Azra*. *Saguenay*'s depth charges exploded and she lost her stern. We were used on that occasion to take some of her crew off. Fairmiles served a lot of useful functions and they were great training ships. You had to know a lot, pilotage, navigation, seamanship; we all knew every detail about the engines, and every other part of the ship. The only thing we didn't know was how to fire the goddamn guns. That's the life and times of McClelland as Fairmile sailor. I loved it and would probably have stayed there. A flotilla was going down to Bermuda and that was an attractive proposition. But volunteers were asked for motor torpedo boats which were faster and more heavily armed and seemed more exciting, so I applied.

"Canada had formed two MTB flotillas, one was under Tony Law and mine had as senior officer a man by the name of Kirkpatrick. Marvellous guy, from Kitchener, Ontario. Law worked out of Dover and we worked out of Brixham, operating mainly in the Channel Islands. Then we moved to Great Yarmouth, this would be after D-Day in Normandy and it was really a lot of fun and a very exciting part of my war. We had a lot of action, it varied, you know, sometimes we'd go weeks without action and then we'd have a lot. We'd get shot up by E-boats and flak ships. I guess the worst incident we had was in fact filmed by the National Film Board; they were doing one of those *Canada Carry On* films.

"I think we had four boats and we picked up a convoy, a small convoy, and bore in for a torpedo attack. Then Kirkpatrick noticed the German ships were so small that they weren't worth torpedoes and changed it to a gun attack. This is less expensive. What we *hadn't* noticed was the amount of fire power they had. We got in to about a hundred yards, beam on to a flak ship, and she opened fire. So we got in and got out bloody quickly. We let them have it first but they had apparently picked us up and they opened fire a few seconds later. I was second boat in line and they really let us have it. It was very gory; we had five hands killed. It was a sad occasion in many respects. One thing we never knew. As we were going out of the action we made smoke. But the third boat which, if my memory serves me correctly, was under the command of Owen Greening (and he was a professional, extraordinary guy, from Hamilton) was following us out. I'm not positive about that but I think it was his boat that was following us out. Anyway, we were firing astern with everything we could; there was smoke and their flak was coming at us and our tracer going the other way but we lost sight of the third boat. Then, suddenly, off to one side a boat emerged out of the smoke, just the bow, and it looked as if it was firing at us. It wasn't. It was the fire from the flak ship behind her. Unfortunately we opened fire on her because we couldn't identify her quickly enough. We let go a couple of bursts and, I think – you know, it's something you never really pin down – but I think we killed a couple of hands on her bow. I was in quite a number of actions but I think that was the hairiest.

"I was in actions where we fired torpedoes but I never claimed a kill from these although some of the other boats did. We'd operate in groups of three or four boats. The other four would go out the next night. Torpedo boats or gunboats would have an area with a frigate or destroyer with advanced radar to direct them onto targets. It was quite interesting because you could see actions going on five or ten miles away but you weren't involved in that. You kept to your area. Some funny things happened. One night we heard on the radio someone calling the senior officer of a British torpedo boat flotilla, 'Hullo, Charlie Dog Able. This is Dog Charlie Baker. We'd like to carry out a communication test. Will you respond, please? Over.'

" 'Hullo Dog Charlie Baker this is Charlie Dog Able. Would *like* to carry out a voice check but could you delay it, please? I'm about to engage the enemy. Out.'

"Then the destroyer directing this Brit flotilla came up, 'Bandits bearing so and so, course so and so, steer so and so, and intercept at full speed.'

"So the leader of the British MTBs called his boats to follow him. Then the guy who wanted to do the voice check called again, in a bored voice, obviously nothing to do. 'Hullo, Charlie Dog Able, this is Dog Charlie Baker, could we carry out a communication check, please?'

" 'No. I'm about to engage the enemy. I'm about to engage the enemy. Port ten. Out.'

"Suddenly all hell broke loose. They'd encountered the E-boats. We were a distance away but on this dark night we could see the starshell and the tracer going back and forth. Just an *unbelievable* action. Then this dope, oblivious to all this, called again, 'Hullo, Charlie Dog Able, this is Dog Charlie Baker, request voice check. Over.'

" 'Am bloody well engaging the enemy. Out.'

"But we thought, 'My God, what a cool guy!' And we could hear the reports going back to their destroyer that they had been badly hit and only two boats could continue the action. All done in such a calm civilized manner – it always struck me as typical of the Royal Navy.

"One action we started into I thought would be the end of us. It was dusk and we came across what we thought were two German Narvik-class destroyers. It scared the hell out of me. We were three MTBs and we were heading out toward this island – I guess it was just before D-Day – and we saw these two destroyers ahead. We hadn't been told there would be any of ours there so they must be German. There was still a bit of light so there we were. Three MTBs. We had no choice. We had to engage them. And if you take *them* on with three MTBs, you're *dead*. We closed the range and flashed the challenge. They replied correctly. Thank God! It was *Haida* and *Athabaskan*. So that was a relief.

"The only other thing I can think of is the time I distinguished myself by carrying out a torpedo attack on our troop carrier, the *Queen Elizabeth*. A lovely target, huge. I'd gone off to pick up a new boat in Scotland and bring her down to Wales, to Holyhead. I went into Greenock to ammunition. It was a fine sunny day and we'd identified ourselves to the port war signal station and we didn't have torpedoes and I thought that everyone knew we were harmless so I decided to carry out a dummy run on this monster, on this great huge ship that was coming out into the stream and moving down-channel towards us. So, full of the joy of youth, I bore in.

"Suddenly lights began flashing and I could see them manning their guns so I thought I'd better break off the attack. And I did. But when I got alongside my berth there was a Lieutenant-Commander and a staff car waiting for me and I was to go to the Admiral's office *immediately*.

Would I have time to change? No. The Admiral was the Flag Officer commanding the area. He ticked me off properly. He told me in front of everyone that I should understand that by this dangerous and frivolous action – scaring everybody – that I had incurred the displeasure of His Majesty or Their Lordships or whoever it was I had offended and that a notation would be made on my file. He absolutely scared the hell out of me. Poor Lieutenant Shakey. But after the ticking off was over and the others were leaving he told me to stay. 'Sit down and have a cigarette and relax.' Then he said, 'You know, in all truth it must have been a pretty inviting target. Tell me about it.' So we had a nice chat and I told him about our work in Fairmiles and MTBs. Then he said, 'Now as far as this other business is concerned, that is just for the record, but I wouldn't recommend that you do anything like that again. I'm not going to take any further action. I'm satisfied that everything that had to be done has been done. You won't hear anything more about it.' And I never did.

Joe Clark joined the RCN as an ordinary seaman at Christmas 1940. Why? "Principally because my father and his brother were old sweats. My father, a newspaperman, used to love telling stories of his time in the infantry and later in the Royal Flying Corps. Like most fathers he did his best to dissuade me from a military career which attracted me so much when I was in my teens. But he revelled in his own. My uncle, Gregory Clark, was the same. I used to go fishing with them and Uncle Greg and my father used to get very competitive in their stories and tell them to my cousins and me. I was absolutely determined that if there was another war I would join. Quite unwittingly, of course, they created a glamorous picture of war. They would swap stories of the Battle of the Somme, Vimy Ridge, Passchendaele, and it sounded marvellous. I have since learned that this is the sort of thing that veterans *do*. Their memories are of the high points, not the grim side of war. Those are the reasons I joined. Here was a war and I was going to emulate these guys I admired so much and I too was going to get in and I would win an MC like my Uncle Greg did at Vimy Ridge and a DFC like Dad did in the Flying Corps.

"I was in the cadet corps at University of Toronto School. In my last year at UTS war was declared and I phoned the navy in Toronto and said I would like to join and I thought I could perhaps be Captain of an MTB. They turned me down, rather rudely; there was raucous laughter, 'How old are you, sonny?' I told them I was seventeen and they said to wait a couple of years. I went to university and brooded about this and then got into the Queen's Own Rifles. So now I was a Rifleman in the QORs. Then I learned that the navy was looking for men from the university to take a 'special course.' They wouldn't tell us what it was but it was asdic. We had six weeks to learn the subject. We had some marvellous instructors, old Chief Petty Officer retreads sent over from the Royal Navy; either that or they had retired in Canada. We were supposed to go to Halifax in March, then it was April, then May, then June. We were going crazy. Here was this wonderful war to be fought and *we* were sitting in *Toronto*.

"A very strange place, the Toronto of those years, very socially conscious. The commanding officer of HMCS *York* was typical of the graduates of the Big Four, the private schools: Upper Canada College, Glendon College School, Ridley, and St. Andrew's. He recruited a large corps of graduates from these schools and put them into uniform – not commissioned, not paid, just wearing uniforms. Toronto was just crawling with these people. The old-boy social thing. They seemed to spend a lot of time here before they went off to become *real* sailors. I knew most of them and here I was a little OD and they Sub-Lieutenants; one night I was on sentry duty and one of the subs I knew came in with his girl friend and I greeted them, 'Hi, Bill, hi, Lucy.' He really gave me hell; he wiped the ground with me. It was humiliating because Lucy just stood there not knowing what to say. It was with some satisfaction that when I got my stripe I found myself senior to him. Another one of the Subs was my divisional officer and he taught us how to play cricket – that was his contribution. Then I went before an interview board for a commission. I didn't know how, but my father becoming Director-in-Chief of Public Relations of the Armed Forces might have had something to do with it.

"I went to *Royal Roads* as an Acting Probationary Tempory Sub-Lieutenant. I met Captain John Grant. I thought he was a marvellous man. I didn't really meet him, actually, until I was in Captain's defaulters. I had run up a bar bill and I wasn't legally old enough to drink. It had never occurred to me I couldn't drink. We lived in the castle, Hatley Castle. Grant was very very kind to me. When he realized how aghast I was that I had erred he sent for me and gave me a fatherly talk. He was respected by all. We did the usual parade ground, pilotage, seamanship, sailing. We had formal mess dinners once a week, learned the protocol, traditions of the service, the responsibilities of officers, that sort of thing. Pearl Harbor was attacked in

December and that night all the Subs were issued with steel helmets, webbing, gaiters, and a rifle and bayonet – no ammunition. We were told to patrol the grounds. Against what I don't know. During our training we were beaten about the ears by the Training Chief Petty Officers and the Training Officers which was right and proper and good for us. Punishments were: doubling around the parade ground with a sixty-pound pack; doubling with your rifle over your head; or standing there and holding the rifle to the firing position with one arm – it was a form of torture to be avoided.

"I had a time after *Royal Roads* in Vancouver in the naval division there; seizing Japanese fishing boats was one thing I did. Not very exciting. I just took over the boat, gave the owners a receipt, and told them to go away. I took boats into the Fraser River, off Annacis Island, there were a raft of them there, and another near the Second Narrows bridge. There must have been two thousand. I was also scheduling training for new entries. I was intensely anxious to get out of this and go to sea so when the Captain asked me what I thought of some plan or other that he had devised, I said, 'I think it's perfectly dreadful.'

"He didn't think a youngster with one ring should talk that way to him with his four rings, but I was completely chock-a-block with all this messing around with paper-work and doing footling jobs ashore when I was now magnificently trained to do battle with the Hun, to go to sea, to join the war. I was afraid it would end before I got my MC and my DFC. What would I tell my children and my nephews? So I was sent away and that's how I got to sea.

"I was sent to Halifax and given a choice of three corvettes but told that *Arrowhead* was commanded by a certain Commander E. G. Skinner and that 'if you can survive under Skinner you will do very well. Not many people can stand up under him.' That got me. I chose *Arrowhead*. She had just come off the St. Lawrence patrols; this would be the end of 1942. U-boats were in the approaches to Halifax and up the St. Lawrence river nearly to Quebec City. Paul Hartwig in U-57 was there, I now know, and Klaus Hornborstel in U-806. There were five or more in total. *Charlottetown* had been sunk. Skinner had been senior officer of that group since 1941. He had *Racoon* also and some Fairmiles. He had taken over the ship after the previous Captain had gone crazy. Skinner was a Newfoundlander who had joined the army in the first war at age fifteen. He was taken prisoner and put to work on a German farm. He killed the farmer with a pitchfork, escaped, got a German sailor's uniform, joined the mutiny of the German navy at Keil, got back to the Allied forces, went back to Newfoundland after the war, resumed fishing, got a Mate's ticket, then his deep-sea Master's ticket, and was Captain of one of the Imperial Oil tankers up to 1939, a senior Captain by then.

"He was a man of considerable intelligence, of enormous physical strength, of strong personality in every conceivable respect. He was marvellous to serve under, a tough son of a bitch. He would never see defaulters; he thought there just never *should* be a defaulter in his ship. He'd say to some burly AB or stoker, 'Do you think you can take me?'

" 'You're goddamn right I can take you, Captain.'

"And they'd fight it out. He always won. He was one of the most incredibly undisciplined officers in some respects; in others he was marvellous. A good seaman. A great seaman. He was always called 'Uncle Eef.' He'd say, 'Eef we do this and eef we then do that, we can do so and so.' 'Uncle Eef.' He had iron-grey hair. He was a handsome man and he loved women. He was never happier than in the presence of women. He loved to eat and he loved to drink; he loved to laugh and he loved to fight. I went to his cabin when I reported on board. He stared at me for quite a while. It was intimidating. I knew he'd make me wardroom wine and tobacco officer; all new boys got that. He was surrounded by the mass of bumph that deluged a Captain every time he put into harbour. Mountains of correspondence, letters, files. He said, 'I'm thinking I might be making you Signal Officer. How good are you at filing?'

" 'Terrible, sir,' thinking I'd get out of that one.

" 'I'll teach you. Get that garbage can over there.'

"He had a great-sized sort of waste basket wedged under his desk. I hauled it out and he proceeded to throw all the correspondence into it and stomp it down. There were papers with receipt slips attached, confidential documents – all degrees of security – booklets, some things not out of their envelopes; all went into this huge basket. He said, 'Never pay attention to that stuff. It's just a lot of nonsense. Now, let's have a drink.'

"He introduced me to the fine art of throwing hands into the chain locker. That's the way of dealing with obstreperous drunks. Don't put them on report. Throw them in the chain locker. If they land on their head, that keeps them quieter. Tomorrow they'll be sober. I was developed by Captain Skinner into The Chief Drafter of All Things. I wrote everything. It was highly improper but I wrote *everything* for

'Uncle Eef.' I got all the necessary documents and wrote all the letters, all the reports. . . . Commander E. G. Skinner, DSC, RD, RCNR, O-57520, Seniority 1, July 1942.

"We were in lots of actions but never sank a U-boat. He had some fine verbal fights with the U-boat Commanding Officers, though. Some of the really historic verbal jousts of the Battle of the Atlantic waged over the radio telephone. I've often wondered if these r/t pleasantries were with Paul Hartwig in U-57. Anyway, one of them would start baiting Skinner. One time there was a dense fog and a U-boat Commander started up and Uncle Eef was enraged. The U-boat Commander was on our r/t frequency and laughing his head off, just having fun you know, and Uncle Eef was roaring back in his inimitable style, cursing him out. He was bloody well *outraged*! In anti-submarine warfare you felt remote from your enemy. And then an incident like this made the whole thing very real. This wasn't the abstract, a sound you pick up on your asdic and you drop your charges. This was a real, honest-to-God, living human being and, what's worse, a man who is superior to you – at the moment anyway.

"I was in *Arrowhead* all of 1943 and some of 1944. I was seasick most of the time. My weight at high school was around a hundred and sixty and I got down to a hundred and twenty-five. I couldn't keep food on my stomach but I used to think of food all the time. I was sick and I thought of food; it got so the thought of food didn't nauseate me any more. I never thought of women. In harbour was the usual drinking and dates, alright for a while but after a few days I wanted to get back to sea again. And I was sick again. It got so I could handle the sickness. I was feeling terrible and my friends said I looked terrible but I could handle it. It didn't bother me. To this day if I get nauseated it doesn't bother me. I learned then that being sick was no problem. A lot of Captains were sick but couldn't get reliefs so they stayed at sea. Alan Easton in *Sackville* was one; he had bad ulcers but there were no trained reliefs; he went on to command a destroyer, took his ulcers with him. Captain Skinner had a gall-bladder attack between Charleston and St. John's. Off Boston Uncle Eef was passing in and out of consciousness; he was in such pain he couldn't talk, so we went in and landed him in this gosh-awful storm. We anchored in the stream and the USN sent a tug out to get him. We lashed him into a stretcher and lowered him over the side. One of the tug's seamen fell overboard and was drowned.

"Yes, Uncle Eef was a great guy. He'd take us anywhere. Once, early on, the first time I'd been in action I guess, he got a contact and chased it right down through the convoy. Everyone was firing. I was Gunnery Officer but the merchant ships were firing and I didn't have a target and a lot of the merchantmen's shells were coming over *us*. My first time in action. I wanted my mommy.

"By 1944 we were talking invasion of Europe and I was frantic to get over to the U.K. All my friends were getting good appointments and here was I where there wasn't much war any more. My new Captain, Les Hickey, said he would get me a command course if I hung on but I didn't entirely believe him. So I got this frigate, *Loch Achanalt*. *Teme* was in our group; she had been cut nearly in half after D-Day by the carrier HMS *Tracker*, but towed two hundred miles to Cardiff by *Outremont*. She was patched up and joined us. *Annan* was another. Ted Briggs of the CBC was the Escort Group Commander in *New Waterford*. He was good. He was bloody good. And he had a great sense of theatre. On a beautiful sunny day we'd steam into Portsmouth at twenty knots, he balanced on the forward edge of the bridge waving to the boating Wrens. But the other side of Briggs was. . . . Well, for example, one night in harbour I made an unguarded remark to the effect that my Captain wasn't the *greatest* in the navy. He didn't say a word, just went on as affable as ever. Then I got a signal I was to report to him. I went to *New Waterford* and knocked on the door of his cabin. 'All right, young fellow,' he said. 'Am I right when I say that you said so and so and such and such?'

" 'Yes, sir.'

" 'All right, tell me about it. I promise you I'm not going to change what I'm going to do to you. You might as well tell me the whole story.'

"So I did. Then he said, 'I've got a problem and you've got a problem. You are going to solve your problem by keeping your bloody mouth shut. I'm going to solve my problem by forgetting this conversation ever took place. But if I have to talk to you again on this, you are dead. You are worse than dead.'

"We thought we sank a U-boat in the Channel in 1944, off the Isle of Wight. I know a post-war chart shows U-676 there but I don't think that's ours. We thought it a "probable." Admiralty gave us a "possible." I was in Ted Briggs's Escort Group – EG6 – until the end of the war. We were a hunter-killer group searching between Plymouth, Scapa, the Faeroes, Portsmouth. This day in the Solent was a Sunday, a gorgeous, sunny Sunday afternoon. We established a submarine contact just after we finished our Sunday sherry. At that time we didn't go to action stations for every asdic echo; it was normal for the cruising watch to handle it. We just kept firing our squid at this thing. We must have fired a hundred mortar bombs. But we just got this "possible." Commander W. E. S. Briggs, DSC, RCNR! He must have lost half his ships in EG6. He lost us for a while. The rest of the group had sailed two days ahead of us and we were flogging along at sixteen knots to catch up and we were between Ireland and Anglesey in a son of a bitch of a gale, banging and pounding right into it. We pounded a hole right in her bottom. The pumps couldn't handle the water pouring in. I went down with the Engineer to look at the damage. We were stopped. It was sloshing right under the forward magazine, just pouring in. The Engineer and I were trying to get this under control but the hole, so help me, was six feet across, you could have rowed a boat through, it was spraying like a geyser. We made it to Holyhead.

"I was ordered to Plymouth by Admiralty as a spare Captain for a landing craft just before the invasion. A landing craft, infantry, large. An LCI (L). The flotilla had sailed and was a couple of miles away. I stood by in Plymouth, waiting for my great moment, hoping someone would get killed so I could command an LCI (L). Not really, I guess. But if he got killed *anyway*, not my fault, I would be Captain of an LCI (L). Next day I wandered up to the officers' club on the Hoe feeling disconsolate – here was another war going on without me – and I met Gib Milne, a photographer from Toronto; he was so dirty it was unbelievable – dressed in a once-white shirt, unknotted tie, and flapping Burberry. He had just come back from France. He had just delivered the first pictures of the invasion of Normandy. He said, 'Well, where the hell have you been?'

" 'I haven't been anywhere.'

" 'I've just been over to France and got my pictures. I'm through for the day. It's time for a drink.'

"He saw more action, that guy! He saw more action than anyone I know. He was always sent where something was expected to happen.

"We got our hole patched up and rejoined Ted Briggs and EG6. But *Teme* took a gnat torpedo up her tail from U-246, off Falmouth. Another of his ships was hit by a glider bomb and I can't remember the details. But I do remember U-1006. October 1944. *Loch Achanalt* and *Annan* were in company. One afternoon we had dropped astern of the others to investigate a contact which faded and were steaming to catch up. That night *Annan* got a radar contact and turned to investigate. We followed. *Annan* closed to about a mile and fired a spread of rockets. There she was! U-1006. *Annan* opened up with her guns. U-1006 replied and shot away some of *Annan*'s radar and bridge and there were several wounded. *Annan* closed more, still firing 4-inch and 20mm's. Then she ran alongside and fired a pattern of depth charges set to shallow. I was told one bounced off the sub's deck and then fell into the water. She settled on an even keel about two minutes later. We came puffing up and helped pick up survivors.

"They were pretty good professionally, these U-boat Commanders. I met a couple of them after the war here in Toronto; they had immigrated to Canada and were working here for Maclean-Hunter. There was a big meeting of the Naval Officers' Association of Canada at the Royal York Hotel, and the guest speaker was the Deputy Chief of the NATO naval forces, Rear-Admiral Otto Kretschmer of U-99 – the Tonnage King. A very nice man, slight, slender, sandy-haired. I was standing with a drink in my hand and I went up and introduced myself to these two strangers who I presumed were two of the Toronto area German ex-naval officers we had invited. I said, 'You're ex-*Kriegsmarine*?'

" 'Yes, I am, and my friend here. We were both U-boat Captains.'

"Out came the wallets and I was shown photos of their boats. They seemed very anxious to talk. They introduced two more ex-*Kriegsmarine* officers; one of them was running a motel north of here and had been in destroyers as their equivalent of our Captain (D). He was shown a great deal of respect by the other Germans. We agreed to dine together. This was all helped when we got a waiter who had been a steward in the German navy. There was much heel clicking and '*Ja wohl mein Kapitan*' and a special bottle of wine appeared. We began to reminisce and, to my delight, the man on my left had been the Captain of a U-boat we had been involved with off the Faeroes in 1944. I said, 'I was in a hunter-killer group in that area. We were supposed to get you guys as you came up from the U-boat pens. Did you ever know the captain of U-1006?

" 'Oh, that son of a bitch.'

" 'Thank Heavens you said it first. We found him a snooty bugger. We tried to treat him properly but he was just a horse's ass.'

" 'I agree. You know, I was there. I was Captain of U-1003 and the two of us were going out on the Atlantic patrol from Norway, from Bergen we sailed."

" 'I remember the occasion quite well. I was in *Loch Achanalt* and we were with *Annan*.'

" 'Yes. We were on the surface and watched you pass.'

" '*Annan* made the initial attack that blew U-1006 to the surface. It was a dark night.'

" 'Yes, it was dark, but we saw you. I submerged when I saw U-1006 engaging one of your ships. It must have been you I had in my sights as you were picking up survivors.'

" 'Yes, among them that horse's ass of a Captain.'

" 'I fired two fish at you.'

" 'Then you missed.'

" 'Or the torpedoes were defective.'

" 'That explains why when we put the prisoners in the tiller flat they looked so nervous. We thought they were afraid of us.'

" 'No. They were afraid of me.' "

Memories. Memories. I could go on. Oh, how I could go on. There are tens of thousands of us in Canada who spin these salty dips. In June of 1985 Vice-Admiral J. C. Wood, CMM, CD, the Commander of Canada's navy, was host to about a thousand of us in the Nova Scotian Hotel in Halifax. He got the full impact of a lot of these yarns, told, towards the end of the evening, in stentorian tones and oracle-like confidence with much waving of arms and, "No, it wasn't like that at all. *We* opened fire first and you. . . ."

Wood has an oak plaque outside his office listing those who came before him as Commanders-in-Chief of the North America and West Indies Station and Senior Officers at Halifax, Nova Scotia, starting with Vice-Admiral The Honourable Edward Boscawen, Royal Navy, in 1755, going through the seventy-two who followed him up to the birth of the Royal Canadian Navy, then closing with the thirty-three Canadian Commanders.

"Told toward the end of the evening in stentorian tones. . . ." Yarns of our youth, now many years past. For five and a half years we had gamboled at the supper dances at the Nova Scotian Hotel. Rum bottles under the table, Coke on top. One group of destroyers and corvettes just arrived; another leaving tomorrow. "Careless Talk Costs Lives." Rushing waiters. The syncopated drums, the smooth, sad saxophones, the confident, soaring trumpets. "String of Pearls." "Moonlight Serenade." "We'll Hang Out Our Washing on the Siegfried Line." "In the Mood." *Do you remember the night Tiger Turner swung from that chandelier?* Beautiful young girls. A score of convoys behind us; a hundred to come.

Sung to the tune of "Road to the Isles,"

It's away outward bound the swinging fo'c's'ls heel,
From the smoking sea's white glare upon the strand.
It's the grey miles that are slipping under keel,
As we're rolling outward bound from Newfoundland.
From Halifax to Newfie John to 'Derry's clustered towers,
Through trackless paths where conning towers roll.
If you know another group in which you'd sooner spend your
    hours,
Ye've never sailed beneath the Barber Pole.

The Barber Pole Brigade. Funnels with white and red bands. *Skeena, Saguenay, Sackville* (Alan Easton, her first Captain, eighty-two now, down from Montreal for the occasion of her rebirth), *St. Laurent* (nicknamed "Sally Rand" or "Sally"), *Assiniboine* (or "Bones"), *Restigouche* ("Rustyguts").

Memories. Memories. A brave Band of Brothers then; a brave Band of Brothers now. But many faces missing; some to their iron coffins then, others to the depredations of time since. Of the rest of us, some stooped, some favouring arthritic joints. But Rear-Admiral Debby Piers as erect and exuberant as when he was Lieutenant Debby Piers commanding *Restigouche,* still able to get into his RMC scarlet jacket; Rear-Admiral Pat Budge as keen of eye as ever. My wife Alma. . .I know we see through the eyes of love, but I swear, she's as entrancing and vivacious now as she then was.

"Told toward the end of the evening in stentorian tones. . . ." But now, to our shame, we find ourselves tending to drift off back to our hotel rooms at an hour when, forty-five years ago, we, after gaining flying speed in the wardrooms of our ships, would have come whooping and hollering in. Oh, well, there are compensations, I suppose.

Intrepid mariners then when that was the be-all and end-all of our existence. The alpha and the omega. To be called "a prime seaman" the highest accolade. Now including in our ranks premiers ("Do you remember when John Robarts. . . ?"), Lieutenant-Governors ("Did Tony Paddon and Dan Hanington write 'The Barber Pole' or was it. . . ?"), QCs galore (hoping some of the stories never reach the ears of junior barristers), business titans who make Bay Street, and sometimes Wall Street, tremble. Bank presidents telling of how, when running the ship's canteen, they couldn't make their books balance (the wardroom wine books were easier; when you were short you watered the 40 per cent overproof rum and nobody noticed). Others. . . so many others.

Memories. Memories. The wives Alma and I had met perhaps forty-five years ago when they were the girlfriends of the young men who went to war. The then-Midshipman Peter Chance and Peggy; Sub-Lieutenant Joe Clark and Pat; Sub-Lieutenant Ralph Hennessy and Connie; Sub-Lieutenant Tommy Pullen and Betty.

There were poignant moments. One evening there was dinner and a ball. Serving officers in their mess dress; officers from eleven navies for the fleet review, retired officers in white or black dinner jackets and medals. I wandered to the lobby for a breather and a rest period. A man in street clothes approached with his wife, "Excuse me, sir. Are you Sub-Lieutenant Lawrence?"

Well, I thought, this *is* going back. "Yes, I am."

"I was a killick when you joined *Moose Jaw* in 1940."

The years disappeared as I searched his face. The lineaments were familar. The way he stood. The cock of the head. "You're Leading Seaman Berry. Wait a minute. . . *Fred* Berry."

Berry coloured with pleasure and nudged his wife, "See, I told you."

I invited them in and got them drinks. He said that a few years ago, in Victoria, he'd seen our Captain, Freddie Grubb. I said Alma had gone to school with Carol Grubb and we saw them from time to time. (I didn't tell him Freddie had died a couple of months ago.) He'd phoned, said Berry, and Freddie had said, "Get your ass over here, Berry, and you and your missus have tea with my missus and me." Now Freddie Grubb was Edwardian in demeanour and Berry has no ear for dialogue. The Captain certainly never used *those* words. But a gentleman was Freddie who had a high regard for those who had served under him. *Noblesse oblige* is a trait not much spoken of today but which Freddie possessed in full measure. So tea they had and they sank the U-501 again. That night Berry and I sank the U-501 one more time. I'd never thought that Freddie Grubb had suitably stressed my role in that action, so, when I left *Moose Jaw*, I had recounted the story as it *really* happened. Apparently both Freddie Grubb and I had got it wrong. It was Fred Berry who was the prime mover in that action. But you can't always trust the memories of these old fellows.

248

Index